THE 10-MINUTE MUSICAL

AN ANTHOLOGY FROM THE SOUND BITES FESTIVAL

PRESTON MAX ALLEN • JONATHAN BAUERFELD • WILL BUCK • TALIA BERGER • DANNY K. BERNSTEIN
BLAIR BODINE • CHRISTIANA COLE • CHRIS CRITELLI • CHRIS EDGAR • GREG EDWARDS • GE ENRIQUE
JOEL ESHER • MICHAEL FINKE • A.J. FREEMAN • DYLAN GLATTHORN • ASSAF GLEIZNER • ERIC GRUNIN
KEVIN HAMMONDS • TALAURA HARMS • KARL HINZE • HOWARD HO • TIMOTHY HUANG
JONATHAN KEEBLER • BOB KELLY • AARON KENNY • CHRIS KERRIGAN • WILL LACKER
DIMITRI LANDRAIN • JONNY LEE JR. • ED LEVY • JUSTIN ANTHONY LONG • CHARLIE O'LEARY
ERIK PRZYTULSKI • KRISTEN REA • ANDY RONINSON • DAVID SHENTON • CINDY SIDERIS
JORDAN SILVERZACH SPOUND • LUKE STEINHAUER • THICKET & THISTLE

Copyright © 2020 Theatre Now New York. All Rights Reserved.

ISBN: 978-1-7350805-0-5 (Paperback)

Cover Design: Andre Padayhag
Layout Design & Production: Ben Van Buren (Yonkers International Press)
Copy Editing: Chris Giordano & Frank Hartley
Cover Photograph: Julia Lennon, Sean Patrick Murtagh, and Alexis Floyd in "Book Lovers" by Talaura Harms & Jonathan Bauerfeld. Photo by Eleah Burman.

Printed by Lulu Press, Inc.

LIVE PERFORMANCE RIGHTS

Take notice that professional/stock, amateur and educational live performance rights in and to the musical stage plays appearing in this volume are administered by Music Theatre International (MTI). To inquire as to the availability of such rights, please visit www.mtishows.com, email licensing@mtishows.com or call (212) 541-4684. All other rights in and to the musical stage plays appearing in this volume, under copyright and otherwise, are reserved by the respective authors thereof. Without limiting the foregoing, this book may not be used to facilitate the live performance of any of the musical stage plays appearing in this volume and the purchase of this volume does not include the right to perform the shows contained herein.

CONTENTS

Foreword ix
Roma Torre

Introduction xi
Thomas Morrissey

About Theatre Now New York xv

Acknowledgments xvii

A MOST AVERAGE MUSICAL 15
Book & Lyrics by Jonathan Keebler, Music by Bob Kelly

A RELATIVE RELATIONSHIP 37
Book, Music, & Lyrics by Timothy Huang

ANT AND GRASSHOPPER 57
Book & Lyrics by A.J. Freeman, Music by Dimitri Landrain

BITTERSWEET LULLABY 71
Book by Will Lacker, Music & Lyrics by Dylan Glatthorn

BOOK LOVERS 85
Book & Lyrics by Talaura Harms, Music by Jonathan Bauerfeld

BYSTANDER 99
Book & Lyrics by Ed Levy, Music by Eric Grunin

COOKIE SOIRÉE 113
Book & Lyrics by Justin Anthony Long, Music by Ge Enrique

COOKING FOR TWO 131
Book & Lyrics by Charlie O'Leary, Music by Karl Hinze

DEAD FLOWERS 147
Book, Music, & Lyrics by Michael Finke

DINOSAUR ... 163
Book, Music, & Lyrics by Zach Spound

END OF THE LINE ... 181
Book by Howard Ho, Lyrics by Chris Edgar, Music by Kristen Rea

FINDING THE WORDS ... 197
Book & Lyrics by Andy Roninson and Chris Critelli, Music by Andy Roninson

FRANKLIN PIERCE: DRAGON SLAYER ... 213
Book & Lyrics by Preston Max Allen, Music by Will Buck

ON YOUR MARK! ... 225
Book & Lyrics by Danny K. Bernstein, Music by Aaron Kenny

PELLETS, CHERRIES, AND LIES: THE PAC MAN STORY ... 243
Book, Music, & Lyrics by Erik Przytulski

RUN THIS TOWN ... 259
Book & Lyrics by Cindy Sideris, Music by Assaf Gleizner

SUPERHOTS! ... 275
Book & Lyrics by Blair Bodine, Book & Music by Joel Esher

THE ALMOST IN-LAWS ... 295
Book & Lyrics by Greg Edwards, Music by Andy Roninson

THE ANSWERING MACHINE ... 311
Book & Lyrics by Kevin Hammonds, Music by Andy Roninson

THE CHARM ... 325
Book & Lyrics by Christiana Cole, Music by David Shenton

THE FACEBOOK FIGHTER ... 345
Book, Music, & Lyrics by Chris Kerrigan

THE HIPSTER SISTER ... 361
Book, Music, & Lyrics by Andy Roninson

THE ONLY THING THAT MATTERS ... 377
Book, Music, & Lyrics by Chris Kerrigan

WHAT'S YOUR WISH? ... 393
Book, Music, & Lyrics by Thicket & Thistle

WELCOME TO RIDGINGTON ... 409
Book & Lyrics by Jordan Silver, Music by Luke Steinhauer

The SOUND BITES festival of 10-minute musicals 2013 to 2019 ... 425

Rights and Permissions ... 431

Contributors ... 433

FOREWORD

Yes it sounds crazy—a ten minute musical! But for every creative team behind a "Fiddler On The Roof" there are thousands of young talents that never see the light of a stage. Inside these pages are short works from among the best of those song-writing talents. Mighty oaks from little acorns grow... and great full-length shows from ten minute musicals flow. This is how it starts.

Full-length musicals are a massive collaborative effort. They take a lot of money, time and effort to come to fruition. Few producers want to take a risk working with new composers, no matter how promising they seem. And let's face it, writing anything is intimidating enough. How many new artists are scared away from even attempting to match the virtuosity of a *"Hamilton"* or a *"Hadestown"*. My husband, playwright Eduardo Lopez, wrote the libretto for one musical early in his career. He loved the experience but was never able to repeat the thrill. The process was just too daunting.

The short musical allows fledgling artists to hone their craft and it gives them a showcase to prove their mettle. It also opens the door to developing bigger productions down the road.

The short musical is also an art form in itself. Much like the one-act play or the short story, they are engagingly concise. We have become a culture with a short attention span and these bite-size works, grouped together can easily satisfy a theatre-going audience hungry for original entertainment.

As a student of the theatre, I know the disappointment of not getting into the school play. We would do two big shows a year in high school. So many kids trying out and so few roles to fill. I can still feel the butterflies waiting for the cast list to be posted and then the tears when someone else got the part, and my name in the ensemble. The short musical is the perfect solution to this age-old school dilemma. So many more roles to cast... and not just in the chorus! Teachers take note.

Given the high stakes on Broadway these days and the reluctance among producers to take a chance on original works, the short musical is a young composer's best chance to be heard. How fortunate that finally, there's an anthology putting the best of these collaborations in one spotlight. Theatre Now has done an invaluable service not only to the creative talents behind these new shows but also to audiences and producers eager to discover the next big thing.

– Roma Torre, Chief Theater Critic, NY1

INTRODUCTION

In 2013, my friends Julie Marino, Stephen Bishop Seely and I sat down to discuss founding a musical theatre company in New York City. We examined our experiences developing new musicals together with a previous theatre company and our time running a professional regional theatre. We couldn't ignore the great divide that exists between the early developmental stages of a musical and the fully produced final production. We recognized the fundamental need to bridge that gap, if we are to secure the future of musical theatre. Out of that need, Theatre Now New York emerged.

Musical theatre writers face a unique problem. Although opportunities exist for early readings, where do you go from there? Readings are a cost-effective and valuable process in the development of new work. They give the authors and others a chance to hear the show, while allowing the audience to envision the final production. But readings are only a first step. The real development of new work happens when the show is on its feet and in production. The question many writers face, and the one we sought to answer: how do we get there?

Producing new works for the purpose of further development is expensive. And the risks involved seldom pay off in the short term. We sought a format that would give musical theatre writers the opportunity to rehearse and perform their work in front of an audience. That's where shows really grow, where writers mature, and where artistic teams discover necessary improvements and next steps. Again, we asked the question: how do we get there?

I give Stephen full credit for the answer. He said, "Let's do a festival of 10-minute musicals!" In that moment, the SOUND BITES Festival of 10-Minute Musicals was born.

We put out a call for submissions from new writers. We published press releases and reached out to musical theatre organizations, musical writing programs, and colleges and universities with established musical theatre writing programs, including BMI, ASCAP and NYU to name a few. We wanted a wide reach with diverse material. So we worked hard to get the word out and to ensure the submission process was open to all. In our first year, we received over 50 submissions of 10-minute musicals! The work was wide-ranging and varied, representing a cross section of styles, stories, and storytellers.

We assembled a group of 12 adjudicators to help us select 10-minute musicals to produce in our first SOUND BITES Festival in 2013. The adjudicators consisted of professional writers, directors, performers, and other theatre artists. We specifically invited musical theatre professionals from different backgrounds, each with different perspectives and aesthetics. Together with the Theatre Now team, this group would choose 10 musicals that represented as wide and diverse a creative range as possible, both with respect to the total submission pool and amongst the selected musicals. In each year thereafter, we have expanded our outreach and have brought in more styles and forms of new musicals. In order to include and expand the definition of what a musical can be, our only submission requirement is that the 10-minute piece must include music.

Each of the shows are helmed by a director and, when dance is involved, a choreographer. We cast the shows with professional actors who rehearse for a two-week period of roughly 18 to 20 hours per musical. As an artist service organization and producer of SOUND BITES, Theatre Now covers the majority of our writing teams' costs and expenses. We produce the festival providing artist honorariums and reimbursements for each musical in the festival to cover expenses.

It all comes together a few days before the big night. The cast and crew assemble in a rehearsal room, and run the shows in the order they will be performed. We add in sound effects, and our crew run set changes using mostly black boxes and chairs with props and simple set decoration. We focus on fine-tuning each writer's material and ensuring the evening moves fluidly between shows. A full day of tech in the actual theatre follows, complete with stage lighting, and the show is performed that evening before an enthusiastic and animated audience. The SOUND BITES festival is fast-paced and electrifying, with no two musicals alike. The originality of musicals presented is astounding and the talent explodes on stage. There is nothing like it!

The first three years, we presented SOUND BITES at the 47th Street Theatre, a 199-seat off-Broadway theatre in the heart of New York's famous theatre district. We sold out each year, and by the third year, we had a waiting list for over 40 people. We knew it was time to expand. But should we expand the festival to multiple evenings and, if so, how many? The logistics of a run seemed almost impossible. Each show was cast with a completely different set of performers and musicians. Add in the writers, directors, crew, and volunteers, and we had over 120 people! How could we possibly assemble those people over the course of a number of performances? We also knew that the exhilarating pace of the festival, like being shot out of a canon, stemmed from the excitement of it being a one-night-only event.

We made the obvious choice and moved to a larger venue. We have since moved twice: first to a 300-seat theatre and then to our current venue seating just under 500 people. As I write this, we are in the midst of the COVID-19 pandemic and all live performances in NYC have been suspended, including our planned April 2020 SOUND BITES 7.0. Of course, this has been a huge disappointment for us, our writing teams, the festival cast and crew, and our loyal audience members. We have rescheduled SOUND BITES for the spring of 2021, when we expect to be at Merkin Hall at the Kaufman Music Center in the Lincoln Center area. We are in the early planning stages of moving again to an even larger venue, likely by 2022, exposing even more audiences to emerging writers and the unique ingenuity of the 10-minute musical.

The 10-minute musical compels writers to create a full story arc with a clear beginning, middle, and end in its most concise form, while developing skills directly applicable to writing a full-length piece. The SOUND BITES festival itself gives a larger number of writers the opportunity to engage in the full production process: working with a director, casting the show, and running rehearsals and tech, culminating with the full performance on stage. Theatre Now works with the writers though the entire process, offering access to accomplished artists, quality rehearsal spaces, and a professional venue. In return, we gain the rare opportunity to support and mentor multiple writing teams while building meaningful, long-term, professional relationships.

And yet, the value in the short musical goes beyond honing the talents of the musical theatre writers involved. It also has the same developmental impact on directors, designers, performers, and all theatre artists. Past SOUND BITES selections have gone on to be part of New York Musical Festival Next Link Project, City Theatre's Short Play Festival in Miami, Florida, and The Samuel French Off Off Broadway Short Play Festival. Indeed, following the success of SOUND BITES, several educational institutions contacted us to request the use of short musicals as training tools in the academic setting. After fielding additional inquiries from other theatres, Theatre Now decided to publish this anthology to introduce our writers' musicals to even more audiences, classrooms, and theatres. We also expanded our support for writers to include the licensing of performance rights, a natural progression of the services we provide our artists. Which brings us full circle to Theatre Now's founding mission of supporting the next generation of musical theatre writers.

This anthology represents some of the best of SOUND BITES, chosen from our first six years of producing ten 10-minute musicals in one sitting. In the festival the musicals are relegated to a strict 10-minute format and most of the twenty-five musicals represented here are exactly 10 minutes in length. We have, however, included all the musicals here as they were originally submitted and a few did run a bit longer before cuts were made in rehearsal for the festival.

Whatever your interest in the short musical, whether as a writer, actor, educator, producer, or theatre enthusiast, we hope that you enjoy the talent, creativity, diversity, and energy of musical theatre represented in these selections.

All the best,

Thomas Morrissey
Theatre Now New York
Founding Producing Artistic Director

ABOUT THEATRE NOW NEW YORK

Theatre Now New York is an artist service organization dedicated to the development, production, publication, and circulation of new short and long-form musicals by providing ongoing support to emerging writers and their work. Theatre Now bridges the gap between early readings and fully-produced theatrical runs by offering developmental productions to pieces that are ready to live on their feet. We nurture diverse storytellers and innovative forms that showcase untold stories and push the boundaries of musical theatre.

Theatre Now's flagship event, SOUND BITES is an annual festival of 10-minute musicals performed before a live audience. Since its inception, SOUND BITES has produced musicals by over 60 new musical theatre writers, utilizing the talents of over 700 performers, musicians, directors, choreographers, interns, and volunteers.

Theatre Now's development programs for writers include our Musical Writing Lab, now entering its second year. Select musical theatre writing teams experience weekly writing sessions, early table reads of new work, readings and cabarets before invited audiences, and staged industry readings in preparation for major production. Our Musical Writing Lab teams may also submit full-length musicals for developmental workshops produced and presented by Theatre Now in an off-Broadway theatre over a two- to four-week run.

Theatre Now furthers the visibility of our alumni writers with opportunities for networking, publication, and future production. In addition, Theatre Now acts as theatrical licensor for musical properties we have produced, offering musicals for production in schools, colleges, community theatres, other professional theatre companies, and venues across the country. By providing long-term support for rising artists and original forms, we entice unexpected audiences to experience the emerging voices of musical theatre.

For more information about Theatre Now and our upcoming shows and programs, visit our website at www.tnny.org.

The company of Theatre Now's SOUND BITES 5.0 at The Irene Diamond Stage at The Pershing Square Signature Center in 2018.

The company of Theatre Now's SOUND BITES 6.0 at Merkin Hall at Kaufman Music Center in 2019.

ACKNOWLEDGMENTS

Theatre is a collaborative endeavor and an extremely intensive labor of love involving many people. This anthology would not be possible without all of those who have been involved with Theatre Now and SOUND BITES throughout the years.

Firstly, thank you to our incredibly talented musical writing teams. Thank you for trusting Theatre Now with your musicals and your artistic growth. Thank you for your inestimable creativity and innovation. Thank you for showing up for each other throughout the development and production process. We are so happy to be a supportive part of your musical theatre journey and cannot wait to see what the future holds for you and your works.

A resounding thank you to the more than 700 writers, directors, designers, choreographers, performers, technicians, producers, administrators, and volunteers who have made SOUND BITES a successful and exhilarating event since 2013. There is no way we could bring SOUND BITES to life year after year without your energy, artistry, and contribution to musical theatre.

Thank you to our faithful donors and members, enthusiastic audiences, gracious industry judges, and the entire Theatre Now family. We are deeply honored by your continued generosity, encouragement, and support of Theatre Now, our writers and programs, and the world of musical theatre.

As a 501(c)(3) non-profit organization, our volunteers are the lifeblood of Theatre Now. We are forever appreciative of the contributions all of our current and former volunteers who gave their time and energy as staff, production personnel, and interns, with special thanks to Mary Andrews, Amy Barrick, Rachel Shayna Bass, Nico Baumgartner, Ashley Elizabeth Benson, Emily Briggs, Angelica Cabrera, Ana Canals, Cory Candelet, Charlese Dawson, Lauren Downie, Liz Doyle, Lauren Draper, Erin Edelstein, Jonathan Freeland, Juan Garcia, Chris Giordano, Mia Haiman, Colleen Harris, Frank Hartley, Ellie Kahn, Joe Kenny, Jonas Klabin, Kaisha Huguley, Cory Ingraham, Lauren Jacobs, Amberlee Lynn, Jordan Moreno, Andre Padayhag. Adriana Pannuzzo, Charles Quittner, Kristen Rea, Ashlee Reed, Rebecca Nell Robertson, Alia Shawa, Cindy Shumsey, Paulina Tobar, Michael Tosto, Matt ZanFagna, and Emely Zepeda.

We are so grateful for our wonderful board of directors, who generously lend their professional and personal time and support to help Theatre Now chart the course for the future of musical theatre: Stan Fishman, Eric S. Goldman Esq., Mark Henry, Jonathan B. James, Melissa Kadir, Jonas Klabin, Eric R. Roper, Ken Suh, Radim Teplitskiy, Richard Vos, Peter Weingard, Camele-Ann White, and Marcus Woollen.

To my Theatre Now co-founders; Julie Marino and Stephen Bishop Seely. I am so proud of what we have accomplished together.

A huge thank you for the guidance and support we've received over the years from Music Theatre International (MTI), Disney Theatrical productions, Jeff Lee, Ken Cerniglia, New York City Department of Cultural Affairs, Lower Manhattan Cultural Council, New York State Council on the Arts, Alliance of Resident Theatres/New York (A.R.T./NY), League of Independent Theatres (LIT), and National Alliance for Musical Theatre (NAMT).

THE 10-MINUTE MUSICAL

an Anthology from the
SOUND BITES festival

A MOST AVERAGE MUSICAL

Book & Lyrics by *Jonathan Keebler*
Music by *Bob Kelly*
Based on a screenplay by *Talia Berger*

Sarah Smithton, Natalie Powers, Neda Lahidji, and Cody Boehm in *A Most Average Musical* at Theatre Now's SOUND BITES 4.0.

SYNOPSIS

It's Jenny's first Friday night at college. While she sits in her apartment, her roommates Liz, Gwen, and Melanie prepare for their exciting evenings *"WHAT A NIGHT"*. Jenny's roommates leave for their thrilling nights of romance, adventure, and productivity.

Feeling quite lonely and all set for a dull night in, Jenny's imagination takes over. She envisions her roommates' perfect nights as she sits at home with nothing to do *"EXTRAORDINARY"*. After this pity party, she hears a knock on the door...

Nerdy neighbor Charlie stops by to ask for a toothbrush *"TOOTHBRUSH"*. Jenny's relieved to meet someone in a similar situation, having a pathetic start to the college experience *"PATHETIC"*. Jenny invites Charlie to stay to watch some Netflix, and they choose a mutual favorite title: Undercover Llama.

Suddenly the apartment door blows open as the roommates return from their nights out *"RETURN OF THE ROOMMATES"*. Liz, Gwen, and Melanie each unpack their disappointing and humiliating evenings.

In the end, they learn that sometimes an average night in is just as extraordinary as an exciting night out *"AVERAGE"*, and they all enjoy the satisfying ending of the Netflix hit film: Undercover Llama.

PRODUCTION HISTORY

A Most Average Musical, written by Talia Berger, Jonathan Keebler, and Bob Kelly, was first presented as a reading in February 2015 at NYU Tisch Graduate Musical Theatre Writing Program in the Black Box Theatre. It was directed by Talia Berger, with musical direction by Bob Kelly. The cast was as follows:

JENNY	Kristen Yasenchak
CHARLIE	Sean Doherty
LIZ	Cody Boehm
GWEN	Aliza Berger
MELANIE	Natalie Powers

In 2015 pre-production on a short film version of the show began, with filming taking place in New York City and at State College, Pennsylvania, featuring the same cast from the previous reading. The film was later submitted into film festivals.

A stage adaptation of the show first premiered at The Irene Diamond Stage at The Pershing Square Signature Center for Theatre Now's SOUND BITES 4.0 on May 28, 2017. The production was directed by Talia Berger, and choreographed by Aliza Berger, with musical direction and arrangements by Bob Kelly. It was produced by Thomas Morrissey, Stephen Bishop Seely, and Chris Giordano. The cast was as follows:

JENNY	Sarah Smithton
CHARLIE	Jack Flatley
LIZ	Cody Boehm
GWEN	Neda Lahidji
MELANIE	Natalie Powers

Sarah Smithton was awarded Best Actress for her role as JENNY in that year's festival.

In March 2019, the short film was released online for the general viewing public.

CHARACTERS

JENNY	18. Female identifying. An average girl who wants her life to be extraordinary.
LIZ	18. Female identifying. A want-to-be sorority girl who craves status.
GWEN	18. Female identifying. An ambitious student who wants to land a prized internship.
MELANIE	18. Female identifying. A romantic who wants her tinder date to be perfect.
CHARLIE	18. Male identifying. Jenny's awkward neighbor who desperately needs to find a toothbrush.

SETTING
A college dorm room, present.

MUSICAL NUMBERS

"What A Night"	Liz, Gwen, Melanie
"Extraordinary"	Jenny
"Toothbrush"	Charlie, Jenny
"Pathetic"	Charlie, Jenny
"Return of the Roomates"	Liz, Gwen, Melanie
"Average"	Jenny

AUTHORS' NOTE

A Most Average Musical started as an idea for my senior thesis film. Something that would have a small cast, and a relatively small amount of locations. Something cheap enough for a student film, but just big enough to stand out. This project would not be what it is today without the brilliant music and lyrics by Bob Kelly and Jonathan Keebler.

    I never imagined I'd be able to pull this off, especially on a tight budget. I'll admit, my film teacher was so skeptical she thought I should write a backup script just in case. That's where Bob and Jonathan came in, giving me a crash course in musical theater writing

101. They helped develop the short film into a fully realized musical. I could not have asked for a better writing team, and I consider myself extremely lucky to have been able to continue working with them on A Most Average Musical over the past five years.

We wanted to tell the story of someone feeling lost and insecure, and gaining a sense of self over the course of a night. It was a reflection of what I felt my senior year of college, nervous about starting a new chapter in my life and career. Bob and Jonathan suggested setting the film on the first Friday night of our roommates' freshman year, and the pieces started falling into place from there.

A Most Average Musical is about finding where you belong and learning what makes you happy. I know that working on this musical with Bob and Jonathan has made me extraordinarily happy. They've written music and lyrics I hold so dear to my heart, and I consider it a win that my family and friends still sing the songs.

- *Talia Berger*

From its beginnings as a short film, we adapted *A Most Average Musical* for the stage for SOUND BITES 4.0. It was a wonderful chance to revisit this lovely little story and make it even better the second go around. And since, despite her humility, this piece could not exist without Talia's masterful storytelling, inspiring enthusiasm, and deep trust, it seemed only fitting that she return to direct the stage version. The piece we ended up with is something I will cherish forever, and I'm so happy it gets to receive a further life.

We hope that you will have fun with the show, lean into its silliness, and let its heart shine through. It might be a most average show, but we really do believe average can be extraordinary.

- *Jonathan Keebler*

I still remember my first few days at college—the thrill of newfound freedom, the promise of new friendships, the grand ambitions to make a mark on the world—and also a great fear that maybe none of it would happen. My hope is that *A Most Average Musical*, in all its brevity, encapsulates the giddy whirlwind of emotions that accompany those first extraordinary/pathetic/average days of college.

- *Bob Kelly*

JENNY sits on a couch in her freshman college apartment, a laptop open in front of her. Liz, her roommate, enters, with a look that screams rich sorority girl. She is searching for the contents of her purse.

Song begins - "What A Night"

LIZ:
FIRST FRIDAY NIGHT AT COLLEGE!
I'M OFF TO A KAPPA SOIREE.
MY LOOK WILL BEWITCH!

GWEN enters looking a bit disheveled, carrying a big backpack. She is throwing every book in sight in the backpack.

GWEN:
NO, YOU LOOK LIKE A BITCH.

LIZ:
SO? IF THAT MAKES THEM LIKE ME, OKAY.

GWEN taps her on the head with a book.

GWEN:
FIRST FRIDAY NIGHT AT COLLEGE!
THE LIBRARY, THAT'S WHERE IT'S AT.
THOSE STEADFAST AND STURDY
GET TENURED BY THIRTY!

MELANIE enters, presenting herself to the girls.

MELANIE:
AND END UP ALONE WITH A CAT.
WELL, NOT ME.
CAUSE I'M MEETING A GUY,
SO HOT I COULD DIE.

LIZ: In that dress? That's like twelve fashion sins.

GWEN: I should change.

GWEN immediately starts changing dresses.

LIZ, GWEN, MELANIE:
    GOTTA GET IT RIGHT!

LIZ:
    'CAUSE TONIGHT IS THE NIGHT…

GWEN, MELANIE:
    TONIGHT IS THE NIGHT…

LIZ, GWEN, MELANIE:
    THAT MY WAY ABOVE AVERAGE LIFE BEGINS!
    WHAT A NIGHT!
    IT'S GONNA BE PERFECT.
    WHAT A NIGHT!
    MY LIFE'S TAKING FLIGHT.
    WHAT A SIMPLY UNBEATABLE –
    SO SWEET, IT'S EATABLE –
    HOPE IT'S REPEATABLE NIGHT!

LIZ, GWEN, and MELANIE make their final preparations before leaving.

GWEN:
    MY WORLD-RENOWNED PROFESSOR
    IS IN NEED OF AN INTERN AND QUICK.
    AND I'LL MAKE HER SEE THAT
    HER CHOICE SHOULD BE ME.

MELANIE:
    THAT'S SO NICE,
    NOW CHECK OUT MY GUY'S PIC.
    THAT'S HIM, WE MET ON TINDER.

GWEN:
    HA! A VERY RELIABLE SOURCE.

MELANIE:
>   I'M GETTING AHEAD...
>   BUT WHAT IF WE WED!

LIZ:
>   WELL, THAT'S SURE TO END IN DIVORCE.
>   YOU'RE ALL CRAY!
>   'CAUSE YOU LOOK LIKE A FREAK,
>   UNLESS YOU GO GREEK.

GWEN: Bitchy.

MELANIE: Rude.

LIZ:
>   JENNY, DON'T YOU AGREE?

JENNY: Leave me out.

LIZ, GWEN, MELANIE:
>   WELL, YOU ALL CAN HATE,

GWEN:
>   BUT IT'S GONNA BE GREAT.

LIZ, GWEN, MELANIE:
>   I AGREE,
>   O.M.G.,
>   I CAN'T WAIT!
>
>   WHAT A NIGHT!
>   IT'S GONNA BE FLAWLESS.
>   WHAT A NIGHT!
>   NO MAYBE OR MIGHT.
>   WHAT A SO-UNFORGETTABLE,
>   BEST-EVENING-YET-ABLE,
>   NEVER REGRETTABLE NIGHT!

LIZ: Hey Jenny, would you please zip me?

GWEN: So, Jenny, what are *you* up to?

MELANIE:
    WELL, DUH, SHE HAS PLANS, RIGHT?

LIZ, GWEN, MELANIE:
    TONIGHT, WHO'D STAY AT HOME?

LIZ checks the time on her phone.

LIZ:
    GOTTA GO NOW!

MELANIE:
    I WISH I COULD HEAR THEM.

GWEN:
    I HOPE YOU HAVE FUN.

LIZ:
    BUT NOW I GOTTA RUN—

GWEN & MELANIE:
    NOW I GOTTA RUN—

LIZ, GWEN, MELANIE:
    TO A NIGHT THAT'S SECOND-TO-NONE!

LIZ:
    WHAT A NIGHT!

LIZ, GWEN, MELANIE:
    WHAT A NIGHT!
    IS COLLEGE NOT EPIC?
    WHAT A NIGHT!
    AND MORE ARE IN SIGHT!

LIZ:
    YOU'LL SEE MY NIGHT IS GREATER, JEN.

GWEN & MELANIE:
  TRY NOT TO HATE HER, JEN.

LIZ:
  BYE, SEE YOU LATER, JEN –

GWEN & MELANIE:
  BYE, SEE YOU LATER, JEN –

LIZ, GWEN, MELANIE:
  GOODNIGHT!

LIZ, GWEN, and MELANIE exit. There's silence. JENNY stares at the door, then her computer, then the door. She tries to type something, but gives up and exhales with frustration, falling back on the couch. She picks up a piece of clothing Liz discarded while getting ready. She holds it up to herself.

Song begins - "Extraordinary"

Acting out the scene she describes

JENNY:
  BET LIZ JUST GOT TO HER PARTY.
  SHE FLIPS HER HAIR AND SHE'S SEEN.
  EACH GIRL WHO'S THERE RUNS UP TO HER, LOVES HER,
  THEY LOOK LIKE THEY'VE CROWNED HER QUEEN.

Suddenly, a fantasy version of LIZ enters and crosses in front of JENNY, taking over acting out what JENNY describes.

  THEY EYE THE BOYS IN THE CORNER.
  THEN DOWN A QUICK VODKA LIME.
  THEY START TO DANCE TO THE HIT SONG PLAYING,
  AND GOD IT'S A PERFECT TIME!

JENNY dances with fantasy LIZ.

  DANCE, DRINK, TALK A LITTLE,

THEN REPEAT IT.
SHE'S MAKING DOZENS OF FRIENDS.
SOON, THEY'RE SISTERS AND HER
LIFE IS SWEET AND IT'S EXTRAORDINARY.
YEAH, IT'S EXTRAORDINARY.

JENNY turns around and sees fantasy GWEN entering and taking a seat in the library. LIZ freezes in mid-dance, while GWEN acts out JENNY's imaginings. JENNY tries to join her, but GWEN doesn't want her, she's just being distracting.

AND GWEN IS PREPPING TO STUDY.
SHE'S BOUGHT A LATTE ONE SHOT.
SHE'S PICKED HER SPOT AT THE PERFECT TABLE.
SHE STARTS AT EIGHT ON THE DOT.
SHE QUICKLY LAYS OUT A GAME PLAN.
THEN BROWSES BOOKS LIKE THE PROS.
AN HOUR IN AND A GREAT THOUGHT HITS HER,
IT'S SOMETHING THAT NO ONE KNOWS.

PLAN, READ, WRITE A LITTLE,
WOW, IT'S THRILLING,
SHE'S OFF AND CHANGING THE WORLD.
SOON, HER LIFE WILL BE SO
DAMN FULFILLING IT'S EXTRAORDINARY.
YEAH, IT'S EXTRAORDINARY.

GWEN freezes, the picture-perfect image of a confident scholar.

OH!
WASN'T THAT SUPPOSED TO BE ME?
WASN'T I THE ONE
WHO DREAMED IN HER BACKYARD
THAT SHE'D GET TO COLLEGE
AND FIND OUT EXACTLY
WHO SHE'S SUPPOSED TO BE?

Fantasy MELANIE enters, acting out Jenny's imagination. JENNY can't even bring herself to look.

JENNY:
>   AND I BET MEL'S ON HER DATE NOW,
>   AND CHAD'S A DREAMBOAT, I'M SURE.
>   AND ALL THE QUESTIONS SHE HAS INSIDE HER,
>   THAT NIGHT IS THE PERFECT CURE.
>   THEY EAT SOME CHOW FROM A FOOD TRUCK.
>   EACH LOOK HE GIVES HER IS BLISS.
>   THE DATE GOES ON AND THEY'RE WALKING, TALKING,
>   'TIL HE LEANS IN FOR ONE GREAT KISS!

>   *MELANIE freezes in a leg-popped kiss pose.*

JENNY:
>   LAUGH, BRAG, KISS A LITTLE
>   CHANGE SPECIFICS,
>   THE THING YOU GET IS THE SAME.
>   LIZ, GWEN, MELANIE, THEIR LIFE'S TERRIFIC,
>   IT'S EXTRAORDINARY.

>   *LIZ, GWEN, MELANIE come alive, shoving their happiness in JENNY's face.*

LIZ, GWEN, MELANIE:
>   EXTRAORDINARY!

JENNY:
>   AND THEN THERE'S JENNY.
>   DREAM, WAIT, BITCH A LITTLE,
>   HOPE LIFE MIGHT BE
>   A LITTLE BETTER REAL SOON.
>   I'M BEGGING, SHOUTING FOR A TIME MY NIGHT CAN BE
>   EXTRAORDINARY.

LIZ, GWEN, MELANIE:
>   EXTRAORDINARY.

JENNY:
>   I WANT EXTRAORDINARY.

LIZ, GWEN, MELANIE:
> EXTRAORDINARY.

LIZ, GWEN, and MELANIE slowly exit...

JENNY:
> GIVE ME EXTRAORDINARY!

We hear a knock at the door! JENNY answers it. CHARLIE, awkward as hell, is standing before her.

Music begins - "Toothbrush/Pathetic"

CHARLIE:
> CAN I BORROW A TOOTHBRUSH?
> I LEFT MINE BACK AT HOME.

JENNY: We've been here a week.

CHARLIE:
> I PACKED FORTY-TWO T-SHIRTS,
> TWO BOXES OF MANGA,
> AND A TWENTY INCH GARDENING GNOME.

His name's Harry.

JENNY: Is that relevant?

CHARLIE:
> BUT I LEFT OUT THE TOOTHBRUSH—

JENNY: Gross.

CHARLIE:
> AND MY ROOMMATE IS GRIM.
> HE STAYS LOCKED IN HIS BEDROOM—
> I THINK I SAW HANDCUFFS—
> I CAN'T REALLY GET ONE FROM HIM.

JENNY: Look, I'll see what we have.

CHARLIE: I'm Charlie, by the way.

JENNY: Jenny.

CHARLIE:
    I SHOULD GO TO THE STORE,
    BUT I'D PROB'LY GET LOST,
    OR GET MUGGED,
    OR I'D TRIP AND FALL DOWN.
    IF IT'S NOT CLEAR TO YOU,
    WELL IT'S SURE CLEAR TO ME
    THAT I SHOULDN'T HAVE LEFT MY HOME TOWN.

    'CAUSE THEN I'D HAVE A TOOTHBRUSH,
    'STEAD I'M HERE AT YOUR DOOR.
    I TRIED ALL OF THE OTHERS,
    BUT THEY'RE OFF HAVING GOOD TIMES,
    NOT LIKE YOU, NOT LIKE ME, SUCH A BORE.

JENNY: I'm not a bore.

CHARLIE:
    ONCE YOU GIVE ME A TOOTHBRUSH,
    MAYBE WE BOTH COULD CHILL.
    SINCE WE'RE BOTH KINDA LOSERS.

JENNY:
    HEY, I'M NOT A LOSER!

CHARLIE:
    OKAY, JUST ME'S A LOSER, BUT STILL…

JENNY: Look, here's the toothbrush. The thing is—and you seem nice, but I don't think we—

CHARLIE: Okay, say no more.

I'VE NEVER HAD A B.F.F.
SO I GET IT.
OR STAYED UP PAST, LIKE, ONE A.M.,
SO I GET IT.
MY CLOTHING'S EITHER BEIGE OR GRAY,
I HAVE TO CARRY NASAL SPRAY,
JUST SAY IT, THAT YOU DON'T DIG THE WAY THAT I'M
PATHETIC.
PATHETIC.
AN AWFULLY SORRY SIGHT.
PATHETIC.
PATHETIC.
PATHETIC, AM I RIGHT?

JENNY:
I'M HERE ALONE ON FRIDAY NIGHT,
SO I GET IT.
I'M JEALOUS OF MY ROOMMATES' LIVES,
SO I GET IT.
I DREAM A LOT, THEN SIT AND WAIT,
I BITCH HOW MY LIFE'S LESS THAN GREAT,
I HATE TO ADMIT IT, BUT FACT OF THE MATTER'S I'M
PATHETIC.

CHARLIE:
PATHETIC?

JENNY:
PATHETIC.

CHARLIE:
PATHETIC?

JENNY:
PATHETIC, JUST LIKE YOU.

CHARLIE:
PATHETIC.

JENNY:
    PATHETIC!

CHARLIE:
    PATHETIC.

JENNY:
    PATHETIC!

JENNY, CHARLIE:
    PATHETIC'S ALL I DO.

CHARLIE:
    OTHER PEOPLE HAVE THINGS FIGURED OUT,
    THEIR LIFE'S A JUBILEE.

JENNY:
    THEY KNOW AND THEY GET ALL THE THINGS THEY WANT.
    THERE'S THEM AND THEN THERE'S ME.

JENNY, CHARLIE
    I'M LOST. I'M SCARED.
    MY HEAD'S A MESS.
    I DON'T KNOW WHAT TO DO.
    SOMETIMES IT FEELS
    LIKE NO ONE OUT THERE
    FEELS THE SAME WAY TOO.

JENNY:
    I DON'T KNOW WHAT I REALLY WANT,
    SO I GET IT.

CHARLIE:
    I ALWAYS FEEL LIKE I'M ALONE,
    SO I GET IT.

JENNY:
    IF I WAS HERE ALONE I'D GO
    SIT DOWN, TURN ON SOME NETFLIX—

CHARLIE:
>SO?
>SOUNDS GOOD TO ME.

JENNY:
>BUT THAT WOULD SHOW THAT WE'RE PATHETIC?

JENNY:
>PATHETIC.

CHARLIE:
>PATHETIC!

JENNY:
>PATHETIC!

JENNY & CHARLIE:
>IT'S LOCKED IN OUR DESIGN!

CHARLIE:
>PATHETIC!

JENNY:
>PATHETIC!

CHARLIE:
>PATHETIC!

JENNY:
>PATHETIC!

CHARLIE: So, how 'bout that movie?

JENNY: Fine.

>*They collapse on the couch and Jenny hits a button on the remote. The lights dim and they freeze.*

VOICE FROM THE MOVIE (*voiceover*): So you were the llama this whole time?

ANOTHER VOICE (*voiceover*): Sí, señora, sí!

We hear credits music for the movie as lights go up.

CHARLIE: So good! Umm... bathroom?

JENNY pauses the movie and points him in the right direction and he exits. Just then, the door swings open and LIZ, GWEN, and MELANIE slump in.

Song begins - "Return of the Roommates"

LIZ, GWEN, MELANIE:
    FIRST FRIDAY NIGHT AT COLLEGE.

JENNY:
    HEY GUYS, HOW'D IT GO?

LIZ, GWEN, MELANIE:
    TAKE A GUESS!

MELANIE:
    I NEED CARBS!

GWEN:
    COMFY SOCKS!

LIZ:
    GIVE ME GIN ON THE ROCKS!

LIZ, GWEN, MELANIE:
    I'LL RECAP THE WHOLE AWFUL MESS.

LIZ:
    SO, THERE I AM AT THIS PARTY.

GWEN:
    I'M SITTING TRYING TO FOCUS.

LIZ:
    I FLIP MY HAIR, PEOPLE STARE.

MELANIE:
    I'M AT MY DATE. CHAD IS LATE.

GWEN:
    SOME GIRL NEARBY HAS A NERVOUS BREAKDOWN.

LIZ:
    THEY WONDER WHY I AM THERE.

MELANIE:
    HE'S TEXTING, WHICH ISN'T GREAT.

GWEN:
    CELL PHONES RINGING, PEOPLE SNEEZING

LIZ:
    SO, I RETREAT TO A CORNER.

MELANIE:
    WE EAT SOME SLOP FROM A FOOD TRUCK.

LIZ:
    I DOWN A QUICK VODKA LIME.

MELANIE:
    HE WOLFS IT DOWN LIKE HE'S HIGH.
    AND WHILE WE'RE WALKING, I GLANCE HIS PHONE,
    AND HE'S TINDERING WITH A GUY!!!
    WHAT A NIGHT!

LIZ, GWEN, MELANIE:
    WHAT A NIGHT!
    A TOTAL DISASTER!
    WHAT A NIGHT!
    IT'S GOT ME UPTIGHT!
    WHAT AN AWFUL, CALAMITOUS,

WORLD SHOUTING DAMN AT US,
DOORS START TO SLAM AT US
TOTALLY, UTTERLY, TERRIBLE, HIDEOUS NIGHT!

The sound of a toilet flushing. CHARLIE returns from the bathroom, singing the credits song of the movie.

CHARLIE: ¿Como se llama, mr. undercover lama?...

JENNY: Roommates, Charlie. Charlie, roommates.

CHARLIE: Hi-dee-ho. How were your nights?

GWEN, LIZ, and MELAINE all give a collective groan.

CHARLIE: Yeah, ours was pretty average too. You guys like undercover llama? It's my fav!

The roommates nod. CHARLIE fires up the movie. JENNY reflects to herself.

Song begins - "Average"

JENNY:
AVERAGE.
GUESS THAT'S WHAT YOU CALL IT.
AVERAGE.
JUST STEP BACK, THAT'S ALL IT
WAS, WASN'T IT?
BUT DOESN'T IT
FEEL LIKE SOMETHING MORE...

THAN AVERAGE?
THAT FEELS LESS THAN FITTING.
AVERAGE?
LOOK AT US ALL SITTING
HERE, WHAT A SIGHT,
WOW, WHAT A NIGHT,
I HOPE THERE'S MORE IN STORE.

THOUGH IT WASN'T THE START OF A GREAT CAREER,
OR A DATE WITH THE LOVE OF OUR DREAMS,
IT WASN'T A GAGGLE OF FRIENDS, THAT'S CLEAR,
BUT IT'S SOMETHING WAY MORE THAN IT SEEMS.
IT'S YOUR COMFIEST SHEETS,
IT'S YOUR CHILDHOOD HOME,
IT'S THE PARK THAT YOU PASS EVERY DAY.
IT'S YOUR FAVORITE PENS,
IT'S A SMALL GROUP OF FRIENDS,
IT'S THE THINGS THAT WE ALL TEND TO SAY ARE

AVERAGE.
PRETTY GREAT AND YET THEY'RE,
AVERAGE.
TO THINK I DIDN'T GET THEIR
WORTH. MAKES ME LAUGH,
'CAUSE SEEMS THAT AFTER
ALL THAT WE'VE BEEN THROUGH,
I SEE THAT SOMETHING'S TRUE:
SOMETIMES AVERAGE IS EXTRAORDINARY TOO.
YEAH, SOMETIMES AVERAGE IS EXTRAORDINARY TOO.

JENNY joins her new friends and they laugh as the lights fade.

END

A RELATIVE RELATIONSHIP

Book, Music, & Lyrics by *Timothy Huang*

Jennifer Blood, Madeline Doherty, and Hansel Tan in A Relative Relationship at Theatre Now's SOUND BITES festival, 2013.

SYNOPSIS

Emerson Junior High Vice Principal's Office. 2:30pm, Thursday. Simon Pang and Carmen Soledad, both aged 15, are in big trouble. It would appear they have been caught cheating on their Bible, Myth and Epic class final. "MY MOM IS GONNA KILL ME" To make matters worse, the sociopathic, villainous, Vice Principal Delancy is on her way to greet them at any moment to mete out their punishment. When their parents find out, in particular, Simon's mom and Carmen's dad, heads will roll.

Vice Principal Delancy, though savage, is not without a sense of compassion. Wait did I say compassion? I meant humor. Not without a sense of humor. As luck would have it, Carmen's father is recently wed to Simon's mother, making her two victims step-siblings. Each with an axe to grind with the other. She offers a simple suggestion: Instead of both of them getting in trouble for cheating, instead of breaking both their parents hearts, only one will be suspended. And only one parent will be devastated. She writes both names on a dry-erase-board. (You're your name is on there, it's on there forever unless she erases it.) She leaves them to decide which it shall be.

Carmen, who is far less studious and organized (and frankly less civil) attempts to convince Simon that it should be he who falls on the sword, given his perfect record. "IT SHOULD BE YOU/I'VE DESPISED YOU FOR SO LONG" In fact, says she, he is so well liked at this school he could probably pull a fire alarm and not get a detention. Simon, on the other hand, maintains that it should be Carmen to fall on the sword because, well, she tried to cheat off him. He's only really guilty by association. An argument ensues. Unrelenting Simon torments his step-sister by calling her a bald-faced cheater, and Carmen, getting more and more irked, accuses Simon of orchestrating their parents' marriage. Had he not done that, it would just be her and her dad, and she wouldn't have to deal with stupid Simon. Simon, on the other hand, doesn't even attempt to deflect. Yes, it was his plan to get their parents to meet and to date. But, he is quick to point out, he wasn't the reason Carmen's mother walked away.

This is a bridge too far. Carmen is hurt deeply by that comment. In fact, she confesses, she feels the guilt of her abandonment every day. "IT HAPPENS EVERY DAY" Every day, in some form or other, she is reminded that she's the reason her parents split up, and she is the reason for her own unhappiness. Simon too, confesses that he feels enormous guilt for the absence of his father. And that the only way he survives is to pretend to be a grown up. They realize they have more in common than they knew. Suddenly Simon has an epiphany. He pulls the fire alarm, causing the sprinklers to go off, washing the entire dry erase board clean and drenching Vice Principal Delancy's office. "RAIN" There may be hell to pay for it tomorrow, but for now, he and his sister will wash their guilt clean.

A Relative Relationship, copyright 2010 by Timothy Huang

PRODUCTION HISTORY

A Relative Relationship, written by Timothy Huang, was originally presented as a reading for the BMI Lehman Engel first year Musical Theater Lab in the Spring of 2010 at Shelter Studios. It was directed by Timothy Huang, with musical direction by Michael Hicks. The cast was as follows:

SIMON_____Timothy Huang
CARMEN_____Jennifer Blood
VICE PRINCIPAL DELANCEY_____Beverly Ward

The following November it was presented at Don't Tell Mama, as part of the *Are You Working On Something New* series produced by Will TN Hall and Emmy Laybourne. It was directed by Rob Baron, with musical direction by Mark T Evans. The cast was as follows:

SIMON_____Timothy Huang
CARMEN_____Jennifer Blood
VICE PRINCIPAL DELANCEY_____Lucy Avery Brooke

In November 2013, it was produced by Timothy Huang and Laura Brandel for Theatre Now's first annual SOUND BITES festival at the 47th Street Theater. It was directed by Laura E Brandel, with musical direction by Mark T Evans. It was produced by Thomas Morrissey and Stephen Bishop Seely. The cast was as follows:

SIMON_____Hansel Tan
CARMEN_____Jennifer Blood
VICE PRINCIPAL DELANCEY_____Madeline Doherty

The 10-Minute Musical: an anthology from the SOUND BITES festival

In December 2013, it was included in the BMI edition of *NYTB in the D-Lounge*, produced and curated by Pat Cook and Rick Freyer of BMI, and Joe Barros and Laura Brandel of New York Theatre Barn. It was directed by Laura E Brandel, with musical direction by Will Shuler. The cast was as follows:

SIMON..Hansel Tan
CARMEN..Jennifer Blood
VICE PRINCIPAL DELANCEY_____Sara Wordsworth

CHARACTERS

CARMEN SOLEDAD[1]	15 years old. 9th grade. Girl. Of Ecuadorian ancestry. Third or fourth generation. i.e., American. A princess to her father, to everyone else, something decidedly less.
SIMON PANG[2]	15 years old. 9th grade. Boy. Korean American. 2nd Generation. Not a band geek, but not really cool either. Likes rules. Studious.
VICE PRINCIPAL DELANCY	Somewhere between Sue Sylvester and Dr. Perry Cox, Professor Moriarty and Wyle E. Coyote. She is the marriage of insensitivity with bitterness, dispassion and sadism all wrapped in a warm, fuzzy poncho of shut the hell up.

Note: While these roles were originally intended to be played by adults, they could be played by actors 15 years and older.

SETTING
Emerson Junior High Vice Principal's Office. 2:30pm, Thursday.

---

[1] From the Spanish, meaning "solitude" or "loneliness", also derived from the Bizet opera, about a chick with a bad, bad temper.
[2] Derived from the english: *anguish, regret* or *heartbreak*. Derived from the Korean: *pəng* meaning *long, large, big, vast* etc.

MUSICAL NUMBERS

"My Mom is Gonna Kill Me" — Simon, Carmen
"It Should Be You/I've Hated You For So Long" — Simon, Carmen
"It Happens Every Day" — Simon, Carmen
"Rain" — Instrumental

AUTHOR'S NOTE

A Relative Relationship was conceived out of a desire to do more work with Jennifer Blood. (*Gentleman's Guide, Violet, Matilda*.) I was finishing my first year of the Lehman Engel workshop, which culminated in a ten-minute musical, and had collaborated with Jen earlier in the year on a short musical for Prospect Theatre called *Crossing Over* where we very quickly became artistic soul mates. So I took her to Kodama and over sushi asked if I could write something new for her and me to do together. As proof of concept I sent her a short story I wrote about two kids in their early teens at summer camp, ditching a group activity. "This isn't what I'm going to write," I said "but it's sort of what I was thinking." Basically, grown-ups pretending to be children, was the aesthetic: The world starting or ending because of a small act, except the audience has the objectivity to recognize its absurdity while it's happening. All of which to say, you may have the urge to cast actual middle schoolers. I... I can't recommend that. I mean, you do you. I believe in you. But personally, as an audience member, I only feel I have permission to laugh at the emotional abuse these two students endure because part of me knows they're not actually children. That's me. Maybe that's not you. But let's be clear- what they are subjected to? That's absolutely emotional abuse. So tread with kindness.

To that end, some of the lyrics in this edition have been altered for the benefit of younger audiences. Basically, I took out a lot of swear words. Like, a lot. The original version exists on the cast album though, so be careful who you share that with. Feel welcome to use either version. What you should not feel welcome to do though, is cast this non-traditionally. Simon and Carmen are Asian and Latinx respectively. They *don't* need to justify their ethnicity in the story. They *do* need to be represented by performers of color.

I once taught a class called "Writing the Ten Minute Musical" wherein my first statement walking in was "Introduce unmovable object to unstoppable force in real time, and you'll always have a successful ten-minute musical." This is obviously not the only way to write in the short-form, but for me it's the most satisfying. The stakes keep amping up until one of them goes too far. When Simon off-handedly says Carmen was the reason her mom left her dad- that's enormous. It is by contrast to all the slapstick of Vice Principal Delancy, an even more nefarious and vile form of emotional abuse. It is, in this context, *the* cardinal sin. I hope you'll afford it that weight and consideration. Small acts. Big ideas. That's what makes a satisfying piece of theater for me.

Thanks,

– Timothy Huang

A Relative Relationship

Emerson Junior High Vice Principal's Office. 2:30pm, Thursday. Office contains a desk, three chairs, a dry erase board on the wall, a clock, fire alarm, windows etc. It could be any office in any school on the eastern seaboard. Seated directly underneath the dry erase board are CARMEN SOLEDAD, aged 15 and SIMON PANG, also 15. On the board behind them in all caps and double underlined is written <u>FUTURE DRAINS ON SOCIETY</u>. CARMEN makes no eye contact, does not stir. SIMON stares at the clock above HIM, stares at the door. Stares at HIS wrist watch, stares at the door.

    Song Begins - "My Mom is Gonna Kill Me"

SIMON:
    CAN SOMEONE PLEASE EXPLAIN
    MY RELATIVE RELATIONSHIP TO TIME?
    LIKE HOW IN CLASS WHEN I LOOK UP TO
    WATCH THE CLOCK
    HOW THE HANDS NEVER MOVE,
    THE HOURS NEVER CHIME?
    BUT WHEN I'M SITTING IN THE OFFICE OF
    VICE PRINCIPAL DELANCY
    I'M SWEATY AND I'M NERVOUS
    I'M FIDGETY, I'M ANTSY.
    THE SECONDS JUST KEEP COMING
    LIKE FORESHADOWING THE KNELL
    THE CLOCK WON'T CEASE IT'S HUMMING
    AS I'M WAITING FOR THAT BELL
    AT THREE O'CLOCK IT'S OVER
    'CAUSE THIS WON'T GO OVER WELL…

    'CAUSE MAN, MY MOM IS GONNA KILL ME.
    SHE CAN. SHE GREW UP NEAR THE DMZ.
    SHE'LL PLAN. THE QUESTION IS "HOW WILL SHE?"
    WILL IT BE THE BAMBOO ROD?
    WILL IT BE THE FIRING SQUAD?
    WILL I HAVE TO EAT HER CODFISH STEW?
    OH MAN. WHAT AM I GONNA DO?

    CARMEN interrupts.

CARMEN: Oh. My. God. Could you be any more drama? Your mom is not gonna kill you.

SIMON: Said the girl who doesn't know my mom at all.

CARMEN: Very nice. Like it's not your own fault we're in this mess to begin with.

SIMON: My fault? My fault?

CARMEN:
> SO NOW SHOULD I EXPLAIN
> MY RELATIVE RELATIONSHIP TO NERDS?

SIMON: That doesn't even mean anything.

CARMEN: Worked for you, pocket protector.

> IT'S PRETTY SIMPLE.
> I'M MORE POPULAR IN SCHOOL,
> NEED AN ANSWER OFF YOUR TEST.
> AND YOU GIVE IT. NOT MINCE WORDS.

SIMON: Who minced wor—

CARMEN:
> OR ELSE WE'RE SITTING IN THE OFFICE OF
> VICE PRINCIPAL DELANCY
> I'LL PROB'LY GET SUSPENDED
> 'CAUSE YOU ARE SUCH A NANCY.
> I'M TRYING NOT TO PANIC
> BUT YOU SPAZ AND THEN YOU YELL
> MY COMPOSURE'S INORGANIC.
> AND IT'S STARTING TO REBEL.
> I SHOULDA BIT YOUR HAND OFF
> WHEN YOU RAISED IT UP TO TELL MISS FORBES.

SIMON:
> YOU ALMOST DID. STILL HAVE IMPRESSIONS OF YOUR TEETH.

CARMEN:
CUFF ME! WHEN DAD FINDS
OUT, I'M DONE FOR.
I SEE, MY LIFE FLASH RIGHT
BEFORE MY EYES.
AT THREE,
THERE'S NOWHERE LEFT
TO CALMLY MAKE A RUN FOR

SIMON:
CUFF ME! WHEN MOM FINDS
OUT, I'M DONE FOR.
I SEE, MY LIFE FLASH RIGHT
BEFORE MY EYES
AT THREE,
THERE'S NOWHERE LEFT
TO CALMLY MAKE A RUN FOR

CARMEN:
    NOT A SINGLE PLACE TO HIDE.

SIMON:
    WE'RE LOOKING AT FILICIDE.

BOTH:
    TELL MY FRIENDS GOODBYE AND IT WAS GRAND.

CARMEN:
    MY DAD WILL NEVER UNDERSTAND.

SIMON:
    FORTY DAYS AND FORTY NIGHTS
    OF RESEARCH AND REGURGITATION
    FORTY NIGHTS...

CARMEN:
    FORTY DAYS AND FORTY NIGHTS
    CONCEALING MY TRUE SITUATION

SIMON:
    THIS TEST WAS GONNA BE MY ACE

CARMEN:
    ONE MORE SCHOLASTICAL DISGRACE
    TO BURN, CONCEAL OR SHUN
    TO KEEP THE PARENTS BLITHELY UNAWARE.

BOTH:
    AND NOW I HAVEN'T GOT A PRAYER.

CARMEN:	SIMON:
'CAUSE WOW! MY DAD IS GONNA SLAY ME THEN POW! LIFE AS WE KNEW IT'S GONE FOR GOOD AND NOW MY DEATH'S MORE THAN A MAYBE	'CAUSE WOW! MY MOM IS GONNA SLAY ME THEN POW! LIFE AS WE KNEW IT'S GONE FOR GOOD. AND NOW MY DEATH'S MORE THAN A MAYBE

BOTH:
    WILL IT BE THE GUILLOTINE?
    SOME MEDIEVAL DEATH MACHINE?
    GROUNDED TILL I TURN SIXTEEN OR GRAY?
    THIS HAS BEEN THE CRAPPIEST DAY.

    I HATE YOU!

The song ends. CARMEN and SIMON return to their respective seats. CARMEN, hands folded, doesn't make eye contact. SIMON again, looks at the clock, looks at the door, looks at his watch, looks at the door.

CARMEN: I can't believe you blew the whistle on me over a stupid test.

SIMON: There are no stupid tests, just stupid people.

CARMEN: It's not like any of it matters in the real world anyway. I mean, it's just BMI.

    HE corrects HER.

SIMON: BME, Carmen, BME. *Bible, Myth, and Epic.* You don't even know what classes you're in.

    They speak over each other.

CARMEN:
Whatever. BME. Stupid Noah's flood.

I don't see what difference it makes because I'll probably be suspended now, thanks to you.

SIMON:

It's Noah's *Ark*, the flood was God's idea. You'd know this if you just applied yourself. If you just cared even a little bit, you'd know this—Thanks to me? What the hell are you doing cheating on a test for, while on academic probation?

CARMEN: (*obviously*) Because I'm on academic probation!! I *thought* you might want to help me out.

SIMON: I *was* helping you out.

CARMEN: How? By ratting out your own sister?

SIMON: Oh so now you're my sister? I love how I'm only your brother when it's convenient for you.

CARMEN: *Step* brother... My dad is gonna be so pissed!

SIMON: Your dad?? My mom!!

CARMEN: Oh, like she's gonna even understand the English.

SIMON: Well she didn't have the benefit of taking it two years in a row.

CARMEN: I will kill you right now.

SHE reaches for SIMON'S shirt.

SIMON: Unhand me!

The office door opens. In walks VICE PRINCIPAL DELANCY. The two kids are deathly silent and perfectly still.

VP DELANCY: Visiting my ex-husband in prison. Being told my cancer came back. Taking a second rate job at a third rate school to afford my nephew's cocaine addiction. These are but three of the things I'd rather be doing right now than having this conversation with you two.

SHE walks to the dry erase board, the kids scootch aside. As they do, we see underneath the heading are several names. VP DELANCY takes the dry erase marker, adds two more. She's saying their names as she writes.

VP DELANCY: Soledad, Carmen... Pang, Simon... Now. One of you, I'm surprised to see up there. The other, I'm surprised wasn't already. So here's how this is going to work. At three o'clock, I'm calling your parents. I am either telling them that their honor roll son is a cheater, or their princess daughter is a failure.

CARMEN: Failure?!?

SIMON: Cheater?!?

VP DELANCY: Hey, one of you getting expelled is better than both, right?

CARMEN & SIMON: Expelled?!?

VP DELANCY: The question for you to figure out, is which do your parents want less:

SHE addresses SIMON.

To lose face?

SHE addresses CARMEN.

Or lose innocence?

SIMON: But that isn't fair!	CARMEN: That's not even how it happened!

Ignoring their pleas, she continues.

VP DELANCY: Sure, there's probably a greater lesson to be learned here, about how everything has to cost something. How for every action there is a relative reaction but the lesson *I* want you both to focus on, and pay attention now because you'll hear this again at your first AA meeting: *you have no power over this.*

SIMON: But you don't understand.   CARMEN: You can't do this!

VP DELANCY interrupts their outbursts.

VP DELANCY: NO POWER! Once your name's on the board, your name's on the board. One of you goes, one of you stays. Back in a half hour.

SHE exits. SIMON and CARMEN sit quietly for a moment, waiting for VP DELANCY'S steps to fade away...

Song begins - "It Should Be You/ I've Hated You For So Long"

CARMEN:
    LIKE OH MY GOD, WHAT A WITCH.
    WHERE DOES SHE GET OFF
    MANIPULATING US LIKE WE'RE HER
    LITTLE PUPPET TOYS OR WHATNOT.

SIMON:
    LIKE WHAT WE DID WAS ALL THAT BAD
    BUT THERE SHE GOES AGAIN ALL
    STIPULATING THIS AND THAT AND
    SHE CAN DO WHATEVER BUT NOT REALLY
    THE BOARD OF EDUCATION COULD HAVE HER ASS.
    IDEALLY, EXPLOITING HER HIGH STATION
    IS GROUNDS FOR TERMINATION

CARMEN:
> HER STUPID THREATS CAN'T BEAT US

SIMON:
> SHE HAS NO REAL FOUNDATION.

CARMEN:
> AND THAT'S NO WAY TO TREAT US.

SIMON:
> I THINK IT'S CLEAR THAT

BOTH:
> THERE'S ONLY ONE STEP THAT WE SHOULD TAKE.
> ONLY ONE ANGLE TO PURSUE
> ONLY ONE MOVE THAT WE SHOULD MAKE.
> AND I THINK IT'S LONG OVERDUE.
> ONLY ONE WAY TO MAKE THIS
> SCREWED UP SITUATION UNSCREW.
> WE'RE JUST GONNA HAVE TO TELL HER IT'S YOU.

Simultaneously:

CARMEN:	SIMON:
Wait—what?	Wait—what?
Why should it be me?	Why should it be me?
It should totally be you.	It should totally be you.
Stop doing that!	Stop doing that!
You stop doing that!	You stop doing that!

CARMEN throws HER hands up as if to indicate all parties should stop talking. SIMON agrees. Gestures for CARMEN to go first.

CARMEN:
> SO FIRST OF ALL, YOU'RE A DICK.
> BUT YOU'RE ALSO REALLY
> SMART AND WELL PREPARED.
> GOT YOUR FUTURE PLANS ALL CALCULATED

BUT LET'S BE FAIR. I'M A MESS.
I'M A STRIKE AWAY FROM CARTIN' OFF YOUR LAUNDRY,
WASHING DISHES OR SOME UNRELATED POORNESS

THE POINT IS I CAN'T HACK IT.
I DON'T HAVE YOUR HARDCORENESS
YOUR DISCIPLINE, I LACK IT.
I TALK BUT I CAN'T BACK IT.

YOUR RECORD HERE IS SPOTLESS
NO OTHER CAN ATTACK IT.
IF ONLY I GOT CAUGHT LESS, I TOO WOULD HAVE
THE FREEDOM TO COMMIT WHATEVER
MISCHIEF I ASPIRED TO
YOU COULD PULL A FIRE ALARM AND
WOULDN'T BE REQUIRED TO
DO TIME.
THAT'S WHY I'M SAYING IT SHOULD BE YOU.

SIMON:
GENIUS! GENIUS! GENIUS! GENIUS!
GENIUS! GENIUS! GENIUS!

CARMEN: Nice.

SIMON:
THERE'S ONLY ONE ERROR TO ADDRESS
ONLY ONE TRUTH HERE TO CONSTRUE
ONLY ONE SINNER TO CONFESS
ONLY ONE LIAR, NOT TWO.
ONLY ONE CRIBBING, THIEVING
TEETH-MARK LEAVING, HATER
THROUGH AND THROUGH
AND THAT GUY WOULD BE ME. NO WAIT, IT'S YOU!

CARMEN overpowers SIMON, begins to strangle him.

CARMEN:
I'VE DESPISED YOU FOR SO LONG

>   THIS WHOLE SCENARIO'S SO WRONG.
>   I CAN'T BELIEVE I'M HAVING THIS DISCUSSION WITH YOU.
>   ARE YOU LISTENING??

SIMON escapes her grip, recovers.

CARMEN:	SIMON:
YOU'RE THE REASON THAT WE'RE HERE. I WISH YOU'D DISAPPEAR AND TAKE THIS WHOLE ENTIRE REPERCUSSION WITH YOU.	THERE'S ONLY ONE ERROR TO ADDRESS. ONLY ONE SINNER TO CONFESS THAT SHE'S A LYING CHEATER. AND SHE REALLY LIKES TO BITE.

CARMEN:
> COME ON, PLEASE!

SIMON:
> CHEATER.

CARMEN:
> LOSER

SIMON:
> CHEATER.

CARMEN:
> TOOL.

SIMON:
> CHEATER.

CARMEN
> DOUCHEBAG.

SIMON:	CARMEN:
CHEATER!	I HATE YOU!

SIMON:
>	CHEATER CHEATER
>	DEAD HORSE BEATER!

CARMEN:
>	THERE'S ONLY ONE DAY THAT I REGRET.
>	AND THAT'S THE DAY BOTH OUR PARENTS MET.
>	THERE'S ONLY ONE PERSON WE CAN THANK FOR THAT:
>	IT'S YOU!

SIMON:
>	I MIGHT HAVE BEEN THE REASON WHY
>	THEY GOT TOGETHER. WON'T DENY.
>	BUT I AM NOT THE REASON YOUR MOM WALKED AWAY.

CARMEN is silent. A look of outrage and shock is slowly but surely replaced with a look of sadness and regret. SIMON has crossed a line. And HE knows it.

CARMEN: Don't talk to me.

SHE turns HER back to SIMON, takes HER seat. Does not engage.

SIMON: That... didn't come out right. Look, Carmen, I... I didn't mean... I'm sorry.

CARMEN weeps.

Song begins - "It Happens Every Day"

CARMEN:
>	IT HAPPENS EVERY DAY
>	I MAKE A STUPID CHOICE.
>	I CHOOSE A STUPID PATH.
>	I THINK I HEAR HER VOICE INSIDE ME.
>	SAYING THAT SHE'S GLAD SHE LEFT
>	SAYING SHE IS SO RELIEVED.
>	SAYING HOW SHE COULDN'T EVEN TRY
>	SAYING IT WAS EASY TO SAY BYE.

IT HAPPENS EVERY DAY.
MY DAD SAYS THAT HE KNOWS.
THAT NO ONE IS TO BLAME.
IT'S JUST THE WAY IT GOES SOMETIMES. AND
SAYING IT OUT LOUD WILL HELP ME.
SAYING HOW IT'S NOT MY FAULT.
HEARING IT WILL WASH AWAY THE DOUBT.
BUT ALL I EVER HEARD
WAS "I WANT OUT."

AND THEN I KNOW I HEAR THE RAIN OUTSIDE
COMING DOWN SO CLEAN, SO PURE
BUT IF I GO, I FEAR THIS PAIN WILL NOT ENDURE.
AND THEN SHE'S GONE FOREVER
SO I HIDE. I HIDE HER DEEP INSIDE
BITE DOWN. AND JUST GO NUMB.
BUT OUTSIDE, THE RAIN STILL
CALLS FOR ME TO COME.
AND MAYBE I'M CLICHÉ.
BUT I DON'T SEE ANOTHER WAY.
AND THAT'S WHAT HAPPENS EVERY DAY.

SIMON:
I TRY TO BE MY BEST.
I STRUGGLE TO ACHIEVE.
PASS EVERY SINGLE TEST FOR HER.
SAYING TO MYSELF "BE STEADY
SUCK IT UP AND BE THE MAN.
GROWING UP WAS BOUND TO HAPPEN ANYWAY."
NO ONE TOLD ME IT WOULD HAPPEN EVERY DAY.

They see each other. Finally.

BOTH:
AND THEN I KNOW I HEAR THE RAIN OUTSIDE.
COMING DOWN SO CLEAN SO PURE.
AND ALTHOUGH IT'S CLEAR IT PROMISES A CURE

SIMON:
I'M NOT SURE I DESERVE IT.

BOTH:
SO I STAY. I STAND AND WATCH FROM FAR
AWAY, DESPITE MY THIRST.
UNPREPARED TO BE OUTSIDE AND UNREHEARSED.

CARMEN:
IS THAT THE STATUS QUO?

SIMON:
IS THAT THE ONLY BALANCE?

CARMEN:
THE TRUTH IS, I DON'T KNOW.
I HAVEN'T GOT YOUR TALENTS.

SIMON:
FUNNY, I WAS JUST ABOUT TO SAY...

SIMON has an idea. HE rotates the dry erase board 90 degrees so the list is facing up, sits CARMEN underneath it.

Hold, please.

CARMEN shrugs HER shoulders, as if to say "Mmkay." SIMON crosses to the fire alarm. Pulls it. The alarm is heard offstage, on the other side of the door.

CARMEN: What... the...

SIMON: Wait for it.

SIMON holds up HIS finger, points to the ceiling. The sprinklers go off. Then,

Music begins - "Rain"

It sounds like rain! Out in the hall, VICE PRINCIPAL DELANCY can be heard screaming.

VP DELANCY (*offstage*): OH, MY—

SIMON dances around the room like a doofus. CARMEN comes out from under the board and does the same. Within moments they are soaking wet. And laughing. VP DELANCY enters.

Which one of you refugees did this?

Neither of them says a thing. They look at each other and just start laughing. VP DELANCY, upset, flips the board back down. The names have all been washed away.

My beautiful dry erase board! I swear to God when I find out who did this someone's gonna get punched in the heart. Agnes!!

SHE runs back out.

CARMEN: Our parents are gonna be so pissed!

SIMON: About what? I don't see our names on this board, do you?

THEY jump around and point and laugh at each other as the dry erase board behind them slowly wipes clean, their names are gone. VP DELANCY enters, soaked.

VP DELANCY: Today was my birthday.

Lights slowly fade on a brother and sister who really couldn't care less.

END

ANT AND GRASSHOPPER

Book & Lyrics by *A. J. Freeman*
Music by *Dimitri Landrain*
Based on the Aesop Fable *The Ant and the Grasshopper*

Sam Balzac and A.J. Freeman in *Ant and Grasshopper* at Theatre Now's SOUND BITES 6.0.

SYNOPSIS

We meet hardworking and miserable Ant as she sings about wishing for more fulfillment in her life *"YOU CAN'T WHEN YOU'RE AN ANT"*. Enter Grasshopper: fun-loving, irresponsible, and full of song *"IF YA WANNA"*. Ant reminds Grasshopper that it is important to be responsible and plan ahead because Winter is coming and food will be scarce *"WINTER"* and Grasshopper despairs *"GRASSHOPPER'S LAMENT"*. They realize that their opposite talents balance each other, and Grasshopper shows Ant how to have a good time and use her talents *"TEACHING SEQUENCE"* while Ant teaches Grasshopper how to gather food. Together, they learn the importance of friendship *"FINALE"*!

PRODUCTION HISTORY

Ant and Grasshopper, written by A. J. Freeman and Dimitri Landrain, first premiered during the Theatre Now's SOUND BITES 6.0 Festival on April 2, 2019 at the Merkin Hall at the Kaufman Music Center in New York City. It was directed by A. J. Freeman and choreographed by Kelcey Matheny, with music direction by Dimitri Landrain. It was produced by Chris Giordano, Thomas Morrissey, and Liz Doyle. The cast was as follows:

ANT	A. J. Freeman
GRASSHOPPER	Sam Balzac

CHARACTERS

ANT	Hardworking, serious, miserable. Always puts duty first, but wishes for more.
GRASSHOPPER	Carefree, fun-loving, irresponsible. Cares more about having a good time than planning for the future.

SETTING

A forest. Tomorrow.

MUSICAL NUMBERS

"You Can't When You're An Ant"	Ant
"If Ya Wanna"	Grasshopper
"Winter"	Ant & Grasshopper
"Grasshopper's Lament"	Grasshopper
"Teaching Sequence"	Ant & Grasshopper
"Finale"	Ant & Grasshopper

AUTHORS' NOTE

Ant and Grasshopper, a ten-minute excerpt from the full length show *Fables*, was created to entertain the young and the young at heart, and tell a timeless tale in a fun and sophisticated way. We love both the Ant and the Grasshopper, different as they are, and we believe that the balance between hard work and using your gifts and talents is important for all ages. We hope that this musical will encourage us all to consider friendships with those we see as opposites, and that we will learn to be creatures who fling up our anthems to the sky and sing of the wonders that go by!

- A. J. Freeman & Dimitri Landrain

Song Begins - "You Can't When You're An Ant"

ANT enters and takes a long, weary look at the audience.

ANT: Hello there, little- what are all of you? *(looks closer)* Oh. Fleas. You're fleas. YOU ARE SO LUCKY! You get to jump around all day, hang out with dogs- Do you have any idea how hard it is to be an ant?

ANT is wearily moving large burlap sacks throughout the song.

SOME CREATURES PRANCE THROUGH A
FIELD WHEN THE MOON IS HIGH
AND SOME CREATURES DANCE WHEN IT'S SUNNY
SOME LIKE TO SPIN IN THE SEA WHEN A WAVE GOES BY
AND SOME CREATURES GRIN WHEN LIFE'S FUNNY

SOME CREATURES TASTE EVERY FLOWER THAT THEY SEE
SOUNDS LIKE A WASTE OF A SET OF WINGS TO ME
MAYBE IT'S SWELL TO MAKE HONEY
BUT YOU CAN'T WHEN YOU'RE AN ANT

EVERY DAY I LIFT, DRAG, AND GATHER
REAP, CLIMB A TREE
EVERY DAY'S A GIFT THAT I'D RATHER
KEEP JUST FOR ME

SOME CREATURES WEAVE WEBS LIKE
PAINTINGS THAT HANG IN SPACE
AND SOME CREATURES LEAVE TRAILS THAT GLISTEN
SOME CREATURES GLOW LIKE A STAR THAT IS IN A RACE
AND SOME JUST DON'T KNOW WHAT THEY'RE MISSIN'

SOME CREATURES FLING UP THEIR ANTHEMS TO THE SKY
CAN'T HELP BUT SING OF THE WONDERS THAT GO BY

WHY CAN'T WE ALL STOP AND LISTEN
BUT YOU CAN'T WHEN YOU'RE AN ANT

I CAN'T 'CAUSE I'M AN ANT
I CAN'T...

Song ends and GRASSHOPPER leaps onto the stage.

GRASSHOPPER: Did somebody say, "Partytime?"

ANT: Oh no. Look, Grasshopper: Winter will be here soon and there is SO much work to do!

GRASSHOPPER: Work? Why would you spend your time working when you could be dancing?

Song begins - "If You Wanna."

GRASSHOPPER does a little dance flourish, points to the audience.

See, these fleas know what I mean! Let's get this party started!

GRASSHOPPER sings to the audience, but dances around and distracts ANT while she continues to work.

IF YA WANNA DANCE, THEN DANCE!
YOU CAN THANK ME IN ADVANCE
DON'T BE LIKE THOSE BORING ANTS
NO, TAKE A CHANCE, CHANCE, CHANCE!

IF YA WANNA PLAY, THEN PLAY!
WORKIN' THROWS YOUR LIFE AWAY
HEY, NO MATTER WHAT THEY SAY
WORK DOESN'T PAY, PAY, PAY!

DON'T YA KNOW THAT WHEN YOU'VE
GOT A GIFT, YOU USE IT

SPREAD THAT NIFTY TALENT
FRIENDS, OR YOU'LL LOSE IT- POOF!

IF YA WANNA BRAG, THEN BRAG!
HUMBLENESS CAN BE A DRAG
GET YOURSELF A TAIL TO WAG
AND GRAB THAT SWAG, SWAG, SWAG!

(*to the audience*) Don't be some sad creature who works all day! Spend your time dancing! Eating! Living! Like me!

DON'T YOU KNOW EACH MAMMAL,
BIRD, AND GASTROPOD
ME-OW, MOO, BLAST, AND CHEER
WHEN THEY ALL APPLAUD ME- CLAP!

He shows a few tap dance moves.

NOW YOU KNOW THE WAY TO BE!
GOTTA LIVE A LIFE THAT'S FREE
NOW YOU'LL BE THE COOLEST FLEA
I GUARANTEE, TEE, TEE

YOU WAIT AND SEE, SEE, SEE
JUST BE LIKE ME, ME, ME!

(*to audience member*)
SORRY IF I DIDN'T INTRODUCE MYSELF, SIR
I'M THE BE-BOPPIN', SHOW-STOPPIN' GRASSHOP-PER!

Song ends.

ANT: All right, all right, enough of this, this fun. Winter will—

GRASSHOPPER: Winter...sounds an awful lot like a winner. And I love to win! In Winter, I shall jump higher and dance smoother and—

She interrupts him.

Song Begins - "Winter"

ANT:
    NOT IN WINTER, NOT A CHANCE
    LIFE IS NOT A SONG AND DANCE
    THINGS SEEM EASY IN THE SUN
    GO TO A PLAY
    OR THE BALLET
    MAYBE A DAY BY THE BAY

    WELL, NOT IN WINTER- I SHOULD KNOW
    INSECTS DON'T DO WELL IN SNOW
    PICTURE GLACIERS
    RAINING DOWN

    EACH MIGHTY FLAKE
    MAKES THE GROUND QUAKE
    GRASSHOPPER, WAKE UP
    DON'T MAKE A MISTAKE

    YOU'D BETTER TAKE IN ALL I'VE SAID
    TIME TO START PLANNING AHEAD

    The world will be COVERED in snow. All the green you see around you will be smothered by white. Do you finally get it?

GRASSHOPPER: Of course I do!

    He sings:

    I BLEND WITH THE KINGDOM
    IN THE SPRING
    WHEN THE WHOLE WORLD IS GREEN
    BUT MY FRIEND, IN THE SNOWFALL
    THEN MY GREEN WILL BE STUNNING!

    THEY'LL ALL COME RUNNING HIP-HURRAH!
    EV'RY ANTENNA ON MOI!

ANT:
    NOT IN WINTER. SOON, BEHOLD:

    EV'RY BUG HAS GOT A COLD

    ONE LITTLE SNEEZE
    YOU'RE IN THE TREES
    GRASSHOPPER, PLEASE! NOW WHEN—

GRASSHOPPER:
    WHEN I AM SEEN IN MY SPLENDOR
    EACH PRETENDER
    WILL BE WISHING THAT HE COULD BE
    GREEN AS A LIZARD
    IN A BLIZZARD
    I'M TERRIFIC, MAGNIFICO—

ANT:
    OH, THE WINT-RY
    THINGS I'VE SEEN
    SNOW ON EVERY EVERGREEN—

GRASSHOPPER:
    GREEN AS A GECKO
    I WILL ECHO LIKE A—

ANT:
    LIKE IT OR NOT
    YOU'LL BE DISTRAUGHT

GRASSHOPPER:
    GOT IT!
    YOU'LL FOCUS A SPOTLIGHT ON ME!

    I will use this tree stump as a stage and sing and—

ANT: Grasshopper! You haven't experienced a Winter yet, but I sure have. In Winter, your resources will disappear!

GRASSHOPPER *(gasp)*: You could sing with me!

ANT *(sighs)*:	GRASSHOPPER:
FIGURE OUT A PLAN	PLANNING IS SILLY!

SILLY MAN	AW, MAN WILL HE
WILL HE EVER LEARN	LEARN TO TWIRL AND TO
DON'T SPEAK OUT OF TURN	TURN AND TO DANCE
DANCING TIME WILL STOP	WHEN IT'S REALLY
REALLY HOPE HE'LL DROP IT	DARK AND CHILLY
CHILLINESS WILL FREEZE	IT'S THE PERFECT TIME
THE NIGHT	TO PROVE I'M RIGHT
AND HE WILL FINALLY SEE	
I'M RIGHT—	

ANT:
    WHEN HARVEST TIME IS DONE
    YOU WILL NOT HAVE ANY FOOD

GRASSHOPPER:
    SINGING HERE WITH YOU IS FUN—
    WHAT DID YOU SAY ABOUT FOOD?

ANT:
    I SAID YOU WILL NOT HAVE FOOD

GRASSHOPPER:
    CUT IT OUT, DUDE!

ANT:
    DON'T BE SO RUDE!

GRASSHOPPER:
    YOU SPOILED MY MOOD!

ANT:
    LET ME CONCLUDE:
    FACE IT: YOU WILL NOT HAVE FOOD!

GRASSHOPPER (*shocked*): But I love food... I love to look at it and smell it and talk about it... but mostly, I love to eat it!

ANT brings her point home.

ANT:
> NOT IN WINTER
> WHAT'S YOUR DEAL?
> CREATURES HAVE TO PLAN EACH MEAL!
> LEARN YOUR LESSON
> WHILE IT'S HOT:
> SOON YOU'LL BEGIN
> LOSING THAT GRIN
> THIS SONG MAY BE FIN-ISHED
> BUT WIN-TER'S NOT!

The songs ends and GRASSHOPPER is terrified.

GRASSHOPPER: Noooooooooooo!! What am I going to dooooooo??? Help, help, I feel myself wasting away! The snow is closing in around me. It's cold! Oh, so cold...

Song begins - "Grasshopper's Lament"

> IF I WANNA DINE-
> IF I WANNA CHEW-
> IF I WANNA SNACK-
> WHAT 'M I GONNA DO??
> IF I WANNA EAT—I CAN'T!

(on his knees, begging)

Please! Please let me help you gather food for the Winter! I'll do anything!

ANT: Well, sure. Actually, I was kind of thinking, if we work together, we will get done a lot faster... and then maybe we could do something fun!? Oh, never mind, I am not really good at anything, other than working.

GRASSHOPPER: *OF COURSE YOU ARE!!*

Music begins - "Teaching Sequence"

Every creature on this planet has a talent; we just need to find yours!

He sings:

SOME CREATURES GUARD AND
SOME CREATURES GUIDE AND
SOME GIVE PROFOUND ADVICE

SOME CREATURES TEACH AND
SOME CREATURES TAP AND
SOME CREATURES SEEM KINDA MEAN AT FIRST BUT IT TURNS OUT THEY ARE ACTUALLY NICE...

ANT (*to herself*):
EVERYBODY HAS A TALENT
MAYBE THIS IS MINE
PLEASE SHOW ME A SIGN...

GRASSHOPPER: Let's try juggling!

GRASSHOPPER takes three juggling balls out of his pocket, and goes first. Juggles pretty well. ANT tries: is unsuccessful.

That's ok! Juggling takes a lot of practice. Just keep working on it! Let's try dancing!

We hear "salsa type" music. GRASSHOPPER dances first. Does it pretty well. ANT tries: is unsuccessful.

That's ok, don't get discouraged! Dancing takes a lot of practice, too. Gosh, well... let's try singing!

GRASSHOPPER scats. ANT scats back. She is so good! They scat together!

See! You have been using your talent all along—you are a wonderful singer!

ANT: Gee, you really think so?

GRASSHOPPER: I sure do! All those fleas out there think so too! And fleas have excellent taste. You know what? You're also great at being a friend! When I picture myself wasting away this Winter-

Song begins - "Finale"

ANT: Hey, Grasshopper? You are a really good friend too. Say, let's get to work! For some reason, I'm excited about it now!

They each grab a burlap sack.

GRASSHOPPER:
SOME CREATURES LEARN
THAT THEY'VE GOTTA WORK EACH DAY

ANT:
SOME CREATURES EARN JUST A LITTLE TIME FOR PLAY

BOTH:
NOW WE CAN DO BOTH TOGETHER
I'M SO GLAD THAT YOU'RE/I'M AN ANT

ANT:
IF YA WANNA SING, THEN SING!
SINGING HELPS WITH EVERYTHING

GRASSHOPPER:
WINTER, SUMMER, FALL, AND SPRING

BOTH:
WE'LL ALWAYS SWING, SWING, SWING!

They work hard together while vocally scatting.

CAN YOU FLIP-FLOP WHEN YOU'RE
OPPOSITES AT FIRST? SURE!
LOOK AT BRAND NEW BEST FRIENDS:
ANT AND GRASSHOP-PER!

END

BITTERSWEET LULLABY

Music & Lyrics by *Dylan Glatthorn*
Book by *Will Lacker*

Michelle Dowdy and Jason Veasey in *Bittersweet Lullaby* Theatre Now's SOUND BITES 6.0. *Photo by Eleah Burman*

SYNOPSIS

Moving boxes are scattered around a cramped New York City apartment. A songwriter (Man) sits at a piano desperately, yet fruitlessly, trying to write the opening of a song *"BOUNCY OPENING"*. A second songwriter (Woman) enters talking on a cellphone. While Woman begins to unpack the moving boxes, Man continues experimenting at the piano; neither one sees the other.

Becoming frustrated by his writer's block, Man begins pacing around the room. Woman, intrigued by the piano, sits down and begins experimenting with a few chords. Without realizing it, they serendipitously begin to compose the beginnings of a song.

Suddenly, an argument from the upstairs neighbor interrupts the mysterious moment. Man and Woman both retaliate by making as much noise as they can. The neighbors end their argument and Man and Woman return to composing their song *"The DUET DEVELOPS"*. As the song continues to take shape, they realize something strange is happening: they are not alone. Woman, a new resident of the apartment living in present day, is composing this song with Man, a resident of the apartment living in 1954.

Pushing through their fear and hesitation—still unable to fully grasp what is happening to them—Man and Woman both lose themselves to the moment and sing their newly completed song together *"BITTERSWEET LULLABY"*. Their voices connect through time and for a brief moment, Man and Woman, can see each other.

The song ends and the two songwriters return to their separate timelines. Both writers struggle to understand what just happened but are overcome with excitement from composing a new song. Man grabs his hat and exits out the door while Woman searches for a piece of paper to write the song onto. Her search takes her to the old piano bench where she finds the sheet music for "Bittersweet Lullaby" dated 1954. As she stares in wonderment and bafflement at the sheet music, beginning to take in what's just taken place, her cell phone rings and she answers the call.

PRODUCTION HISTORY
Bittersweet Lullaby, written by Will Lacker and Dylan Glatthorn, premiered at Theatre Now's SOUND BITES 6.0 Festival on April 2, 2019 at the Merkin Hall at the Kaufman Music Center in New York City. It was directed by Will Lacker, with music direction by Dylan Glatthorn. It was produced by Chris Giordano, Thomas Morrissey, and Liz Doyle. The cast was as follows:

MAN	Jason Veasey
WOMAN	Michelle Dowdy

It was awarded for Best Book, Best Director (Will Lacker), Best Actor (Jason Veasey), and Best Actress (Michelle Dowdy).

The following June it was presented at The Players Theatre Short Play Festival in New York City with the same creative team, where it won Best Play. The cast was as follows:

MAN	Paul Scott Pilcz
WOMAN	Michelle Dowdy

CHARACTERS
MAN   Aspiring composer/lyricist living in the 1950's.

WOMAN   Aspiring composer/lyricist living in the present day.

SETTING
A small apartment in New York City. Simultaneously 1954 and present day.

MUSICAL NUMBERS
Bittersweet Lullaby is a musical sequence that also functions as one song. However, music cues can be broken down into the following sections:

"Bouncy Opening"	Man
"Less Bouncy"	Instrumental
"Less Bouncy Continued"	Instrumental

"Woman Plays Chords"	Instrumental
"Woman Continues"	Instrumental
"A Duet Emerges"	Man, Woman
"Woman Plays Bouncy"	Instrumental
"The Duet Develops"	Man, Woman
"Bittersweet Lullaby"	Man, Woman

AUTHORS' NOTE

All attempts should be made to maintain the appearance of a single shared space. While these characters exist in two separate time periods, the audience should discover this over the course of the play. The lines and stage directions are designed to maintain this illusion until the characters begin to bridge the gap between timelines through composing their duet. Because of this, much of the meaning and timing of the piece depends on the piano. This piece does not require actors to actually play the piano. It can easily be performed with the actors miming to live or recorded accompaniment. If an accompanist is being used, it is encouraged that they participate in the creative process as a third actor would.

- Will Lacker & Dylan Glatthorn

Lights rise on a studio apartment in New York City. The room is sparsely furnished with items that show their age. Moving boxes are scattered around the room. An upright piano is the space's main focus. A door leads out to the hallway. At the piano sits MAN. He stares intently at the piano keys. Finally, he takes a breath and begins to play.

Music section - "Bouncy Opening"

MAN:
>IF I WERE DREAMING
>HOW WOULD I...?

(yelling) That's not it!

MAN puts his head on piano in frustration.

Ok, take a breath, focus... the tempo is wrong. What if I change up the time? Make it less... bouncy.

MAN begins to play at a different tempo.

Music cue - "Less Bouncy"

The piano's sustain pedal sticks.

MAN (*addressing the piano*): You have got to be joking. I'm trying to pour my soul into this song, and you want to get cheeky with the pedal?!

MAN strikes the top of the piano. The pedal releases.

That's better. Now behave yourself, or I swear I will put you on the curb.

WOMAN enters through the front door. She carries a large moving box and talks on a cell phone. MAN doesn't notice WOMAN.

WOMAN: I've got the last box now.

MAN: Let's take it from the top.

>   *MAN begins to play the piano.*
>
>   *Music cue - "Less Bouncy Continued"*

>   *WOMAN puts down the box.*

WOMAN: Sorry, what did you say? I can barely hear you.

MAN: I'm sorry I lost my temper. I would never put you on the curb.

WOMAN: I get terrible reception here. Must be something about these old buildings.

MAN: Getting you down the stairs would be a nightmare.

WOMAN: The apartment is... fine. I'm going to have to get used to the walk-up.

MAN: Who am I kidding? I can't blame an inanimate object for my lack of talent. This song is garbage, and so am I.

WOMAN: The hallway definitely has a smell to it.

MAN: Rancid trash roasting on a summer day!

>   *MAN bangs the keys and stands up from the piano in frustration. He grabs the sheet music and begins to pace.*

WOMAN: It's not necessarily a bad smell. Just sort of like the place has been lived in.

MAN: What is wrong with me?

WOMAN: You know what I mean? It's like, food, and people, and pets, and time.

MAN: Inspiration will come in time.

WOMAN: Don't laugh at me. It's really not that bad. Besides, I can't afford much else right now.

MAN: You can't control it so don't even try.

WOMAN: There is one silver lining.

MAN: The music is there, you just have to listen.

> *MAN sits down at the piano, willing himself to be inspired. WOMAN crosses to the piano.*

WOMAN: There's a piano! Yeah, an upright.

MAN: Ok, take a breath, focus...

WOMAN: The landlord said it would be a nightmare getting it down the stairs, so it can stay.

MAN: Should I go back to bouncy? People like bouncy. Bouncy sells.

WOMAN: Maybe this is a sign I should start writing again.

MAN: What am I doing with my life?

> *MAN walks away from the piano in frustration.*

WOMAN: I should go. If I don't unpack these boxes, no one will. I'll call you later.

> *WOMAN ends her call. She considers the boxes but instead sits down at the piano. She begins to experiment with a few chords.*

> *Music cue - "Woman Plays Chords"*

MAN: I'm washed up. I have nothing left to give.

> *After a moment, the piano's sustain pedal sticks.*

WOMAN: Poor old piano. You have seen better days.

MAN: I'm just a hack with a piece of junk piano!

MAN bangs on the top of the piano and the pedal unsticks.

WOMAN: See, all you need is a little encouragement.

WOMAN goes back to playing the piano.

Music cue - "Woman Continues"

MAN (*addressing the piano*): I'm sorry, I shouldn't have called you a piece of junk. The stress is getting to me. I've got the lyrics, why can't I figure out the damn melody? It's like the music is playing through the walls. I hear it, but I can't make out the notes.

WOMAN stops playing.

WOMAN: I should unpack.

WOMAN crosses to a box and begins to unpack.

MAN: It's maddening! As soon as I think I have something, it disappears.

WOMAN begins to hum a song.

Music cue - "A Duet Emerges"

MAN and WOMAN conclude their duet. They share a brief moment of contemplative silence. Suddenly, a muffled argument is heard from the upstairs neighbors.

WOMAN: Oh, this better not be a regular thing.

MAN: Not again!

WOMAN: Why does every apartment in New York have loud neighbors? It's like they're built into the lease.

MAN: I'm trying to create art down here, you simpletons!

WOMAN crosses to the piano.

WOMAN: At least I don't have to worry about playing too loud.

WOMAN begins to play the same bouncy tune man originally played.

Music cue - "Woman Plays Bouncy"

MAN: No, that's too bouncy.

WOMAN: How do you like this bouncy bullshit, neighbor?!

Finally, the argument from upstairs stops.

WOMAN: That's better!

MAN: Finally!

After a moment, WOMAN begins to play the melody she began earlier.

MAN: I don't mind that.

WOMAN: I like that a lot.

MAN: It's got a sweetness to it.

WOMAN: It's sort of sad.

MAN: And a little melancholy.

WOMAN: But at the same time hopeful.

MAN and WOMAN begin to lose themselves in the music.

Music Cue - "The Duet Develops"

MAN:
    IF I WERE DREAMING...

WOMAN:
    DO DO DO DO...

MAN:
    WOULD I STILL FEEL YOU...?

WOMAN:
    DO DO DO...

MAN:
    YOUR GENTLE VOICE...

WOMAN:
    DO DO DO DO...

MAN AND WOMAN:
    SINGING SWEETLY AS THE WORLD DISAPPEARS...

MAN: That was it!

WOMAN: That was...strange.

MAN: I heard it.

WOMAN: Like I heard–

MAN: Music.

WOMAN: A man singing.

WOMAN begins to search the small apartment for intruders.

Hello, is someone there?

MAN: What are you doing?! Don't let this slip away, write it down!

WOMAN: I've got mace! I just don't know what box it's in.

MAN: Was that second chord minor? I never write with minor chords.

WOMAN: Must have been the neighbors.

MAN: But, how did it end?

WOMAN: But, something felt...

MAN: I'm losing it!

WOMAN: Strange.

MAN: I can't believe I'm losing it!

WOMAN: I must be losing it. Still...

>   *WOMAN cautiously approaches the piano.*

MAN: Ok.

WOMAN: Don't think.

MAN: Take a breath.

WOMAN: Just let the music happen.

MAN: Focus...

>   *WOMAN begins to play.*
>
>   *Song begins - "Bittersweet Lullaby"*
>
>   *MAN writes on the sheet music. They both lose themselves to the moment.*

MAN:
>	IF I WERE DREAMING HOW WOULD I KNOW?
>	WOULD I STILL FEEL YOU HAUNT ME SO?
>	YOUR GENTLE VOICE RINGS IN MY EARS
>	SINGING SWEETLY AS THE WORLD DISAPPEARS
>	EACH WAND'RING NOTE
>	AN ACHING CRY
>	IN YOUR BITTERSWEET LULLABY
>
>	IF I WERE DREAMING

WOMAN:
>	IF THIS ALL WERE A DREAM

MAN:
>	HOW WOULD I KNOW?

WOMAN:
>	HOW WOULD I KNOW?

MAN:
>	WOULD I STILL FEEL YOU HAUNT ME SO?

WOMAN:
>	YOU HAUNT ME SO

MAN:
>	YOUR GENTLE VOICE

WOMAN:
>	I HEAR YOUR VOICE

MAN:
>	RINGS IN MY EARS

WOMAN:
>	PASS THROUGH THE YEARS

MAN AND WOMAN:
    SINGING SWEETLY AS THE WORLD DISAPPEARS
    EACH WAND'RING NOTE
    AN ACHING CRY
    IN YOUR BITTERSWEET LULLABY
    IN OUR BITTERSWEET LULLABY

The duet ends.

MAN: That was it!

WOMAN: What the hell was that?!

MAN: Holy hell, I actually did it!

WOMAN: What just happened?

MAN: I listened, and I heard...

WOMAN: I swear, I heard...

MAN: The song.

WOMAN: A song.

> *WOMAN stands from the piano and crosses the room in disbelief. MAN puts the sheet music in the piano bench. The noise of the bench lid shutting startles WOMAN. He places a hand on top of the piano.*

MAN: Baby, I'm sorry we fought.

> *MAN crosses to the door and pauses. For the first time MAN and WOMAN look directly at each other.*

Good work today.

WOMAN: Same to you.

MAN exits.

WOMAN (*coming to her senses*): I've got to write this down. Paper, where did I pack the paper?!

She begins searching for something to write on. After a moment, something compels her to look in the piano bench. She removes a page of sheet music worn with time.

What is this? These notes, this is my song. But where did these lyrics...

WOMAN turns the sheet music over and reads the back.

Bittersweet Lullaby, 1954.

WOMAN's cell phone rings. She is startled by the noise. She answers the call.

Hey, the strangest thing just... I think I wrote a song?

Blackout.

END

BOOK LOVERS

Book & Lyrics by *Talaura Harms*
Music by *Jonathan Bauerfeld*

The cast of *Book Lovers* in Theatre Now's SOUND BITES 6.0.
(Left to right): Julia Lennon, Sean Patrick Murtagh, Katie Emerson, Mark Schenfisch, Sam Balzac, Alexis Floyd, and Talaura Harms.

SYNOPSIS

Charlotte sits at a library table surrounded by stacks of books. She peers over a book at something offstage, or rather, at someone offstage. Dewey, the librarian, enters with a stack of books and tells Charlotte that he's just shelved some new romance novels. (Is he flirting?) She shudders at the idea of reading a ridiculous romance. Dewey leaves, feeling stupid that he suggested it. Charlotte declares in "ROMANCE IS..." that love is a "silly old convention" and that she prefers the intrigue and excitement of other literary genres.

Charlotte's protestations of love awaken three ghosts from the bookshelves. Cyrano de Bergarac, Helen of Troy, and Juliet Capulet materialize, announcing themselves as "literature's greatest lovers" who have been summoned to help Charlotte in her affairs of the heart. With a little convincing from the Book Ghost Trio, Charlotte realizes that she is in love with Dewey, but doesn't have any notion what to do about it. The Book Ghost Trio advises with *"WOO HIM MY WAY,"* each giving Charlotte (really bad) advice from their own love stories.

Charlotte recognizes that their advice is terrible and led to the end of each of their tragic romances, and refuses to do anything. The Book Ghost Trio sings *"REWRITE THE STORY"* to nudge Charlotte to take a chance on love and show each of them that love can, indeed, have a happy ending. Dewey enters just as Charlotte is almost persuaded to go for it. She awkwardly flirts, and in a panic begins to woo using the Book Ghost Trio's initially suggested (terrible) ways. Dewey is charmed, and a surprise entrance from his own Book Ghost reveals that he's been getting bad advice all along, too.

PRODUCTION HISTORY

Book Lovers, by Talaura Harms and Jonathan Bauerfeld, was written as a final presentation for the First Year BMI Lehman Engel Musical Theatre Workshop. It was presented as a reading with limited costumes and movement at BMI in New York City, May 2018. Music direction was by Jonathan Bauerfeld. The cast was as follows:

CHARLOTTE	Katie Emerson
DEWEY	Mark Schenfisch
CYRANO DE BERGERAC	Jason Weisinger
HELEN OF TROY	Deborah Berenson
JULIET CAPULET	Melissa Weisbach
HESTER PRYNNE	Talaura Harms
SIR LANCELOT	Sam Balzac

The following year it had its first professional production during Theatre Now's SOUND BITES 6.0 festival on April 2, 2019 at the Merkin Hall at Kaufman Music Center in New York City. It was directed and choreographed by Erin Thompson, with music direction by Jonathan Bauerfeld. It was produced by Chris Giordano, Thomas Morrissey, and Liz Doyle. The cast was as follows:

CHARLOTTE	Katie Emerson
DEWEY	Mark Schenfisch
CYRANO DE BERGERAC	Sean Patrick Murtagh
HELEN OF TROY	Alexis Floyd
JULIET CAPULET	Julia Lennon
HESTER PRYNNE	Talaura Harms
SIR LANCELOT	Sam Balzac

CHARACTERS

CHARLOTTE	A book lover. She probably drinks tea and has cats.
DEWEY	A librarian. No one understands the jokes on his t-shirts.
CYRANO DE BERGERAC	Puts on airs. Big nose.
HELEN OF TROY	Brassy. Beautiful.
JULIET CAPULET	Innocent. Obsessed with death.
HESTER PRYNNE	A loose woman.
SIR LANCELOT	Oh man. This dude.

SETTING
A library in your town. The present.

MUSICAL NUMBERS

"Romance Is..."	Charlotte
"Woo Him My Way"	Cyrano, Helen, Juliet
"Rewrite the Story"	Company

AUTHORS' NOTE
Book Lovers is a simple fantasy about love and taking chances. It is our hope that it is played with a little bit of heart and a great deal of fun. Please feel free to cast whoever tells the story best—all ages, races, genders encouraged.

- Talaura Harms & Jonathan Bauerfeld

Lights up on CHARLOTTE sitting at a table in the library. Bookshelves behind her. She is reading a large book. She isn't really reading. She is hiding behind a large book. She peers over the top. DEWEY enters.

DEWEY: Hi, Charlotte.

CHARLOTTE (*awkward, suspicious, and weird*): ... Hi...

DEWEY: I just catalogued and shelved some new Harlequin romances if you're interested.

CHARLOTTE: Ew. Gross. No.

DEWEY: Oh, yeah. Heh. Of course. I don't know why I said that. Heh. (*while exiting, to himself*)...So stupid.

Song begins - "Romance Is..."

CHARLOTTE: Romance. Heh.

She sings:

I LIKE WHODUNITS.
WITH A BODY, A SUSPECT, A CLUE.
I'LL FIGURE WHO DONE IT, WHO DID IT,
BEFORE THE BOOK IS THROUGH.
GIVE ME AGATHA CHRISTIE OR ARTHUR CONAN DOYLE
BUT ROMANCE?

(*spoken*) Ha!

ROMANCE IS A MYSTERY TO ME.

OR MAYBE SCI-FI
WITH SOME ROBOTS OR MONKEYS IN SPACE
ALL SORTS OF DESTRUCTION, AND MAYHEM,
THAT ENDS THE HUMAN RACE.
GIVE ME ATWOOD, AND BUTLER, AND ISAAC ASIMOV
BUT ROMANCE?

(*spoken*) Blech!

ROMANCE IS SO ALIEN TO ME.

ROMANCE IS …SUCH A BLATANT CONDESCENSION
I'M FAR TOO CLEVER FOR THAT TRAP
I NEED EXCITEMENT. I NEED INTRIGUE.
BUT LOVE JUST MAKES ME WANT TO NAP.

She yawns.

HOW 'BOUT ADVENTURE?
WITH SOME MAGIC, A DRAGON, A QUEST
I'D RATHER HAVE HOBBITS THAN PRINCES,
UNLESS THE KINGDOM'S FAR WEST.
I WANT TOLKIEN AND MARTIN AND ALL
THEIR EXTRA "R"S
BUT ROMANCE?
ROMANCE IS JUST FANTASY TO ME.

(*spoken*) Blechhhhh!!!!!

CHARLOTTE *makes loud gagging sounds and gestures. She is shushed by offstage library patrons.*

ROMANCE IS… SUCH A SILLY OLD CONVENTION
WHERE LOVERS PICK HEATHER IN WUTHERING WEATHER
THEY SIMPER, THEY SIGH
THEY ASK THE STARS WHY
THEY WISH AND THEY WONDER
TIL HEARTS TEAR ASUNDER.
HA! IT'S JUST A SPELL THEY'RE FALLING UNDER.

GIVE ME A THRILLER
MAKE ME SCREAM OUT, AND CRY OUT, AND SQUEAL
I WANT TO FEEL SOMETHING, FEEL SOMETHING,
EVEN IF IT ISN'T REAL
PICK ME UP AND SHOCK ME AND

SHAKE ME TO MY
CORE
BUT ROMANCE?

She shakes her head simply, silently.
ROMANCE IS TOO FRIGHTENING...
SO ALIEN, JUST FANTASY,
YES, ROMANCE IS A MYSTERY TO ME.

CYRANO, JULIET, and HELEN OF TROY appear magically from the bookshelves.

Song begins - "Woo Him My Way"

CYRANO, HELEN, & JULIET: Woooo... Woooo... Wooooo...

They sing:

WOO HIM MY WAY

JULIET: Methinks that lady doth protest too much.

HELEN: Awww, she's in love.

CYRANO: My dear lady, fret no longer.

CHARLOTTE (*jumping*): Oh gosh! Um. Who are you?

CYRANO: Literature's most famous lovers!

JULIET: Juliet. Pleased to meet you.

HELEN: Helen.

CHARLOTTE: Of Troy? Wow. You are beautiful.

HELEN: Yes, I know.

CHARLOTTE: And you're Cyrano!

CYRANO: I see my nose isn't the only thing that precedes me.

CHARLOTTE: What are you doing here?

CYRANO: Summoned here to help you in some matter of the heart.

CHARLOTTE: I don't have any matters of the heart.

JULIET: Then wherefore art thou so sad?

    CHARLOTTE doesn't answer. She's still confused.

CHARLOTTE: I'm not sad.

HELEN: Where is he?

CHARLOTTE: Over there in the periodicals. Ooooh. I'm in love!?! What do I do?

CYRANO: You woo.

CHARLOTTE: I what?

HELEN & JULIET: Woo.

CHARLOTTE: Whoa.

JULIET: Oh, it's easy.

CYRANO, HELEN, & JULIET:
    WOO HIM MY WAY...

CHARLOTTE: Noooo.

CYRANO:
    JUST BE WITTY.
    USE YOUR WORDS TO SHOW YOU'RE CLEVER.
    POUR YOUR HEART OUT, MAKE IT SMART.
    WRITE A LETTER FULL OF FLAIR AND PRETTY

NOTHINGS, BUT DON'T SIGN IT. HIDE YOUR HEART.

WITH A LITTLE INK AND A FLOURISH OF YOUR PEN.
YOU COULD WIN A HUNDRED MEN.
HIDE IN A BUSH. DON'T SHOW YOUR FACE.
BE FUNNY AND CUNNING TO MAKE HIS HEART RACE.
BUT HOMELY AND UGLY
AND MONSTROUS AND BEASTLY
SENDS THEM CHASING FAR FROM YOU.
SO, BE WITTY.

HELEN: Shh. She's a perfectly lovely girl. Don't listen to him.

She sings:

WOO HIM MY WAY...

JUST BE PRETTY.
FLIP YOUR HAIR AND BAT YOUR LASHES.
GIVE A SHIMMY. THAT'S THE PLAN.
THEN YOU GIGGLE.
PINCH YOUR CHEEKS AND STIR UP TROUBLE.
JUST BE PRETTY, GET YOUR MAN

WITH A LITTLE WINK
AND A PUCKER OF THE LIPS
YOU CAN SINK A THOUSAND SHIPS
WATCH THE MEN FIGHT, SEE HOW THEY BRAWL
ALL SWEATY AND DIRTY
AND CAUGHT IN YOUR THRALL
CLASHING AND BASHING AND SPITTING AND BITING
AND CRAWLING AFTER YOU.
IF YOU'RE PRETTY.

ALL:
    WOO HIM MY WAY

HELEN:
    AND HE'LL WHISK YOU OFF TO PARIS FOR A WEEKEND

JULIET: Paris?? Ew.

    WOO HIM MY WAY

HELEN: Well, what's your way?

JULIET:
    JUST KILL YOURSELF

There's silence, a beat.

    WITH A LITTLE DRINK
    OF A POISON FROM A PLANT
    YOU CAN STOP YOUR HEART

HELEN & CYRANO react.

JULIET:
    FIRST THE COUGH
    THEN THE CHOKE
    THEN THE GASPING
    THEN YOU CROAK
    BUT IF NOT

    Here's a dagger!

CYRANO & HELEN (*pulling JULIET away from CHARLOTTE*): No. No. No. No. No.

    WOO HIM MY WAY

HELEN:
    AND HE'LL WHISK YOU OFF TO PARIS FOR A WEEKEND

ALL:
    WOO HIM MY WAY

JULIET:
    AND YOUR LOVE WILL LIVE FOREVER IT'S A KNOT
    THAT CAN'T

(*spoken*) can't be severed.

SHE mimes a throat slit.

ALL:
    WOO HIM MY WAY

CYRANO:
    AND YOUR LOVE WILL BE A SECRET FOR THE KEEPING

ALL:
    WOO HIM MY WAY

CYRANO:
    JUST BE WITTY

HELEN:
    JUST BE PRETTY

JULIET:
    JUST BE DEAD

Another BOOK GHOST appears from the bookshelves. She has a scarlet letter A on her chest.

HESTER:
    WOOO WOOOO WOOO HIM MY WAY

CYRANO: Hester Prynne! Get back in your book!

HESTER gives CYRANO a dirty look and exits muttering.

ALL:
    MY WAAAAAAAY!

Song ends.

HELEN: Now, go get him!

CHARLOTTE: But that's all such terrible advice. *(beat)* Cyrano, Roxane loved you. All you had to do was tell her that you wrote those letters. And Juliet, you didn't have to die.

JULIET: But my love lives forever.

CYRANO: It looks like someone's been reading all those romances after all.

CHARLOTTE: That's not romance. That's tragedy. You all made terrible decisions.

HELEN: I didn't make a decision. I was stolen away. Love doesn't have to be a tragedy. You get to decide how your story goes.

Song begins - "Rewrite the Story"

HELEN sings:

YOU COULD REWRITE THE STORY
GIVE US ALL A NEW CHANCE
WE DESERVE A BETTER ENDING
TO OUR TRAGIC ROMANCE
MAYBE LOVE ISN'T STOLEN
OR A HOPE THAT FALLS THROUGH
WANNA SEE A HAPPILY AFTER
CUZ IT'S LONG OVERDUE

CYRANO:
IF YOU REWRITE THE STORY
MAYBE LOVE DOESN'T HIDE
SHOVE IT RIGHT OUT IN THE OPEN
LOOK WITH EYES OPEN WIDE

JULIET:
WITH A LITTLE REVISION
MAYBE LOVE DOESN'T SLAY
IF YOU LET IT BLEED A LITTLE
WELL, I GUESS THAT'S OKAY

CHARLOTTE:
> WHAT IF HE DOESN'T RETURN MY AFFECTIONS?
> OH GOSH! WHAT IF HE LAUGHS IN MY FACE?
> SO WHAT! NO BIG DEAL! IT'S COOL. I'M GREAT!
> I'LL JUST TURN AROUND, WALK OUT THE DOOR,
> CHANGE MY NAME, MOVE OUT OF STATE.

HELEN: You can do this!

CYRANO, HELEN, & JULIET:
> SO YOU REWRITE THE STORY
> JUST TAKE HOLD OF THE PEN
> IF YOU DON'T GET WHAT YOU'RE AFTER
> THEN REWRITE IT AGAIN

CHARLOTTE:
> GONNA REWRITE MY STORY
> GONNA SWITCH UP THE PLOT
> GONNA TAKE A CHANCE ON ROMANCE
> IF I'M READY OR NOT

DEWEY enters. CHARLOTTE freezes and looks at the BOOK GHOST TRIO, who gesture encouragements to her.

DEWEY: Hi Charlotte.

CHARLOTTE: "There comes one moment, once—and God help those Who pass that moment by!"

The BOOK GHOST TRIO look on. This is a disaster.

DEWEY: What?

CHARLOTTE: Nothing, I just...

CHARLOTTE giggles and flips her hair.

CYRANO: Oh dear.

CHARLOTTE (*giggles*): I'm so sweaty! Hahaha.

HELEN: Oh dear.

CHARLOTTE: Don't look at me. I'm a monster!

> She starts to faint. DEWEY catches her. JULIET cheers because it looks like dying.

DEWEY: Are you ok?

CHARLOTTE: Yes.

> Awkward silence. DEWEY looks over his shoulder. He takes a golden goblet out of a burlap bag.

DEWEY: Um... I got you this chalice.

> LANCELOT enters.

LANCELOT: Well done, Squire!

> LANCELOT and DEWEY celebrate with their own secret weirdo handshake.

ALL:
    WHEN YOU REWRITE THE STORY
    AND PURSUE A ROMANCE
    THEN YOUR HAPPILY EVER AFTER
    WON'T BE JUST CIRCUMSTANCE
    SOMETIMES LOVE CAN BE MAGIC
    SOMETIMES MYST'RIES ARE SOLVED
    SO IT'S A LITTLE BIT SCARY
    BUT TAKE THE CHANCE
    TAKE THE CHANCE!

CHARLOTTE: Is this thing dishwasher-safe?

DEWEY shrugs. Everyone strikes a final tableau pose. HESTER PRYNNE runs onstage and attaches herself to LANCELOT on the final chord of the song.

END

BYSTANDER

Book & Lyrics by *Ed Levy*
Music by *Eric Grunin*

Neda Lahidji, Mikki Sodergren, and Danny Kornfeld in *Bystander* at Theatre Now's SOUND BITES 5.0.

The 10-Minute Musical: an anthology from the SOUND BITES festival

SYNOPSIS

While riding the New York City subway (Q TRAIN), Anna, a terribly shy young woman, is obsessing on an assignment her therapist has given her: to talk to a stranger. At the next subway stop, Doug gets on the train and attempts to draw Anna's attention to the fact that her purse is unzipped. Anna flinches, and Doug resents what feels like a snub. Last to enter the train is Niaz, a Muslim woman wearing a hijab. She accidentally bumps into Anna, and apologizes; but her apology is ignored, leaving Niaz resentful.

The train jolts to a stop. Doug, noticing that Niaz is wearing a hijab and studying a chemistry book, jumps to the conclusion that she is a terrorist. He questions her, aggressively, and she explains that she is a nursing student. He doesn't believe her, and his level of tension escalates. Anna is afraid for Niaz and feels she has to do something, *"ANNA'S DECISION"*, but cannot imagine what. Finally, Anna turns to Niaz and strikes up a seemingly irrelevant conversation. After a moment of hesitation, Niaz catches on to Anna's strategy and converses, thus successfully frustrating Doug's attempts to provoke her.

The train once again jolts, the lights dim. Doug's anxiety and rage give way to a full panic attack. Niaz recognizes Doug's symptoms, and she reaches out to him with a Farsi song she learned from her mother *"RUMI"*. Anna improvises a counterpoint (in English), and the song succeeds in calming Doug.

After he recovers, Doug asks Niaz to forgive him for harassing her. Niaz tells him she won't forgive him, not until she knows he has changed his behavior in the future.

The train lights come back to normal, and it resumes its journey. Doug exits at the next stop. Anna asks Niaz if she will go to the movies with her this coming weekend. Niaz says no—but only because it's Ramadan. They agree to go to the movies sometime in the future *"Q TRAIN (reprise)"*.

PRODUCTION HISTORY

Bystander, written by Ed Levy and Eric Grunin, was originally produced in 2017 by Summerfest! at the Hudson Guild Theater in New York City. It was directed by Caitlin Wees, with musical direction by Cynthia Meng. The cast was as follows:

ANNA	Mikki Sodergren
DOUG	Codie Milford
NIAZ	Neda Lahidji

The following year a revised version was produced in Theatre Now's SOUND BITES 5.0 at The Irene Diamond Stage at The Pershing Square Signature Center for on May 28, 2018. It was directed by Rachel M. Stevens, with music direction by Adam Wiggins. It was produced by Thomas Morrissey, Chris Giordano, and Stephen Bishop Seely. The cast was as follows:

ANNA	Mikki Sodergren
DOUG	Danny Kronfeld
NIAZ	Neda Lahidji

The musical was awarded Best Music at that year's festival.

CHARACTERS

ANNA	Woman, nervous, frightened.
NIAZ	Woman, a nursing student, confident, wears a hijab.
DOUG	Young man, nervous, scared, and belligerent.
SUBWAY ANNOUNCER	Subway worker, unseen.

SETTING

New York City, the Q train. The present.

MUSICAL NUMBERS

"Q Train"	Company
"Anna's Decision"	Anna
"Rumi"	Niaz, Anna
"Q Train (reprise)"	Company

AUTHORS' NOTE

We wrote *Bystander* in response to the rising tide of hatred flooding the world; we experienced some of it firsthand, in situations analogous to the one depicted in our story. In addition, we took practical inspiration from tactics presented by Jewish Voice for Peace in their "Bystander Training Workshop." We hope you find it resonant.

    Niaz sings in Farsi. In the score, this text is notated using IPA, with the original text shown in an appendix. If your actor doesn't speak Farsi, we suggest using a coach to ensure that the actor feels the connection between the sense and the sound. In our experience this makes a huge difference.

    Though the text of a play must never be changed without the writer's affirmative consent, here we encourage you to change the movie named when Niaz responds to Anna's question "Have you seen any good movies lately?", so that it remains current. Your choice should be specific to the character of Niaz (as it is here), and of course Anna should then respond by naming the leading actor (as she does here).

    One final note: the character of Doug is bad, but not evil; if he's merely a hard-core psychopath, his abusive behavior is too easy to dismiss.

- Ed Levy & Eric Grunin

APPENDIX
The text is from Rumi, Divan-e Shams-e Tabrizi: Quatrain 1325:

ماییم که گه نهان و گه پیداییم
گه مومن و گه یهود و گه ترساییم
تا این دل ما قالب هر دل گردد
هر روز به صورتی در می آییم

From time to time, we are visible and/or invisible
From time to time, we are either a Muslim, a Jew or a Christian
Until our heart would fit all other hearts
Every day we [have to] form into a different shape

Transliteration (IPA):
/mɒːʔm/ /ke/ /gæh/ /næhɒːno/ /gæh/ /pejdɒːʔm/
/gæh/ /moʔmeno/ /gæh/ /jæhuːdo/ /gæh/ /tærsɒːʔm/
/tɒː/ /iːn/ /dele/ /mɒː/ /ɣɒːlebe/ /hær/ /del/ /gærdæd/
/hær/ /ruːz/ /be/ /suræti:/ /boruːn/ /miːʔɒːiːm/

Lights up on the interior of an empty subway car.

Song begins - "Q Train"

The train doors open. ANNA enters the car.

ANNA:
SO LONELY! THERE'S A SIMPLE REASON WHY!
MY SHRINK SAYS "PATHOLOGICALLY SHY".
I'M SHAKING SHAKING RIGHT HERE ON THE Q TRAIN!

SHE TOLD ME PICK A STRANGER OUT TODAY!
MAKE CONTACT! DOESN'T MATTER WHAT YOU SAY!
THANK GOODNESS!
NO ONE ELSE IS ON
THE Q TRAIN! (YEAH!)
THE Q TRAIN (YEAH!)
THE Q TRAIN!

FIGHT TO SURVIVE
HERE IN THIS CITY,
RIDING THIS TRAIN,
SWEATING AND GRITTY.
HARD AS IT FEELS,
I'VE GOT TO TRY
MAKE A CONNECTION.
CAN'T LET LIFE PASS ME BY.

SUBWAY ANNOUNCER: This is a Brooklyn Bound Q local train. Next stop is Lexington and 63rd Street. Stand clear of the closing doors, please.

DOUG enters the car, notices ANNA.

DOUG: Miss? Miss? Your purse is unzipped. The zipper? Of your purse? Somebody might steal something.

ANNA shies away, but sees her purse is, indeed, unzipped. DOUG sings:

>   I TRY TO BE POLITE,
>   BUT IT'S LIKE I'M JUST NOT HERE.
>   WHEN THEY LOOK AT ME
>   AND ALL THEY FEEL IS HATE AND FEAR!

ANNA:
>   FIGHT TO SURVIVE
>   HERE IN THIS CITY
>   RIDING THIS TRAIN
>   SWEATING AND GRITTY
>   HARD AS IT FEELS
>   I'VE GOT TO TRY

DOUG:
>   I TRY TO
>   BE FRIENDLY
>   GET TREATED
>   LIKE A MONSTER
>   CAN'T CALL ME
>   A MONSTER

ANNA:
>   MAKE A CONNECTION

ANNA AND DOUG:
>   CAN'T LET LIFE PASS ME BY

SUBWAY ANNOUNCER: This is a Brooklyn Bound Q local train. Next stop is 57th Street, 7th Avenue. Stand clear of the closing doors, please.

NIAZ enters. The train lurches.

NIAZ: Pardon me.

ANNA doesn't acknowledge NIAZ's apology.

NIAZ:
>   I TELL HER "PARDON ME",

AND SHE LOOKS THE OTHER WAY.
I GUESS IT'S MY HIJAB.
WELL, THAT'S JUST THE PRICE I PAY!
THERE'S NO RESPECT!

ANNA:
MY SHRINK SAYS I SHOULD SAY HELLO
AM I BROKEN? WHAT'S SO HARD?
WHAT WOULD GO SO AWF'LLY WRONG?
I CAN'T DO IT!
I CAN'T LET DOWN MY GUARD
CAN'T TALK TO HER!
MY SHRINK SAYS THIS WILL SET ME FREE.
IT'S CALLED "EXPOSURE THERAPY".
BUT I DON'T THINK IT'S RIGHT FOR ME.

ANNA:	NIAZ AND DOUG:
GETTING ANXIOUS ON THE Q TRAIN (YEAH!)	WHAT'S HER PROBLEM PROBLEMS ON THE
THE Q TRAIN, SO WHAT'S MY PROBLEM?	
Q TRAIN	Q TRAIN
THE Q TRAIN	THE Q TRAIN
I'M STUCK WITH MY PROBLEMS ON THE Q TRAIN	I'M STUCK HERE ON THE Q TRAIN

ALL:
STUCK WITH EACH OTHER ON THE Q TRAIN

The lights change in tandom with a music cue to indicate the train is stalled.

SUBWAY ANNOUNCER: Ladies and gentlemen, we are being held by the dispatcher.

NIAZ sits down. She puts her Chemistry book down on the seat beside her and starts reading the Quran.

DOUG: It's so hot in here! I wish I could open a window!

NIAZ: Yeah. Too bad.

DOUG: What? (*beat*) That's a lot of books you've got there!

NIAZ: For school. Mostly chemistry.

DOUG: That's not a chemistry book!

NIAZ: It's a Quran. It's Ramadan.

DOUG: Wait. What kind of school?

NIAZ: Nursing school.

DOUG: Then why aren't you wearing scrubs?

NIAZ: We only wear scrubs when we go to the hospital. Today was just classes.

DOUG: Nah, you're not a nurse!

Song begins - "Anna's Decision"

DOUG turns to ANNA.

Does she look like a nurse to you?

DOUG starts pacing.

ANNA:
    THIS GUY IS NUTS.
    THE WAY THAT HE STANDS.
    HE POINTS WITH HIS FINGER,
    THEN CLENCHES HIS HANDS.

DOUG: "If you see something, say something!" *Don't look at me like I'm weird!*

NIAZ: What do you see that concerns you?

ANNA:
    WHAT SHOULD I DO?
    I CAN'T MAKE THIS STOP.
    I AM NOT A COP.
    WHAT SHOULD I DO?
    WHAT SHOULD I DO?

DOUG: I see a Qu'ran, a Chemistry book, a backpack, and that thing on your head.

NIAZ: It's a hijab.

DOUG turns to look at ANNA.

DOUG: What if she does have a bomb in there?

ANNA:
    COULD IT BE A BOMB?
    THAT DOESN'T MAKE SENSE.
    I'VE GOT TO STAY CALM,
    I'M FEELING TOO TENSE.

NIAZ: You have no reason to be afraid of me.

DOUG: I'd rather be wrong than get blown up!

NIAZ: No one is getting blown up.

ANNA:
    I'VE GOT TO DO SOMETHING.
    SHE COULD GET HURT.
    I COULD SIT ON THE FENCE ...
    OR I COULD SIT WITH HER.
    I COULD DO THAT.
    I COULD SIT WITH HER,
    RIGHT NEXT TO HER.

ANNA sits down next to NIAZ.

DOUG: Whose side are you on anyway?

ANNA: Have you seen any good movies lately?

NIAZ: What? OOOH! (*understanding the game*) The Big Sick!

ANNA: I loved Kumail/—Nanjiani.

DOUG: Open the backpack! (*to himself*) I am not gonna let this happen! This isn't happening!

NIAZ: Are you OK?

ANNA: Oh my god, is he OK?

NIAZ: He's having a panic attack. Sir! Sir! You have nothing to be afraid of. There is nothing dangerous in my pack.

    NIAZ lifts the backpack, holding it open.

    See?

    Song begins - "Rumi"

    NIAZ begins to sing. [NOTE: An English translation is available on page 105 of this book.]

    ماییم که گه نهان و گه پیداییم

ANNA: What does it mean?

NIAZ: It's hard to translate. It means something like "Until your heart becomes the world, it has to change its shape each day."

    NIAZ sings again. ANNA sings in counterpoint.

NIAZ:	ANNA:
ماییم که گه نهان و گه پیداییم	MY HEART'S CLOSED.
گه مومن و گه یهود و گه ترساییم	LET IT OPEN.

تا این دل ما قالب هر دل گردد
هر روز به صورتی در می آییم

NOW I THINK I SEE THE WAY.
LET A FLOWER BLOSSOM.
SAY A WORD, AND
SPEAK WHAT'S IN YOUR HEART.

> DOUG'S tension eases.

NIAZ: Are you all right?

DOUG: Well. Uh. Yes. I guess so. *(to NIAZ)* Thank you. I mean, I don't know how to thank you.

NIAZ: You said I had a bomb. That's like yelling "Fire!" in a crowded theater. Someone could get hurt.

DOUG: So, why did you help me?

NIAZ: You needed help.

DOUG: I'm sorry. I screwed up. Forgive me.

NIAZ: No.

DOUG: No?

NIAZ: No.

DOUG: But I said I was sorry.

NIAZ: You know, you can go out, and you can be nicer to other people like me, and if you do that for a good long time, then you can know in your heart that I forgive you.

SUBWAY ANNOUNCER: Ladies and gentlemen, the obstruction on the tracks has been cleared and we will be moving shortly. We apologize for any inconvenience.

> *LIGHTS return to normal. DOUG, ANNA, and NIAZ retreat to their separate spaces.*

ANNA:
> TALK TO HER!
> IT'S NOW OR NEVER.
> TALK TO HER!
> THIS IS YOUR CHANCE!
> IF I DON'T SPEAK UP,
> SHE'LL GO AWAY.
> I CAN'T STAND BY!
> I'VE GOT TO TRY!
>
> Are you OK?

NIAZ: Yeah.

ANNA: You were so brave!

NIAZ: Brave?! I was terrified!

ANNA: Do you want to go to the movies with me?

NIAZ: I can't.

ANNA: Oh.

NIAZ: It's Ramadan.

ANNA: When Ramadan is over... ?

NIAZ: You know, I'd like that! I'm Niaz.

ANNA: I'm Anna.

NIAZ: Thanks for what you did back there.

ANNA: It's just what any decent person would do.

NIAZ: That's not what I see.

ANNA: Did it really do any good?

NIAZ: It restored my faith in humanity.

ANNA: You know what? I think it did the same for me.

The lights brighten. ANNA and NIAZ laugh.

Song begins - "Q Train (reprise)"

LEFT MY OLD SELF BEHIND.

NIAZ:
NEVER KNOW WHAT YOU'LL FIND.

DOUG:
IT'S A SWIRL IN MY MIND.

ALL:
GOT TO LEARN TO BE KIND
BE KIND BE KIND
FIGHT TO SURVIVE
HERE IN THIS CITY,
RIDING THIS TRAIN,
SWEATING AND GRITTY.
AS HARD AS IT FEELS,
I'VE GOT TO TRY
MAKE A CONNECTION.
CAN'T LET LIFE PASS ME BY.
ON THE Q TRAIN,
KNOCKING DOWN THE WALLS ON THE Q TRAIN!
KNOCKING DOWN THE WALLS ON THE Q TRAIN!
KNOCKING DOWN THE WALLS ON THE Q TRAIN!

END

COOKIE SOIRÉE

Book & Lyrics by *Justin Anthony Long*
Music by *Ge Enrique*
Concept by *Jonny Lee Jr.*

Amber Coartney, Katie Boren, and Desireé Rodriguez in *Cookie Soirée* at Theatre Now's SOUND BITES 2014.

SYNOPSIS

Raquel, Gretel, & Sandy are three twelve-year-old girl scouts in Sugarland, Texas. Today, they're selling their cookies in a Walmart parking lot. *"COOKIES FOR SALE"* They need to sell at least two hundred dollars worth of cookies by 3pm to earn their cookie badges!

They're on track to earn their new badge when two local teen troublemakers, Brody & Marcus, spot the scouts and decide to teach them a lesson by robbing them. *"HEY GIRLS"* As the troublemakers drive off with their money, the scouts are devastated, left in the parking lot to ponder the cruel world they live in and how, as kids, they are helpless…*"WE'RE JUST KIDS"*…or are they?

On the road, Brody & Marcus count their money and celebrate. Little do they know, the scouts are hot on their trail, scooting after them on scooters, whip and bow and arrow in hand. They're ready to fight for what is rightfully theirs. They chase the troublemakers and teach THEM a lesson they'll never forget. *"GIRL SCOUT GUERRILA ATTACK"*

With the troublemakers defeated, the scouts stand triumphant with their money in hand. They may just be kids, but they are strong! *"WE'RE JUST KIDS (reprise)"* The troublemakers run off and the girls celebrate their accomplishment.

The next day, the scouts all have cookie badges and are once again selling cookies in the Walmart parking lot. *"COOKIES FOR SALE (reprise)"* When two new troublemakers, Billy & Derek, try to rob them, the scouts whip out their new guns, issuing a warning. The troublemakers run away. The girls celebrate their collective power.

PRODUCTION HISTORY

Cookie Soirée, written by Justin Anthony Long and Ge Enrique, with concept by Jonny Lee Jr. first premiered in 2012 in Ken Davenport's 10-Minute Play Contest at Davenport Studios. The production was directed by Justin Anthony Long and Jonny Lee Jr., choreographed by Jelani Remy, with musical direction by Ge Enrique. Christopher Bediones was on the crew. The cast was as follows:

RAQUEL	Desireé Rodriguez
GRETEL	Amber Coartney
SANDY	Kate Lippstreu
BRODY/BILLY	Joe Conti
MARCUS/DEREK	Justin Gregory Lopez

The show was the 2012 contest winner.

Two years later it was presented at The 47th Street Theater in New York for Theatre Now's SOUND BITES 2014 on December 8, 2014. The production was directed by Justin Anthony Long and Jonny Lee Jr., choreographed by Jelani Remy, with musical direction by Andrew Wheeler. It was produced by Thomas Morrissey, Rebecca Nell Robertson, and Stephen Bishop Seely, with associate producer, Charles Quittner. Christopher DeProphetis was on crew. The cast was as follows:

RAQUEL	Desireé Rodriguez
GRETEL	Amber Coartney
SANDY	Katie Boren
BRODY/BILLY	Joe Conti
MARCUS/DEREK	Eddie Egan

The show was awarded both the Audience Choice Award and Best Actress (Desireé Rodriguez) in that year's festival.

CHARACTERS

RAQUEL	Latinx or Black/African American. 12 years old. Leader of the girl scouts. She takes her job seriously and keeps the other girls on task. Raquel helps the girls "do the right thing" when they get robbed.
GRETEL	Caucasian. 12 years old. She's usually seeking the group's approval doing whatever she can to fit in. Gretel has a lot of heart, but won't hesitate to kick you in the face with her combat boots if you mess with her or her friends. She's crushing hard on Sandy and may or may not realize.
SANDY	Asian-American or Pacific Islander. An enthusiastic scout with wacky marketing ideas. She's an excellent shot with a bow and arrow and won't hesitate to kick your butt if you get in between her and her friends or money box.
BRODY/BILLY	Any ethnicity. 18 years old. He's a local troublemaker who wants to teach the girl scouts that life isn't always sweet and sunny. Billy is another troublemaker.
MARCUS/DEREK	Any ethnicity. 18 years old. He's Brody's friend, who steals the girls' money box. A troublemaker. Derek is another troublemaker.

For the Girl Scouts, performers should be femme identifying, not limited to binary; gender conscious. For the Troublemakers, performers should be masc identifying, not limited to binary; gender conscious.

SETTING
Various locations in Sugarland, Texas. April, 2012.

MUSICAL NUMBERS

"Cookies For Sale"	Raquel, Gretel, Sandy
"Hey Girls"	Company
"We're Just Kids"	Raquel, Gretel, Sandy
"Girl Scout Guerrilla Attack"	Company
"We're Just Kids (reprise)"	Raquel, Gretel, Sandy
"Cookies For Sale (reprise)"	Company

AUTHORS' NOTE

This should be fun. Yes, the girl scouts are getting robbed. However, how absurd, that of all the people to rob on this day, two troublemakers pick three do-gooder scouts? In life, perhaps a little scary. Onstage, let's milk the absurd irony of it for all it's worth in comedy gold.

In re: casting. Raquel's character breakdown says she is either Latinx or Black/African American and Sandy's character breakdown says she is Asian American or Pacific Islander. This group of girls should reflect the diversity of America. Could Raquel or Sandy be Indian or Middle Eastern or Native American? Yes. Could Gretel be played by a non-caucasian actor? Yes. My intention in designating different ethnicities for each girl is so that each is visually different. And so that a representation of three visually different best friends who work together and have the same goals can live and breathe onstage for the world to see. And in regards to the gender identities, the characters of the Girl Scouts and the Troublemakers should read as gender opposite.

In re: Billy & Derek's car. In previous productions, we used two office chairs on wheels. The actors mimed a steering wheel, opening and closing car doors. Feel free to create the car however you like. Sound effects were used for engines revving up or cars peeling away. The sound effect of a car window rolling down paired with an actor miming pushing the car window button had great comedic effect. I invite you to explore what's funny for you and your group, but do know that sound effects and miming can add great comedic effect to what's already on the page.

In choosing to do this show, you probably have a great sense of humor. Thank you and enjoy!

-Justin Anthony Long

SCENE 1: WALMART PARKING LOT. Outside a Walmart in Sugarland, Texas. A cute and simple Girl Scout Cookie booth is setup. A money box sits on the booth. GRETEL, a solid & sturdy scout, is busy stacking boxes of cookies, trying not to look awkward. RAQUEL, a natural born leader, holds a clipboard and takes attendance.

Song begins - "Cookie For Sale"

RAQUEL:
    ROLL CALL!
    GRETEL?

GRETEL:
    HERE!

RAQUEL:
    SANDY?

SANDY, an enthusiastic scout, runs in as her name is called.

SANDY:
    HERE!

RAQUEL:
    YOU'RE LATE.

RAQUEL hands the clipboard off to GRETEL.

GRETEL:
    AND RAQUEL?

RAQUEL:
    THAT'S ME!

THE GIRLS:
    AND NOW OUR COOKIE JAMBOREE!

GRETEL & SANDY drum on the cookie stand or upside down buckets. RAQUEL addresses the audience.

RAQUEL:
> PEOPLE OF WALMART,
> TAKE A LOOK IN YOUR SHOPPING CART
> AND SEE WHAT YOU ARE LACKING;
> IT LOOKS LIKE YOU'VE ALL BEEN SLACKING!

GRETEL & SANDY:
> HERE COMES YOUR LUCKY DAY.
> SOON YOU CAN SHOUT

THE GIRLS:
> HIP HIP HOORAY!

RAQUEL & SANDY:
> NEED SOMETHING FOR YOUR SWEET TOOTH?

GRETEL:
> WE'VE GOT WHAT YOU NEED RIGHT IN OUR BOOTH!

THE GIRLS:
> AND THAT'S THE TRUTH!

> *THE GIRLS each grab a box and are ready to sell!*

> COOKIES,
> COOKIES FOR SALE!

SANDY:
> IF YOU EAT TOO MANY, YOU'LL LOOK LIKE A WHALE!

THE GIRLS:
> COME GET YOUR GIRL SCOUT COOKIES TODAY!
> DID YOU HEAR THE NEWS?
> THERE'S A COOKIE SOIRÉE!

RAQUEL: Girls, tell everyone about our fabulous selection!

GRETEL:
> SAVANNAH SMILES

>   IN PILES
>   THAT LAST EVEN LONGER THAN THE NILE!

SANDY:
>   WE GOT SAMOAS,
>   YOU KNOW-A
>   THEY'RE DOPER THAN EDGAR ALLEN PO-A!

RAQUEL:
>   THANKS A LOT
>   BANKS A LOT!

SANDY:
>   IF YOU EAT TOO MANY, YOU'LL GET SHOT!
>   BANG, BANG, BANG! BANG! BANG! BANG! BANG!!!

RAQUEL: Sandy! Just stick to the regular script.

SANDY: But I have so many good marketing ideas!

RAQUEL: To get our cookie badge, we need to sell at least two hundred dollars worth of cookies by three and it's already two-fifteen! Just stick to the script!

GRETEL: Game faces, girls! C'mon!!!

SHE slaps their butts and they turn on the charm.

THE GIRLS:
>   COOKIES,
>   COOKIES FOR SALE!

SANDY starts shoving cookies in her mouth.

SANDY:
>   ONCE THEY HIT YOUR LIPS,
>   IT'S LIKE YOU FOUND THE HOLY GRAIL!

THE GIRLS:
>COME GET YOUR GIRL SCOUT COOKIES RIGHT HERE!
>BETTER HURRY AND CHOOSE
>BEFORE THEY ALL DISAPPEAR!
>
>COOKIES,
>COOKIES FOR YOU!

GRETEL:
>CAN'T DECIDE ON ONE? YOU BETTER BUY TWO!!!

THE GIRLS:
>COME GET YOUR GIRL SCOUT COOKIES!
>COME GET YOUR GIRL SCOUT COOKIES!
>COME GET YOUR GIRL SCOUT COOKIES!
>WE'RE ALMOST OUT!

A Toyota Camry pulls up alongside the booth. Inside are MARCUS and BRODY, two local teen troublemakers with Texan accents. They think they're so cool, but they're giant losers.

MARCUS: Brody, look. Girl Scouts selling cookies in the parking lot.

BRODY: They think they're so great with their bright vests and their do-gooder smiles.

MARCUS: Someone ought to teach those girls that life isn't always sunny and sweet.

BRODY: I'm on it, Marcus.

HE rolls down the car window.

Song begins - "Hey Girls"

BRODY:
>HEY GIRLS...
>I LIKE YOUR SONG...
>HOW MUCH FOR THOSE
>TAGALONGS?

RAQUEL:
>HEY YOU...
>WHAT'S YOUR NAME?
>FOUR BUCKS A BOX,
>THEY'RE ALL THE SAME.

BRODY:
>HE'S TED
>AND MY NAME'S BOB.

MARCUS:
>THEY HAVE NO CLUE
>THEY'RE GETTING ROBBED.

BRODY: What are your friends' names?

RACHEL: That's Sandy and this is Gretel.

>*RACHEL goes to grab a box of Tagalongs. GRETEL shakes BRODY'S hand aggressively.*

GRETEL: Pleased to meet you, sir.

BRODY: Mighty strong grip you got there.

GRETEL: Yup.

>*GRETEL grabs her crotch and crosses to the other girls. Then, MARCUS slips out of the car, goes around the back of the stand, snatches the money box, and crosses back to the car. RAQUEL makes her way back to the car with the Tagalongs.*

RAQUEL: That'll be four dollars...

SANDY: Hey, where's our money box?

>*MARCUS gets back into the car.*

MARCUS:
    HEY MAN...
    IT'S TIME TO GO!

BRODY:
    YOU BUCKLE UP!

SANDY:
    THEY TOOK OUR DOUGH!

BRODY: Thanks a lot, kid!

    HE grabs the Tagalongs from her hand, shakes the box, and the GUYS cackle as they peel away.

SANDY: They're getting away!

GRETEL: We'll never get our cookie badges now.

    In slow motion, MARCUS flips off the girls. They are mortified. GRETEL & SANDY collapse to the ground. RAQUEL stands paralyzed.

    Song begins - "We're Just Kids"

RAQUEL:
    WHAT KIND OF PERSON WOULD STEAL
    FROM A GIRL SCOUT?
    WHAT KIND OF WORLD DO WE LIVE IN?

GRETEL:
    IS THERE NO JUSTICE?
    ARE WE TO SUCCUMB TO THE CHAOS?
    JUST SIT HERE AND GIVE IN?

SANDY:
    BUT WE'RE JUST KIDS.
    WHAT CAN WE DO?
    I WEAR A SIZE SEVEN SHOE...

>   AND A KICK FROM A SHOE AS TINY AS THAT
>   WOULDN'T HURT A FLEA.

RAQUEL:
>   WE'RE JUST KIDS,
>   BUT WE ARE THREE;
>   THERE IS YOU-A AND YOU-A AND ME!
>   AND TOGETHER WE CAN MAKE THINGS RIGHT!

THE GIRLS:
>   IT'S TIME TO FIGHT!!!

RAQUEL: Girls, do you still have your scout emergency packs?

> *THEY nod "yes." All hands in and salute. Blackout.*

> *SCENE 2: ON THE ROAD. Lights up. MARCUS counts the stolen money as BRODY drives while eating Tagalongs.*

MARCUS: We got out with almost two hundred bucks, man!

BRODY: I wish we took more cookies.

MARCUS: Now we can afford what we've always wanted.

BRODY: Tickets to the—

BOTH: Christian Wrestling Federation throwdown!

> *Song begins - "Girl Scout Guerrila Attack"*

> *BRODY turns the radio up and the two rock out to the music and eat cookies as the GIRLS appear on scooters. RAQUEL has a whip and SANDY has a bow and arrow.*

RAQUEL:
>   THEY DON'T GIVE BADGES OUT
>   TO GIRLS WHO ARE BAD,
>   BUT IN ALL MY TWELVE YEARS

I HAVE NEVER FELT

ALL GIRLS:
SO FREAKING MAD!!!

SANDY:
FIN'LLY, I CAN PUT
MY ARCHER BADGE TO USE.

SANDY takes out an arrow.

GRETEL:
TOGETHER WE'LL PUT A STOP
TO THIS WRETCHED ABUSE!

SANDY:
PULL IT BACK,

RAQUEL:
HOLD YOUR BREATH,

GRETEL:
ELBOW GREASE,

THE GIRLS:
THEN RELEASE!

SANDY releases the arrow. It flies in slow motion and hits the Camry's rear tire.

THE GIRLS: Yes!

MARCUS:
WHAT THE HELL WAS THAT?

THE GIRLS:
THIS IS A
GIRL SCOUT GUERILLA ATTACK!
YOU BETTER WATCH YOUR BOOTY

'CUZ WE'RE LAYIN' THE SMACK—

GRETEL:
    DOWN!

THE GIRLS:
    WE'RE GIRL SCOUT GUERILLAS!
    WE'LL WRECK YOUR FACE!

MARCUS & BRODY:
    WE NEVER SHOULD HAVE ROBBED THOSE GIRLS
    IN THE FIRST PLACE!

RAQUEL:
    PULL OVER AND WE SWEAR
    YOU WON'T GET HURT.
    WE KNOW HOW TO SETTLE DISPUTES!

RAQUEL cracks her whip.

BRODY:
    OH GOD, IT'S SO UNFAIR!

GRETEL:
    I REASSERT:
    STOP NOW OR IN YOUR BUTT,
    YOU'LL FIND MY COMBAT BOOT!!!

MARCUS: Why are you slowing down?

BRODY: I can't go any faster with this tire blown!

The GIRLS catch up to the car.

RAQUEL: Let 'em have it, girls!

SANDY: Show no mercy!

GRETEL: Time for a boot sandwich! Eat it! I said eat it!!

GRETEL kicks MARCUS in the face with her boot. The GIRLS grab the GUYS out of the car and attack.

THE GIRLS:
> THIS IS A
> GIRL SCOUT GUERILLA ATTACK!
> YOU KNOW WHAT THEY SAY
> ABOUT "PAY BACK"!
> NOW GIVE US BACK OUR MONEY
> OR YOU DIE!

BRODY hands over the moneybox to RAQUEL.

> NOW HEAR OUR BATTLE CRY!

SANDY: Take that!

Hit!

GRETEL: And that!

Hit!

As the GUYS stumble, SANDY slow motion flies through the air and kicks both BRODY and MARCUS in the face. RAQUEL & GRETEL punch the GUYS. The GIRLS win!

THE GIRLS:
> WE'RE GIRL SCOUT GUERILLAS!!!

Out of breath, the Girls stand triumphant.

> *Song begins - "We're Just Kids (reprise)"*

SANDY:
> WE MAY JUST BE KIDS,
> BUT WE'RE STRONG.

GRETEL:
> WE KNOW THE DIFFERENCE BETWEEN RIGHT AND
> WRONG!

THE GIRLS:
> TODAY WE ARE PROOF THAT THREE LITTLE GIRLS
> CAN BEAT UP TWO SHIT HEADS!

RAQUEL:
> WE MAY JUST BE KIDS,
> HERE WE STAND,
> TOMORROW, THOSE COOKIE BADGES
> WILL BE IN OUR HANDS!

THE GIRLS:
> AND IF YOU GUYS MESS WITH US AGAIN,
> YOU'LL END UP DEAD!!!

> *BRODY & MARCUS run off.*

SANDY: That's right! You better run! RUN!!!

GRETEL: Sandy! It's over...

> *The GIRLS hug.*

> *SCENE 3: WALMART PARKING LOT; The next day. The GIRLS put on their cookie badges. GRETEL sticks an "OPEN" sign on the cookie booth.*

GRETEL: Another day, another dollar!

RAQUEL: Get your cookies!

SANDY: The perfect shnack!

> *Song begins - "Cookies For Sale (reprise)"*

THE GIRLS:
    COOKIES,
    COOKIES FOR SALE!

SANDY:
    IF YOU EAT TOO MANY,
    YOU'LL BE TIPPIN' THE SCALE!

THE GIRLS:
    COME GET YOUR GIRL SCOUT COOKIES TODAY!
    DID YOU HEAR THE NEWS?
    THERE'S A COOKIE SOIRÉE!

RAQUEL: Girls, tell everyone about today's selection!

SANDY:
    DULCE DE LECHE-IAN,
    DON'T BE SKETCH-IAN,
    THEY'RE THE FAVORITE OF KIM KARDESHIAN!

RAQUEL:
    WE GOT LEMONADES
    FOR ALL YOUR ESCAPADES!
    YOU CAN EAT THEM WHILE YOU PLAY CHARADES!

GRETEL:
    DON'T FORGET DO-SI-DOS,
    THEY'RE JUST FOR PROS,
    YOU CAN EAT THEM AND TAKE OFF ALL YOUR CLOTHES!!!

RAQUEL: Why? Why would we do that, Gretel?

GRETEL: It's hot out...

RAQUEL & GRETEL (*ad libsy*): "No." "Not really." "Nuh uh."

    BILLY & DEREK walk over to the booth.

BILLY:
>	HEY GIRLS...
>	NICE DISPLAY.
>	HOW MUCH ARE THOSE "LEMONADES"

RAQUEL:
>	HEY THERE...
>	WHAT'S YOUR NAME?
>	FOUR BUCKS A BOX,
>	THEY'RE ALL THE SAME.

BILLY:
>	I'M REG
>	AND THAT GUY'S STEVE.

Just as DEREK is about to put his hands on the money box, THE GIRLS whip out their new guns and aim at the GUYS.

GRETEL: Hands off the money box MOTHERFATHER!!!

BILLY & DEREK run away. The girls are proud about their newfound confidence and swagger. During the following, SANDY adds vocal embellishments and ad libs.

THE GIRLS:
>	COME GET YOUR GIRL SCOUT COOKIES!
>	COME GET YOUR GIRL SCOUT COOKIES!
>	COME GET YOUR GIRL SCOUT COOKIES!
>	FOR SALE!

END

COOKING FOR TWO

Book & Lyrics by *Charlie O'Leary*
Music by *Karl Hinze*

Stephan Amenta, Robert Berliner, and Bettina Bresnan in *Cooking For Two* at Theatre Now's SOUND BITES 5.0.

SYNOPSIS

In a television studio at Chelsea Piers in New York City, it's almost time for the live season finale of "Tasty Time with Jenny and Brett," everyone's favorite cooking show co-hosted by everyone's favorite real-life married couple.

Brett takes in the darkened studio before the cameras turn on, *"OPENING"*, until he's interrupted by Nameless PA and the hustle and bustle begins. Nameless PA energizes the studio audience while Brett and Jenny fight quietly, and then not so quietly. The problem? He never wants the TV show to end, and she hopes this will be their final episode ever.

The cameras start rolling and the couple is forced to put on their cheery on-air personas. They begin preparing the special meal from the night they got engaged, *"IT TAKES TWO"*. But things go off the rails as they can't keep their off-screen tensions under wraps: during a commercial break, Jenny tells Brett the show is ruining their marriage. She wants to end the TV show and move back home to Connecticut. Brett storms offstage.

Jenny is left onstage as we come back from commercial and has to prepare the dessert alone, *"SIMPLEST THING"*. Brett slips on and watches from the wings, and her cooking becomes what it originally was: an act of love between them.

They both apologize, and Brett agrees, they'll move back to Connecticut, *"IT TAKES TWO (reprise)"*. The cameras turn on once more and Brett announces to the world: they're moving the show to Connecticut! And... they're pregnant! Brett is pleased. Jenny is horrified. The audience cheers.

PRODUCTION HISTORY

Cooking for Two, by Charlie O'Leary and Karl Hinze, was first presented as a staged reading in The BMI Lehman Engel Musical Theatre Workshop on May 28, 2014. The cast was as follows:

BRETT .... Christian Duhamel
JENNY .... Kate Anderson
NAMELESS PA .... Jack Mitchell

Selected material was then performed in concert on November 10, 2014 at the Duplex in New York City. It was produced by Charissa Bertels, and directed by Thomas Caruso with musical direction by Joseph Bates. The cast was as follows:

BRETT .... KJ Hippensteel
JENNY .... Charissa Bertels
NAMELESS PA .... Arlo Hill

A fully-staged production premiered at The Irene Diamond Stage at The Pershing Square Signature Center for Theatre Now's SOUND BITES 5.0 on May 28, 2018. The production was directed by Tasha Gordon-Solmon with musical direction by Karl Hinze. It was produced by Thomas Morrissey, Chris Giordano, and Stephen Bishop Seely. The cast was as follows:

BRETT .... Robert Berliner
JENNY .... Bettina Bresnan
NAMELESS PA .... Stephan Amenta

CHARACTERS

BRETT — 30s, male identifying. Favorite dish: grilled salmon steak with hoisin BBQ.

JENNY — 30s, female identifying. Favorite dish: anything with chocolate.

NAMELESS PA — 20s, any gender. Favorite dish: Cymbalta.

SETTING

Present. Spring. Chelsea Piers: a TV studio for a cooking show.

MUSICAL NUMBERS

"Opening"	Jenny, Brett
"It Takes Two"	Jenny, Brett
"Simplest Thing"	Jenny
"It Takes Two (reprise)"	Jenny, Brett

AUTHOR NOTE

A double-slash (//) indicates that the next line of dialogue should begin. Beats are moments of negotiating, searching, action—finding the words. Silences are moments of absorbing, reflecting, stillness—there are no words. In general, these characters think and speak very quickly. Beats and silences should be brief (1-3 seconds).

> "I love my husband like a pig loves s**t."
> Julie Powell, *Julie and Julia*

– Charlie O'Leary and Karl Hinze

Chelsea Piers: a TV studio for a cooking show. It's the good kind of show that moms watch. Usually, the studio is really bright and cheery and LOUD. But right now, it's super quiet. All the lights are off, and no one's here. It's a little creepy.

Song Begins - "Opening"

BRETT:
> THIS IS MY FAVORITE PART.
> JUST BEFORE THE LIGHTS TURN ON,
> THE CROWDS COME IN,
> THE CAMERAS AND THE CHAOS...
> IT'S JUST ENERGY, ANTICIPATION.
>
> IT'S LIKE RIGHT BEFORE YOU BITE INTO A CHICKEN WING,
> AND YOUR MOUTH ALREADY FEELS LIKE IT'S ON FIRE.
> 'CAUSE YOU KNOW WHAT'S COMING,
> YOU KNOW WHAT'S COMING:
> THAT'S ENERGY, ANTICIPATION.
>
> SURE, THE OVEN DOESN'T WORK, THE KITCHEN WALLS ARE FAKE,
> BUT IT'S STILL THE REALEST PLACE I'VE EVER BEEN.
> AND YOU KNOW WHAT'S COMING,
> YOU KNOW WHAT'S COMING:
> THAT'S ENERGY, ANTICIPATION.
>
> *NAMELESS PA rushes frantically onstage.*

NAMELESS PA (*deadpan*): Brett, you're supposed to be in wardrobe.

BRETT: I'm in my wardrobe!

NAMELESS PA: You need to be in your dressing room.

BRETT: Why do I // need to—?

NAMELESS PA (*still deadpan*): Sir, I am literally begging you, *please, just do me this solid, just please, just...* GO TO YOUR DRESSING ROOM.

Beat. BRETT exits. NAMELESS PA rushes around the studio. Lights start to click on. Cameras move into place. You see, for the first time, a colorful sign overhead: "TASTY TIME WITH JENNY AND BRETT!" And in front of your eyes, in a matter of seconds, the soundstage has totally jumped to life.

NAMELESS PA: THREE MINUTES TO AIR!

JENNY: Because I thought we were—

JENNY and BRETT have wandered back onstage. They settle in a far corner, mid-conversation. Meanwhile, NAMELESS PA addresses the audience.

NAMELESS PA:	JENNY:
So! Who's excited for our show tonight? Tasty Time with Jenny and Brett! Wow, it's gonna be a good one! Can I get a—?	—making dinner last night and I arranged my evening around that, // I'm not saying it's the end of the world, I just would've appreciated—
They try to coordinate a wave.	
Like a, like a, let's do like a wave, like—	BRETT: It's called taking a little break, Jenny, it's called uh: We can't spend every moment of every day together.
They check their phone for the time.	
Yas, wave it up… Ummmmmm… Jenny, Brett! We're at two— Could you, um—?	JENNY: I'm just saying you can tell me your plans, you can send me a text.
BRETT!	BRETT: I SEE YOU EVERY DAY!

BRETT and JENNY finally hear NAMELESS PA.

NAMELESS PA: We're at two.

Lights snap. Everyone freezes except for JENNY.

JENNY:
>IT'S THE MOMENT WHEN YOU'RE WAITING WITH HIM ON THE SET,
>'CAUSE THE BIG EXCITING SHOW'S ABOUT TO START.
>AND YOU KNOW WHAT'S COMING,
>YOU KNOW WHAT'S COMING:
>IT'S FAKING IT, IT'S IMITATION.
>
>And sometimes you catch a glimpse of him, the real him, and you remember when things were easy.
>
>BUT YOU KNOW WHAT'S COMING,
>YOU KNOW WHAT'S COMING:
>IT'S APATHY, DISINTEGRATION.
>
>And I just...

Lights snap. Time returns.

NAMELESS PA (*back to the audience*): So, I heard some of you all camped out overnight? Who camped out overnight? Anybody? Somebody?

JENNY and BRETT whisper-fight.

Um. We here at the Food Network are really excited to feature a real married couple—It really shows you the power of how, like, love and stuff, and working together, and it's just really all about // sharing a meal for two.

JENNY and BRETT make their way downstage.

JENNY:	BRETT:
I HATE THIS JOB,	I LOVE THIS JOB.
BUT I LOVE MY HUSBAND.	I LOVE MY WIFE.
I WANT HIM.	SO YOU KNOW WHAT'S

I MISS HIM.	COMING,
FORGET THIS SHOW.	YOU KNOW WHAT'S COMING:
I KNOW WHAT'S COMING,	ONE MORE SEASON.
I KNOW WHAT'S COMING:	TEN MORE SEASONS!
THE END OF THIS—	WE'RE NEVER GONNA END THIS,
END OF THIS SHOW!	NEVER NEVER NEVER
	NEVER NEVER
	GONNA END THIS SHOW!

NAMELESS PA: Alright, we're on in: Ten. Nine.

BRETT: // Alright, folks!

NAMELESS PA: Eight. Seven.

BRETT (*to JENNY*): // Behave.

NAMELESS PA: Six. Five.

JENNY (*to BRETT*): // Are you talking to me?

NAMELESS PA: Four.

> *NAMELESS PA counts down with their fingers: Three. Two. One. And the show begins! The energy totally shifts once we're on-air. JENNY and BRETT sing the show's theme song.*

JENNY & BRETT:
    TASTY TIME WITH JENNY AND BRETT!

BRETT: Hey there everyone. Boy, do we have a show for you today! Don't we, Jenny?

JENNY: We sure do, Brett, it's gonna be a real humdinger.

BRETT: Yeah it is! I love you, Jenny.

> *Canned audience response: "Awwwww!" (BRETT continues.)*

BRETT: You know, before I met Jenny, I didn't even know how to boil an egg!

Canned audience laughter.

JENNY: Actually we met in culinary school and were both independently talented! Today we'll be making the meal we made together the // night I proposed.

BRETT: —the night I proposed! Right.

JENNY: But before we begin this exciting finale, I want to share // with you all—

BRETT: This exciting season finale, now before we get too deep, let's get ourselves warmed up with the one thing every good proposal needs: a drink!

Song Starts - "It Takes Two"

JENNY: Mhm, so.

She sings:

JENNY:
    ONE OF US POURS THE BRANDY AND SPICES.

BRETT:
    DA DA DA

JENNY:
    ONE OF US CUTS THE MANDARIN SLICES.

BRETT:
    DA DA DA DA

JENNY:
    I CAN SHAKE,

BRETT:
   AND I CAN STRAIN, 'CAUSE

JENNY & BRETT:
   IT TAKES TWO

BRETT:
   TO MAKE CHAMPAGNE.

JENNY: Cocktail. It's not just, it's called a Champagne // Cocktail.

NAMELESS PA: We're at commercial!

BRETT (*to JENNY*): Baby, loosen up.

JENNY: Why are you being such a cheeseball? We were screaming at each other five seconds ago, how do you just turn it off like that, I mean we're having // Real Issues, Brett

BRETT: It's our show, Jenny. I'm being professional. This is what we worked for.

JENNY (*"Do you really not get this?"*): Brett, this show is ruining us.

NAMELESS PA: And we're back!

   JENNY & BRETT sing.

JENNY & BRETT:
   TASTY TIME WITH JENNY AND BRETT!

BRETT: Welcome back! For our next dish, we'll be giving you something a little bit tart, and a lot bit tasty...!

JENNY: ...Bubba Brett's Barbecue Shrimp. Why don't you start this one, Brett?

BRETT: I'd love to!

He sings:

ONE OF US PREPS THE LEMON AND OIL.

JENNY:
    MM MM MM

BRETT:
    ONE OF US BRINGS THE WATER TO BOIL.

JENNY:
    MM MM MM MM

BRETT:
    I CAN CHOP,

JENNY:
    AND I CAN PEEL, 'CAUSE

JENNY & BRETT:
    IT TAKES TWO

JENNY:
    TO MAKE A MEAL.

NAMELESS PA: That's comm- // -ercial!

BRETT: What does that even mean, "ruining us"?

JENNY: Do you remember the year we bought the restaurant? Working seven days a week, and when we thought we would collapse we'd go up on the roof and drink whiskey out of coffee cups.

BRETT: Yeah, 'cause we were broke.

JENNY: I miss our life. I miss planning the future, thinking about kids, do you remember when that was a conversation we were—?

BRETT: Are you serious.

JENNY: I'm moving back home, Brett. I'm quitting the show.

NAMELESS PA: Alright, we're live in three—

>   *NAMELESS PA mimes: "two! one!" The theme music plays, but no one sings. And we're vamping into the entrée.*

JENNY: Hey folks! So, for our big entrée, we're going to show you how to make // Bistro Roast Chicken!

BRETT: Make chicken! We sure are!

>   *They sing:*

JENNY & BRETT:
  ONE OF US

BRETT:
  RIPS THE BONE OFF THE CHICKEN.

>   *He grunts like an animal tearing into raw meat.*

JENNY & BRETT:
  ONE OF US

JENNY:
  LETS THE SAUCE OVER-THICKEN.
  LA LA LA LA

>   *She turns the heat on the stovetop ALL THE WAY UP.*

BRETT:
  I WORK HARD,

JENNY:
  AND I REPRESS, 'CAUSE IT TAKES TWO TO MAKE A—

BRETT:
> IT TAKES TWO TO MAKE A—

BRETT & JENNY:
> IT TAKES TWO

NAMELESS PA: Commercial!

JENNY & BRETT:
> IT TAKES TWO

NAMELESS PA: // Commercial!

BRETT: —to do this, this thing. What am I gonna just do the show alone? Microwave Meals with Bachelor Brett?

JENNY: It's not my fault you decided your brand was Helpless Idiot Husband.

BRETT: I thought you liked that.

JENNY: I can't spend twenty-four hours a day with you, Brett, not here, not like this. Please believe me when I say that this is for the sake of our marriage.

BRETT (*quietly and calmly*): Here's the thing: I remember why I love this show.

Beat. BRETT storms off. NAMELESS PA scampers off behind him. JENNY's alone. Silence.

JENNY: Hey folks, we're back. Um. Brett's not feeling well, so I'm gonna show you the dessert on my own. It's a Chocolate Chunk Cookie for Two. Big enough to share. And this is the dish I—it feels so silly to call it a dish, it's a cookie, it's just, um—This is the dish I made for Brett the night we got engaged? So gather your... Ingredients. Um.

Song begins - "Simplest Thing"

She sings:

IT'S THE SIMPLEST THING IN THE WORLD,
FLUFFY AND WARM AND SWEET.
STIR IN THE BUTTER AND MIX IN THE EGG,
DROP ON THE SHEET.

IT'S THE SIMPLEST THING IN THE WORLD.
NOW THAT YOU'VE MADE THE DOUGH,
PREHEAT TO THREE HUNDRED FIFTY DEGREES,
THEN WATCH IT GROW—

BRETT comes back onstage, listening.

INTO THIS THING YOU DON'T EXPECT.
NOT QUITE SURE HOW ALL THE PIECES CONNECT.
BUT IF YOU JUST—
...AND GIVE AND HOPE AND LOVE AND WAIT,
YOU'LL SEE:

IT'S THE SIMPLEST THING IN THE WORLD,
MAKING A TREAT TO SHARE.
BUT IT DOESN'T JUST HAPPEN. YOU STILL HAVE TO WORK.
YOU STILL HAVE TO CARE.
'CAUSE THE SIMPLEST THING IN THE WORLD
IS JUST BEING THERE.

JENNY sees BRETT. A moment.

NAMELESS PA: Commercial!

They head offstage, and speak into their headset.

Does anyone have Immodium?

BRETT: Hey.

JENNY: Hey.

BRETT: ...I'm sorry. I'm // really.

JENNY: No, I mean I know how happy the show makes you.

BRETT: Cookie bear. I love you, okay?

JENNY: Okay.

BRETT: And if you wanna move back home...

JENNY: I do.

BRETT: Okay. Then we're moving.

Song begins - "It Takes Two (reprise)"

They sing:

JENNY:
ONE OF US IS A LITTLE BIT CRAZY.

It's me. I'm the—

BRETT:
ONE OF US IS A LITTLE BIT CRAZIER.

JENNY: I missed you.

A tender moment between them.

NAMELESS PA: Back for the tag!

Theme music. They sing again, and maybe this time the entire audience joins.

JENNY/BRETT/NAMELESS PA/EVERYBODY:
TASTY TIME WITH JENNY AND BRETT!

JENNY: Well hey, thanks so much for joining us for this exciting finale of Tasty Time with Jenny—

BRETT: —and Brett! If I can just get real for a minute: We had a lot of fun cooking with you guys this year.

JENNY: It has been a wonderful year. But we have some news.

BRETT: Yes, Jenny and I wanted to share with you that we're moving the show to our home in… Connecticut!

JENNY: …Brett?

BRETT: Because… We're pregnant!

Horrified beat. BRETT cradles JENNY's stomach.

So we can't wait to see you all this fall for the next season of: Tasty Time with Jenny and Brett… And Baby!

BRETT hugs JENNY. The audience cheers.

END

DEAD FLOWERS

Book, Music, & Lyrics by *Michael Finke*

The cast of *Dead Flowers* in Theatre Now's SOUND BITES 5.0.
(Left to right): Jo Walker, Corey Desjardins, Robbie Torres, Andrew Lee, Ben Yahr, and Daniel Bender Stern.

SYNOPSIS

Polly Patolsky is an 84-year-old woman, reliving the worst day of her life. After coming *"HOME FROM THE GROCERY STORE"*, she finds her husband, Charlie, in bed with her best friend, Ethel. As Polly scolds and chastises the two of them, Charlie and Ethel belittle and demean Polly by reminding her that "stress is never healthy for a woman her age." Needing a drink to calm her nerves, Polly goes to the only bar she knows of that's open early in the day; a bar that her nephew told her about. What she didn't know was that it's a gay dive bar called "The Raging Bull".

Polly is sitting and crying at the bar until a young and vibrant Hispanic drag queen named Javier Delarosa turns to Polly to ask what's wrong. She tells him the tale of Charlie and Ethel and how Charlie has pulled this stunt before. And whenever he does, he always apologizes by taking Polly out to a fancy dinner, buying her a Bloomingdales gift card, and giving her flowers. There's always flowers.

Repulsed by this story, Javier tells Polly of the time he dated a man who then publicly wronged him. Javier then reacted by making a theatrical statement that was *"LOUD AND CLEAR"* which involved stuffing the man's car with sex toys and a goodbye note. Polly says she could never do a thing like that to Charlie, to which Javier responds, "Don't give me that bull." As Javier and a Gaggle of Gays sing to Polly, encouraging her to start a riot and let her husband know the marriage is over, Polly becomes inspired with an idea.

She sends Javier and the Gaggle of Gays to a florist to pick up a very special order. When she returns home to a seemingly apologetic Charlie, she tells him that the time has come for her to leave. And in case he doesn't believe her, Polly directs Charlie to look outside and see the hundreds of *"DEAD FLOWERS"* lying on their lawn (as we watch Javier and the Gaggle of Gays drop dead flowers on the stage). Charlie begs for her to stay. Polly reminds him that he needs to calm down because "time is running out and all his doctors can tell." She hands him dead flowers and says, "This will be you."

Javier and the Gaggle of Gays sing about how Polly walked out of the house with her head held high. And Polly says she tried, "until the day he died to send dead flowers once a year."

PRODUCTION HISTORY

Dead Flowers, written by Michael Finke, premiered as part of Theatre Now's SOUND BITES 5.0 on May 28th 2018 at The Irene Diamond Stage at The Pershing Square Signature Center in New York, NY. The production was directed by Aaron Simon Gross with music direction by David Aaron Brown and choreography by Sidney Erik Wright. It was produced by Thomas Morrissey, Chris Giordano, and Stephen Bishop Seely. Krissy Delahanty was the stage manager. The cast was as follows:

POLLY PATOLSKY	Jo Walker
JAVIER DELAROSA	Robbie Torres
CHARLIE PATOLSKY	Jim Brochu
ETHEL WEINBLATT	Sheilagh Weymouth
THE GAGGLE OF GAYS	Corey Desjardins, Andrew Lee, Daniel Bender Stern, and Ben Yahr

It was awarded Best Choreography (Sidney Erik Wright) in that year's festival.

CHARACTERS

POLLY PATOLSKY	82 years old, timid housewife, the hero and protagonist of the story.
JAVIER DELAROSA	24 years old, a young and vibrant Hispanic drag queen.
CHARLIE PATOLSKY	84 years old, Polly's domineering husband.
ETHEL WEINBLATT	72 years old, Polly's "closest" friend.
GAGGLE OF GAYS	Small queer ensemble of all ages and genders.

SETTING
Polly's Home in Boca Raton and a gay dive bar, modern day.

MUSICAL NUMBERS

"Home From The Grocery Store"	Polly, Charlie, Ethel
"Loud and Clear"	Javier, Polly, Gaggle of Gays
"Dead Flowers"	Polly, Charlie, Javier, Gaggle of Gays

AUTHOR'S NOTE

Dead Flowers was written after a colleague of mine came back from a village in France and told me about a florist she had met. The florist was asked, "What's the strangest bouquet of flowers you've ever arranged." The florist responded with, "A bouquet of my deadest roses... The customer just found her husband cheating." Fast forward to taking the parts of that anecdote that thrilled me most and putting them under a magnifying glass and you have this script and score for *Dead Flowers*.

The story is inherently a little outrageous. There's the visual of a seemingly small and frail senior woman who is ready to unleash hell. There's a drag queen who seems to have back-up singers wherever she goes. And of course there's the theatricality of the titular moment of the play. But with only a short period of time to tell the story, and the rapidity of the story, the audience is left with no choice but to go along with Polly and her rather unexpected journey.

A couple practical notes about casting: Casting need not be age-appropriate. However, considering the absence of roles for senior citizens, it is encouraged to cast seniors for the roles of Polly, Charlie, and Ethel when possible. The role of Javier must be cast with a Latinx actor. While the Gaggle of Gays was written with Baritone and Tenor harmonies, the Gaggle of Gays can include other voice parts (Soprano, Alto, etc...) that simply drop or raise an octave when needed and can sing the score as written.

Lastly, the goal of *Dead Flowers* is to gain greater empathy for those who came before us in a denser, crueler patriarchal society. It's easy to judge those, like Polly, who have followed the social structures that have been laid before them. But the ability to unlearn those structures and behavioral patterns is what makes individuals like Polly and Javier transform from victims to heroes who smash the patriarchy. And may one day the patriarchy be as dead as the flowers in this musical.

- Michael Finke

Song begins - "Home From the Grocery Store"

> *Lights are at black. After a few heavy downbeats, a solo light shines above our heroine, Polly Patolsky. While somehow strong in presence, Polly is fumingly angry and visibly torn. You see, she is 82 years of age and just had the worst morning of her life. Polly addresses the audience.*

POLLY:
> I HAD JUST COME HOME FROM
> THE GROCERY STORE
> GRABBED A COUPLE OF BAGS
> AND WALKED THROUGH THE DOOR
> WHEN I SEE... WHERE I FIND...
>
> I HAD JUST COME HOME FROM THE GROCERY STORE
> WHEN I SCREAMED AND I FELL ON THE LINOLEUM FLOOR
> AND SAW MY HUSBAND

> *CHARLIE, 84, appears in his trousers and undershirt.*

> AND MY BEST FRIEND

> *ETHELl, 72, appears in a nightgown.*

> INTERTWINED

ETHEL & CHARLIE:
> CALM DOWN POLLY
> CALM DOWN POLLY

POLLY:
> AN OBEDIENT WIFE
> FOR FIFTY-NINE YEARS
> DOESN'T GIVE UP NOW, DOESN'T LOSE HER MIND
> DOESN'T LOSE HER MIND
> BUT I SPENT MY LIFE
> JUST HOLDING BACK TEARS

    WITH THE CLUES OF LOVERS YOU'VE LEFT BEHIND
    AND TERRIFIED OF THE BULLSHIT I'D FIND!

ETHEL: I promise, Polly, it's not what you think it is.

POLLY:
    ALL OF THESE YEARS AND WHAT WERE THEY FOR?

CHARLIE (*to ETHEL*): You can't reason with her when she acts this way.

POLLY:
    THERE WERE COUNTLESS TIMES I CHOSE TO IGNORE

CHARLIE: There's a good explanation for all of this.

POLLY:
    BECAUSE I NEVER THOUGHT YOU WOULD EVER
    BREAK MY HEART

ETHEL: Polly, it's not as bad as it looks—

POLLY:
    ETHEL, PLEASE DON'T START!

    (*to CHARLIE*)
    I KNEW THERE WERE OTHER WOMEN
    IN THIS HORRIBLE PARADIGM!
    AND I KEPT MY MOUTH SHUT, LIKE YOU WANTED
    EVERY SINGLE TIME!

CHARLIE and ETHEL begin to corner POLLY.

CHARLIE & ETHEL:
    CALM DOWN, POLLY
    DON'T GET UPSET
    DON'T SAY SOMETHING NASTY
    THAT YOU'RE BOUND TO REGRET

    CALM DOWN, POLLY

DON'T SHOW YOUR RAGE
STRESS IS NEVER HEALTHY
FOR A WOMAN YOUR AGE
CALM DOWN, POLLY

POLLY addresses the audience

POLLY:
I BOUGHT WINE AND BEER AT THE GROCERY STORE
BUT THIS MORNING I KNEW I'D NEED A BIT MORE
THAN PUMPKIN CIDER AND CHEAP ROSÈ

CHARLIE and ETHEL disappear as POLLY continues addressing the audience.

THERE'S ONE BAR IN BOCA THAT'S OPEN THIS EARLY
WHERE THE PRICES ARE CHEAP
AND YOUR GLASS IS ALWAYS FULL
MY NEPHEW SAID HE GOES THERE
WITH HIS FRIENDS ON THE WEEKENDS
IT TURNED OUT TO BE A GAY BAR...
CALLED, "THE RAGING BULL"

Lights shift to reflect the interior of a gay dive bar. A house remix starts playing and reverberates throughout the theater. A bar with a martini on top appears center stage with two stools behind it. POLLY very reluctantly and despondently crosses to one of the stools and has a seat. After a moment of defeatedly sitting at the bar, POLLY starts crying.

A young twenty-something Latinx man, JAVIER DELAROSA, comes dancing into the bar (although not singing along) while texting on his phone. He's texting with a wide grin on his face as his head bops to the music. He sits in the stool next to Polly. JAVIER looks up and calls out for the bartender.

JAVIER: Good afternoon Ronnie! A Tequila Sunrise when you have the chance!

He goes back to texting. After a moment he sternly looks up again

Ronnie! ¡Quiero un Tequila Sunrise en estos momentos!

He continues to text on his phone. He hears POLLY crying, with her face buried in her arms. He stops texting and looks at her. Javier slides his stool a little bit away from her as he angles himself away from POLLY. Her head comes up.

POLLY (*to herself*): What did I do wrong?!

She puts her head down. Javier is startled by her outburst. His back is still turned.

How could a man be so cruel, so vile!

JAVIER slowly turns to POLLY.

JAVIER: Oh honey... What did he do?

POLLY (*startled by his presence, and still crying*): Who the hell are you?!

JAVIER: Well excuse me, Sophia Petrillo!

POLLY: I'm sorry... I'm really sorry.

JAVIER: I'm Javier Delarosa. By day, that is. But at night, I'm... Maria Richman!

POLLY stares in confusion.

... I'm still working on the name.

POLLY: I don't understand...

JAVIER: Don't worry about it. And you are...

POLLY: Polly. Polly Patolsky.

JAVIER: Patolsky...

POLLY: I've never been to a place like this.

JAVIER: So what drove Miss Daisy to the Raging Bull?

POLLY: Well... This morning I caught my husband, Charlie...

JAVIER: No...

POLLY: ... In bed...

JAVIER: No...

POLLY: ... With my best friend, Ethel Weinblatt.

JAVIER: No!

POLLY: Yes!

JAVIER: Fuck that shit!

POLLY: And when I get home, he'll just do what he always does; take me out for a fancy dinner and buy me a Bloomingdales gift card. And flowers. He always gets me flowers...

JAVIER: That's disgusting.

POLLY: But for now... I'm here...

Song begins - "Loud and Clear"

JAVIER: Oh honey, men are dogs. With little, little balls.

He sings:

I ONCE SAW THIS GUY IN DEERFIELD BEACH
(TALK ABOUT A BOTTOM IN DENIAL)
WE WERE HAPPY FOR A YEAR

> BUT THEN I STARTED TO HEAR
> HOW HE'D BEEN GIVING OUT SOME BJ'S ALL THE WHILE
> I DIDN'T CARE
> THAT HE'S THE HOTTEST, RICHEST GUY IN TOWN
> IT WASN'T FAIR
> FOR HIM TO LIFT ME UP THEN TEAR ME DOWN
>
> I COULD HAVE SCREAMED
> I COULD HAVE CRIED
> I COULD HAVE TRIED TO DISAPPEAR
> BUT INSTEAD I GOT CREATIVE
> AND MADE A STATEMENT
> LOUD AND CLEAR

POLLY: What did you do?

JAVIER: Wouldn't you like to know...

> WHEN I HEARD THE TRUTH I SAID, "WE'RE DONE!"
> BUT I WANTED HIM TO REALLY KNOW
> SO WHEN HE LEFT THE DOOR AJAR
> I PUT A HUNDRED DILDOS IN HIS CAR
> WITH A NOTE THAT SAID, "GO AHEAD AND BLOW!"

POLLY: No!

JAVIER:
> CRYSTAL CLEAR
> AND THEATRICAL IN EVERY SINGLE WAY
> IT WAS FIERCE
> TO STAND ASIDE AND WATCH THE BASTARD PAY

A GAGGLE OF GAYS burst onto the stage, backing up Javier.

JAVIER:	GAGGLE OF GAYS:
I COULD HAVE SCREAMED	HE COULD HAVE SCREAMED
I COULD HAVE CRIED	HE COULD HAVE CRIED
I COULD HAVE TRIED TO DISAPPEAR	TRIED... DISAPPEAR
BUT INSTEAD I GOT CREATIVE	INSTEAD HE GOT CREATIVE

AND MADE A STATEMENT	AND MADE A STATEMENT
LOUD AND CLEAR	LOUD AND CLEAR

POLLY: But I can't make a statement like that! I can't even leave Charlie. I don't have a choice.

JAVIER: Bullshit!

> FOR CENTURIES WE'VE BEEN TOLD TO STAY QUIET
> AND NEVER SAY JUST HOW WE FEEL
> BUT HONEY, TIMES HAVE CHANGED
> YOU SHOULD LEAVE AND START A RIOT
> IT'S NOT LIKE YOU'RE TWENTY WITH A KID
> AFTER ALL, LOOK AT WHAT MARIA RICHMAN DID

POLLY:
> YOU DIDN'T SCREAM
> YOU DIDN'T CRY
> YOU DIDN'T TRY TO DISAPPEAR

JAVIER:
> IT'S YOUR TURN TO MAKE A GROWN MAN LEARN
> THAT HE'S A DICKHEAD
> LOUD AND CLEAR, LOUD AND CLEAR

GAYS:
> LOUD AND CLEAR, LOUD AND CLEAR
> WHOA...

JAVIER: Come on, one more time!

JAVIER:	GAGGLE OF GAYS:
I COULD HAVE SCREAMED	HE COULD HAVE SCREAMED
I COULD HAVE CRIED	HE COULD HAVE CRIED
I COULD HAVE TRIED TO DISAPPEAR	TRIED... DISAPPEAR
BUT INSTEAD I GOT CREATIVE	INSTEAD HE GOT CREATIVE
AND MADE A STATEMENT	AND MADE A STATEMENT

ALL:
    MAKE A STATEMENT
    MAKE A STATEMENT!

    JAVIER and the GAGGLE OF GAYS surround POLLY who is deep in thought.

    Song transition - "Dead Flowers"

POLLY:
    ALL THESE YEARS
    I THOUGHT I HAD TO STAY
    BUT I THINK
    I WAS CHOOSING TO LIVE THIS WAY
    SO IT'S TIME
    TO LET MY CHARLIE GO
    BEST OF ALL, I GET TO LET HIM KNOW

    JAVIER and the GAGGLE OF GAYS scurry offstage. POLLY addresses the audience.

    So I asked my new friends for some help. They picked up an important order from Petals of Boca and delivered it to my house, where they'd find me... and Charlie.

    CHARLIE appears. POLLY stares at him intently while holding a bouquet of dead flowers.

CHARLIE: Polly, I'm glad you're home. Can we finally talk about this?

POLLY:
    ON THIS DAY
    FOR THE REST OF YOUR LIFE

CHARLIE (*as if POLLY's a child*): What are you doing...

POLLY:
    YOU'LL BE REMINDED
    OF A WOMAN WHO WAS YOUR WIFE

CHARLIE: What?

POLLY:
> LOOK OUTSIDE
> ON THE LAWN YOU'LL SEE
> HUNDREDS OF DEAD FLOWERS FROM ME

> *CHARLIE looks out in shock and horror. The GAGGLE OF GAYS appear and proudly start throwing dead flowers on the stage while walking to the beat of the music.*

CHARLIE: Jesus, Polly! What did you do now?!

POLLY:
> FOR EVERY TIME I TOOK THE BLAME
> FOR EVERY TIME YOU YELLED MY NAME
> YOU'LL SEE COLD DEAD FLOWERS
> CRINKLING DEAD FLOWERS
> ON YOUR LAWN

CHARLIE: You didn't have to make a mess like this.

POLLY:
> IN YOUR SHED

CHARLIE: Come on, Polly...

POLLY:
> IN YOUR CAR

CHARLIE: ... I'm not going to clean that up.

POLLY:
> IN YOUR BED!

CHARLIE: We know you're not going anywhere. And you know why you can't.

POLY:
  FROM NOW ON
  ON THIS VERY DAY
  EXPECT A PRESENT
  LIKE THIS BOUQUET
  'CAUSE WE KNOW
  TIME IS SHORT FOR YOU,
  MY DEAR
  NOW I CAN REMIND YOU
  ONCE A YEAR

  I REMEMBER BEING
  TAUGHT
  A LADY COULD BE
  TRAINED OR BOUGHT
  BUT WITH THESE DEAD
  FLOWERS
  I'LL KNOW HOW TO
  COUNT THE HOURS
  'TIL YOU'RE GONE
  LOST AT SEA

  I'LL BE FINE
  I'LL BE FREE

JAVIER AND THE GAYS:
  FROM NOW ON
  ON THIS VERY DAY
  AH...

JAVIER:
  LIKE THIS BOUQUET

JAVIER AND THE GAYS:
  AH...
  AH...
  AH...
  I'LL BE...

CHARLIE: You know you have to help me... Polly?

POLLY:
   CALM DOWN CHARLIE
   YOU ARE NOT WELL
   TIME IS RUNNING OUT
   AND ALL YOUR DOCTORS CAN TELL

   CALM DOWN CHARLIE
   DON'T GET UPSET
   DYING ALL ALONE
   IS NOT A REASON TO FRET
   GOODBYE, CHARLIE

CHARLIE: No... you can't...

POLLY slowly turns around. She crosses to CHARLIE. She grasps his hands and gives him a kiss on the cheek. She places a dead flower in his hands.

POLLY: This will be you.

JAVIER AND THE GAYS:
WITH NO MORE FEAR
AND NO MORE DOUBT
SHE THEN WALKED OUT A PIONEER

POLLY addresses the audience a final time.

POLLY:
AND I TRIED UNTIL THE DAY HE DIED
TO SEND FLOWERS...
BEAUTIFUL DEAD FLOWERS...
ONCE A YEAR

POLLY drops one more dead flower.

She smiles.

Blackout.

END

DINOSAUR

Book, Music, & Lyrics by *Zach Spound*

Brooke Wetterhahn, Tristan J. Shuler, Zach Spound, and Emily Gardner Hall in *Dinosaur* at Theatre Now's SOUND BITES 5.0.

SYNOPSIS

Ben is at a bar celebrating his birthday with his sister, Sara, and her Fiancé, Mark, but as of late, he's been miserable over a recent breakup that's turned his life upside down. When Mark discovers that Ben has been using a dating app on his phone for the whole night, he steals his phone and tells him that he's not getting it back until he strikes up an in-person conversation with someone at the bar, just to get him out of his shell. Ben goes up to a girl, and the first thing that pops into his head is, "What's your favorite dinosaur?" Ben rambles on, and the effort fails spectacularly. Sara then tells Ben to try again, but to actually listen. Again, the effort fails.

Ben decides to ditch his friends and sit at the bar by himself, where he is approached by Julie, a similarly neurotic and heartbroken person, who tries to strike up a conversation with him. They challenge each other at first, but then they start to bond over their surface-level insecurities and end up really connecting with each other. They decide to ditch the bar and go somewhere else. A proud yet dumbfounded Mark and Sara look on as they leave, and Mark finally throws Ben his phone back.

PRODUCTION HISTORY

Dinosaur, written by Zach Spound, has its first production at Rockwell Table & Stage in Los Angeles, CA on December. 8, 2015. It was performed as an excerpt from the musical "Leap" as part of the A Little New Music concert series. It was directed by Zach Spound. The cast was as follows:

BEN	Zach Spound
JULIE	Shelley Regner
MARK	Luke Klipp

The following year it was performed as an excerpt from the musical Leap as part of the annual "Got Musical? Concert" at Colony Theatre in Burbank, CA on May 15, 2016. It was directed by Zach Spound. The cast was as follows:

BEN	Zach Spound
JULIE	Gabrielle Wagner
SARA	Andrea Wildner
MARK	Curtis Mopp

It was performed as its own short musical at The Irene Diamond Stage at The Pershing Square Signature Center for Theatre Now's SOUND BITES 5.0 on May 28, 2018. The production was directed by Rebecca Kenigsberg. It was produced by Thomas Morrissey, Chris Giordano, and Stephen Bishop Seely. The cast was as follows:

BEN	Zach Spound
JULIE	Emily Gardner Xu Hall
SARA	Brooke Wetterhahn
MARK	Tristan Shuler

It won the Audience Choice Award in that year's festival.

CHARACTERS

BEN — Male identifying, mid 20s, heartbroken, neurotic, his nature is to apologize for who he is but has the ability to let go in make-or-break situations.

JULIE — Female identifying, mid 20s sincere, vulnerable, raw honesty is her default but she sees the best in everyone, her empathy is boundless.

SARA — Female identifying, late 20s, Ben's sister, caring, joyous, a people-pleaser who lives with abandon.

MARK — Male identifying, late 20's Sara's Fiancé, goofy, mischievous, desperately wants Ben to come out of his shell.

SETTING
A bar in New York City, late at night.

MUSICAL NUMBERS
Dinosaur is a musical sequence that also functions as one song.

AUTHOR'S NOTE
Dinosaur is based on a true story. I was at a bar in LA and was just getting over a terrible heartbreak. My friend was trying to encourage me to let go and meet someone else, so he told me to go up to a girl and ask, "What's your favorite dinosaur?" While I don't condone this tactic, I wrote this piece to highlight the ridiculousness and random lengths we'll go to just to find human connection, when all we have to do is just be ourselves.

    This is meant to be a fun piece, but the one thing to really watch out for are the rhythms. They can be really tricky because they were written to reflect human speech patterns. When trying to nail these down, put rhythm before melody, and it's totally fine to speak a lyric rather than sing it here and there. Acting first, always. Have fun!

- Zach Spound

At Friar Tuck's, a neighborhood dive bar, three friends, BEN, SARA, and MARK, all in their late 20's, sit at a table together. The bar itself is a center stage. SARA and MARK, recently engaged, have whiskeys, and BEN, wearing assorted birthday accoutrements (likely against his will), has a beer. He is downing the absolute crap out of it. We hear dubstep music playing underneath.

MARK: Ok, you ready?

BEN: Yeah, just gimme a second.

> *BEN takes another swig.*

SARA: Don't be so nervous. All you're doing is going up to someone and starting a conversation.

BEN: I just ended a six-year relationship. Forgive me if I need some social lubricant.

> *He drinks again.*

MARK: And what is with this music?

SARA: I hate it. Does that make us old?

> *BEN finishes his drink.*

BEN: Okay, I'm gonna do this!

SARA: Yeah, Ben!

MARK: Birthday sex!

> *BEN takes out his phone and buries his face in it. MARK and SARA can only stare in amazement.*

SARA: What are you doing?

BEN: Starting up a conversation with someone.

SARA looks over at BEN's phone.

SARA: Are you actually on Tinder right now?

BEN: It's Bumble.

MARK: What?

SARA pins BEN's hand, with the phone, down on the table and reads from it.

BEN: Hey!

SARA: Alicia. 26. Looks like she's in front of the Louvre.

MARK: What were you gonna say?

SARA: Is that important?

BEN: "I Louvre your pic." (*beat*) "Not gonna liEiffel." (*beat*) "That was emParissing."

SARA: Ben. Why are you using a dating app?

BEN: It's Monday night. Look, nobody's here.

SARA: We could go somewhere else.

BEN: It's still more comfortable this way. We both know the reason we're talking to each other in the first place, so it cuts the small talk in half... I have more time to formulate witty responses. And if I set the radius to only match people within a couple miles or so, she could easily come here!

MARK grabs BEN's phone from him and gestures towards the bar. The music shifts. MARK points to a girl he sees at the bar.

MARK: Ok. See that girl over there?

BEN: Yeah.

MARK: Go talk to her.

BEN: About what?

MARK: Anything.

BEN: What if she doesn't want me to?

MARK: She probably does.

BEN: How do you know?

MARK: Because you haven't said anything yet.

BEN: Come on.

> *BEN makes a grab for his phone.*

MARK: Nope. You are not getting your phone back until you interact with a real person. For your sake. Ask her a question.

BEN: Like...

MARK: I don't know. Up to you. Just go.

> *MARK pushes BEN towards the girl at the bar. He eventually gets over to her.*

BEN: Excuse me.

> *He sings:*

> WHAT'S YOUR FAVORITE DINOSAUR?
> NO, I MEAN IT, IS IT ONE THAT ROARS?
> OR IS IT SILENT, THEY DON'T TEACH
> PTERODACTYLS COULDN'T SCREECH
> THAT'S A FACT YOU'LL LEARN FROM

WIKIPEDIA

DO YOU WANT ANOTHER BEER?
I'LL GRAB ONE FOR YOU AT THE BAR OVER HERE
YOU WANT A STELLA OR A CRAFT BREW
ANY AWESOME DRAFT, TWO DOLLARS OFF FROM
SOCIAL MEDIA

JUST LOOK AT ALL THE PEOPLE IN THIS CITY
THEY ALL THINK THEY'RE SUPER COOL AND PRETTY
BUT DON'T HAVE ANY DOUBTS OR FEARS
'CAUSE YOU ARE BOTH,
SO, CHEERS.

She walks away. BEN goes back to the table.

BEN: So dumb.

SARA: Well, you talked her face off. You gotta give people a chance to respond.

BEN: But the whole thing felt so dishonest.

SARA: Well, what would have made it honest?

BEN: If I had just said "Hi. Will you have sex with me?"

MARK: Then just say "Hi. Will you have sex with me?"

BEN: No! That's horrible!

SARA: Ok, I'm taking over.

She points to another girl on the other side of the bar.

Go up to her and just notice something. Clothes. Drink. Anything. Go. Now!

BEN goes up to her. He sings:

BEN:
>HEY, I REALLY LIKE YOUR SHIRT
>SEE, THAT'S THE ONLY WAY THAT I CAN FLIRT
>I'M REALLY CLEVER BUT IT NEVER SEEMS TO FUNCTION
>AND I LOSE ALL THE GUMPTION TO SAY
>WHAT I REALLY THINK
>
>WHEN I'M CONFRONTED WITH A GIRL, AT A BAR
>IT'S A PLACE, HERE WE ARE
>AND I'M DRINKING SO I THINK I'M SINKING RIGHT
>INTO THE TAR
>LIKE A DINOSAUR!
>HOPING THAT YOU'LL WALTZ INTO MY BED
>JUST BY SPEAKING FROM MY HEART
>THOUGH I'M REALLY IN MY HEAD
>I'M KIND OF STRANGE, YEAH, YOU CAN TELL
>I MISS MY EX-GIRLFRIEND, I'M IN HELL
>
>BUT I'M NOT THE KIND WHO WANTS TO WHINE OR TO DINE
>FINE— FUCK IT—
>WILL YOU HAVE SEX WITH ME?

An awkward silence. He goes back to the table.

BEN: It seems to me like you're the expert, Mark.

SARA: He's been off the market for three years, why would you listen to him?

BEN: Ok, you know what? I'm just gonna go sit at the bar. By myself. Where you guys can't manipulate me into humiliation. Eat some peanuts. Get another beer.

MARK: Right. 'Cause that's not humiliating.

BEN: I'll take a shot then.

MARK: Onward, lusty gentleman!

> *BEN goes to sit at the bar a couple of seats away from JULIE, who, during the above, has made her way to the bar. BEN starts eating from a bowl of beer nuts. He notices her. As she looks back at him, he quickly turns away. She sings:*

JULIE:
> HOW 'BOUT A PEANUT?

BEN
> NO.

JULIE:
> OH.

BEN:
> THEY'RE MINE.

JULIE:
> K FINE.

> *A beat.*

BEN:
> YOU WANT A PEANUT?

JULIE:
> THAT'S KIND

BEN:
> KINDA STALE

JULIE:
> EPIC FAIL.

BEN:
> OH WELL.

JULIE:
> WHATEVER.

BEN:
>	NEVERMIND.

JULIE:
>	WHAT'S IT LIKE?

BEN:
>	WHAT'S WHAT LIKE?

JULIE:
>	TO BE A LITTLE BITCH.

BEN:
>	I'M NOT A BITCH!

She gestures to Ben's birthday sash.

JULIE:
>	YES YOU ARE.

BEN:
>	NO I'M—

BEN looks down at his sash and realizes it reads "The Birthday Bitch."

>	WELL I WANTED TO SAY SOMETHING

JULIE:
>	WELL YOU WANTED TO SAY SOMETHING
>	BUT YOU WOULDN'T TAKE A SHOT
>	I SEE THAT A LOT

BEN:
>	BUT—

JULIE:
>	YOU'RE A BORE

A beat.

BEN:
    WHAT'S YOUR FAVORITE DINOSAUR?

JULIE:
    WHAT'S YOURS?

BEN:
    I DON'T KNOW.

JULIE:
    WHY'D YOU ASK?

BEN:
    IT'S A WAY TO START A CONVERSATION.

JULIE:
    WHAT AN EXTRAORDINARY OBSERVATION

BEN:
    COME AGAIN?

JULIE:
    WHAT ABOUT ME
    SAYS THAT I'M EVEN THE SLIGHTEST BIT
    REMOTELY INTERESTED IN DINOSAURS

BEN:
    YOU'RE FEROCIOUS.

JULIE:
    THAT'S ATROCIOUS.

BEN:
    THIS IS DUMB!

JULIE:
    WE'RE SO DUMB!

BEN:
    WE'RE JUST TALKING ABOUT TALKING—

JULIE:
    WE DON'T KNOW WHAT WE'RE SAYING 'CAUSE WE BULLSHIT A LOT

BEN:
    AND IT'S NOT LIKE I'M RUDELY INTERRUPTING

JULIE:
    NO YOU'RE NOT

A vocal counterpoint begins.

BEN (*simultaneous*):
    BUT IT'S RARE TO HAVE A FASCINATING TALK
    ABOUT NOTHING
    I'M A TOOL, YOU SEEM COOL
    EVEN THOUGH YOU'RE BLINDLY RAGING
    IN A SENSE- WAIT- NO OFFENSE
    ALTHOUGH YOU'RE THOROUGHLY ENGAGING
    AND ALSO NOT A PHONY
    BY MAKING AN ATTEMPT TO GET TO KNOW ME
    I DON'T EVEN SURE I EVEN KNOW ME
    BUT NOW I KNOW YOU
    I HEAR THE MOMENT KNOCKING
    GOTTA WAIT 'TIL WE STOP TALKING—

JULIE (*simultaneous*):
    NO!
    COMMUNICATING NOW A THING WE DO ALONE
    IN THE CITY
    BECAUSE WE ALWAYS HAVE OUR HEADS IN THE
    CLOUDS
    AND BY CLOUDS I MEAN PHONES
    I'M GLAD YOU FEEL THAT WAY, SEE
    I'VE BEEN TOLD I COME OFF CRAZY
    WHICH ISN'T ACCURATE 'CAUSE

>   MOST GUYS DON'T REACT TO WIT
>   YOU'RE ON THE CUSP OF BURSTING
>   SO ONE OF US WILL HAVE TO SHUT UP FIRST THING
>   OR WE COULD STOP—

Vocal counterpoint ends.

BOTH:
>   —AT THE SAME TIME

They cut off at once. An awkward silence. The lights in the bar start to come on.

BEN: Lights are coming on.

JULIE: Just their time to, I guess.

BEN: Probably trying to kick us out early.

JULIE: Yeah. It's a Monday. Slower.

>   *A beat.*

BEN: What's your name?

JULIE: Julie.

BEN: I'm Ben.

>   *They do an awkward handshake.*

>   *Another beat.*

BEN: So are you, uh, driving home?

JULIE: I don't have a car. Actually I live, like, right around the corner!

BEN: Oh! Nice. I live in Sunnyside, so I'm probably gonna take the 7 train back.

JULIE: Oh, do you want a ride?

BEN: You just said you don't have a car.

JULIE: Oh, wha—yeah! I did! That—I just—that's so... *(starts laughing)* Wow. La-di-da. La-di-da.

Another beat.

BEN: So, what's your number?

JULIE: My number? HA!

BEN: "Ha?" Why "ha?"

JULIE *(trying to embarrass him)*: You don't need my number.

BEN: But I wanna stay in touch.

JULIE: Why?

BEN: Because I like you! I'm trying to, you know, connect!

He makes a suggestive gesture with his hands that is supposed to imply "connection."

JULIE: EW! GOD!

BEN: Wha—what? What did I...

She starts cracking up at him.

BEN: Ok. I'm just embarrassing myself now. Good night and good luck.

He starts to go.

JULIE: Wait.

He stops.

JULIE: Do you wanna come over? Just for a drink. Like a nightcap.

BEN: You just laughed at me for asking for your number.

JULIE: I know. I just… (*says this extremely quickly*) I get uncomfortable really easily and it's not you it usually never is but I'm getting to the point where I wanna meet someone who's not totally a jerk so when I meet someone who might not be totally a jerk I get nervous and when I get nervous I tend to—

BOTH: Push.

They look at each other with a mix of apprehension, trust, and attraction.

BEN: Look, you're cool, but I'm gonna take a pass tonight. I got a busy day tomorrow and I gotta get up early and figure some stuff out.

JULIE: Like what your favorite dinosaur is?

She starts to leave the bar.

That'd be a nice start.

After a moment, Ben calls after her.

BEN:
WHAT'S MY FAVORITE DINOSAUR?
HARD TO SAY 'CAUSE I CAN ONLY NAME, LIKE, FOUR

VELOCIRAPTORS, 'CAUS THEY'VE GOT THOSE
COOL WINGS THAT OPEN UP ON THEIR FACES
AND THIS BADASS SCREECH LIKE "GAHHHH"
WHEN EMIT THIS COOL POISON TOXIC SPRAY….
THAT'S HOW THEY BRING THEIR BABIES FOOD
EVERY DAY

(*spoken*) Yours?

JULIE:
>   TYRANNOSAURUS REX WERE QUEENS AND KINGS
>   THE MOST UNSTOPPABLE OF THINGS
>   BEFORE COMETS WIPED THEM AWAY...

BEN:
>   IT'S LIKE THEY SAY
>   "LIFE WILL FIND A WAY"

JULIE: You mean—

She sings:

"LIFE FINDS A WAY"

BOTH:
>   I LOVE JURASSIC PARK

BEN: I've seen it so many times.

JULIE: Have you seen Jurassic World?

BEN: No.

JULIE: Me neither.

BEN: Wanna... give it a shot?

> *She smiles. They begin to leave together. BEN quickly turns around to a dumbfounded yet proud MARK and SARA. MARK throws him his phone. Ben drops it.*
>
> *Blackout.*

END

END OF THE LINE

Book by *Howard Ho*
Lyrics by *Chris Edgar*
Music by *Kristen Rea*

David Scott Curtis, Elyse Beyer, Kalia Lay, and Patrick MacLennan in *End of the Line* at Theatre Now's SOUND BITES 5.0.

SYNOPSIS

It's Squirt's first day on the job as a Worker Ant and he's eager to complete his first mission: to retrieve tasty morsels for the Queen from the nearby 7-11 parking lot. But, as we learn in "*THE FEW, THE PROUD, THE ANTS / STEP OUT OF LINE*," Squirt is more eager to explore the world above the Ant Colony. The wizened old Worker Ant, Stacy, teaches Squirt the life or death importance of their #1 rule: "A.N.T. - Always. Never. Transcend"—never get out of The Line (the revered pheromone trail). With the rules of the job established, Stacy counts off "*THE FEW, THE PROUD, THE ANTS (REPRISE)*" and leads the no-nonsense Alex, the ever-fearful Taylor, and Squirt.

However, Stacy smells something of mythical proportions: a Twinkie! In "*LEGENDARY STUFF*," Stacy recounts the days when their Ant-cestors feasted on the holiest of Hostess cakes, until they vanished. But, though generations had passed, some Ants believed in the prophecy that if all ants learned to stay In Line, the Gods would smile upon them with the second coming of the Twinkie. Stacy pushes forward, renewed at the prospect of returning a hero, but the team is halted by a giant object blocking their pheromone path—a fork.

Alex, now in charge and convinced that Stacy was smited by the Gods for stepping out of Line, demands they return to the colony. But Stacy and Squirt believe the Twinkie is more important than the rules. Stacy starts to climb over the fork... and dies. His final words in "*MAKE YOUR OWN FATE*" are, "Your new mission is to keep going until you find the Twinkie." Alex is now in charge and is convinced that Stacy was smited by the Gods for stepping out of Line and demands they return to the colony. Squirt, determined to honor Stacy's legacy and their new mission, refuses to go back. Tensions mount in "*ANT-POC-ALYPSE NOW*" and the three find themselves in a complete standstill.

Squirt takes a brave stand in "*STEP OUT OF LINE (REPRISE)*" and walks over the fork, discovering that the pheromone line continues on the other side—they've found the line again! Alex and Taylor reluctantly follow Squirt over the fork and reunite with a new-found sense of purpose—to find the sacred snack cake and return victoriously to the colony with the Twinkie as their trophy! They joyfully end the show with "*THE FEW, THE PROUD, THE ANTS (FINAL REPRISE)*."

PRODUCTION HISTORY

End of the Line, written by Howard Ho, Chris Edgar, and Kristen Rea, was developed in association with New Musicals, Inc. (NMI) and first produced by NMI at the Lonny Chapman Theatre in North Hollywood, California on June 29th, 2015. The production was directed by Scott Guy with music direction by Ron Barnett. The cast was as follows:

STACY	Louis Silvers
TAYLOR	Conchita Belisle Newman
ALEX	Shannon Martinous
SQUIRT	David Crane

It was subsequently produced Off-Broadway at Signature Theatre's Irene Diamond Stage as part of Theatre Now's SOUND BITES 5.0, on May 28, 2018. The production was directed and choreographed by Kristen Rea with music direction by Meggan Herod and Jason Liebson. It was produced by Thomas Morrissey, Chris Giordano, and Stephen Bishop Seely. The cast was as follows:

STACY	David Scott Curtis
TAYLOR	Kalia Lay
ALEX	Elyse Beyer
SQUIRT	Patrick MacLennan

The following year it was produced in NYC at The Vineyard's Dimson 15th Street Theatre as part of the 44th Annual Samuel French Off-Off-Broadway Short Play Festival on August 21, 2019. The production was directed by Heather Arnson with music direction by Jason Liebson, choreography by Jacob Wasson. The production Stage Manager was Luke H. Woods. The cast was as follows:

STACY	Bill Dyszel
TAYLOR	Kalia Lay
ALEX	A. J. Freeman
SQUIRT	Erik Jonathan Shuler

CHARACTERS

STACY	A senior worker ant. Wise and disciplined with a youthful optimism.
TAYLOR	A young worker ant. Naive and fearful. Loves the Queen.
ALEX	An experienced worker ant. Second in command. No funny business.
SQUIRT	A new worker ant. First day on the job.

SETTING

A parking lot outside a 7-11 store. July 2013, shortly after the commercial reintroduction of Twinkies.

MUSICAL NUMBERS

"The Few, The Proud, The Ants / Step Out of Line"	Company
"The Few, The Proud, The Ants (reprise)"	Company
"Legendary Stuff"	Company
"Marching Underscore"	Instrumental
"Make Your Own Fate"	Stacy, Squirt
"Ant-pocalypse Now / Step Out of Line (reprise)"	Squirt, Alex, Taylor
"The Ants Transcend Underscore"	Instrumental
"The Few, The Proud, The Ants (Final reprise)"	Squirt, Alex, Taylor

AUTHORS' NOTE

When this show was in development, the tumultuous fall and resurrection of the Twinkie was part of American pop culture. Hostess Brands filed for bankruptcy on January 11, 2012, suspending the production of the beloved stack cake for 10-months. After some corporate restructuring, production resumed and Twinkies returned to store shelves on July 15, 2013. These ants lived during the later part of that 10-month Twinkie production hiatus.

While the show was originally written for ALEX and TAYLOR to be played by women, and STACY and SQUIRT to be played by men, actors of any sex, capable of singing the part in an appropriate octave, may be cast in any role.

For staging: The Line is a live-or-die part of the ants' mythology. Blocking and choreography should highlight The Line and their fear of getting out of Line. The ANTS should also be in order of their rank, with STACY leading the line, followed by ALEX, then TAYLOR, and finally, SQUIRT.

- Howard Ho, Chris Edgar, & Kristen Rea

We hear the sound of early morning birds in the suburbs. Lights up on FOUR ANTS marching together in single file. In front is STACY who is a veteran and has an avuncular presence although is still in good shape. Next is ALEX with a stern face followed by TAYLOR, who seems annoyed at everything, and finally SQUIRT, who is looking up and around or off-stage altogether.

STACY (*to the group*): Attention, Ants! Smell that pheromone line.

    ALEX and TAYLOR sniff.

Our mission, by order of the Queen…

TAYLOR: I love her! Sorry.

STACY: Ahem! Our mission is to seek the food at the end of the line and to decompose it. Alex!

ALEX: Sir, yes, Sir!

STACY: Taylor!

TAYLOR: For the Queen! Sir!

STACY: Squirt!

    SQUIRT is too distracted to respond.

Squirt!

SQUIRT (*recovering*): Reporting for the first day of work, Sir!

STACY: Just say "yes, Sir!"

    Song begins - "The Few, The Proud, The Ants /Step Out of Line"

SQUIRT: Yes, Sir!

STACY: Move out!

THEY begin marching.

STACY, ALEX, TAYLOR & SQUIRT:
    RELENTLESSLY WE ROAM
    IN SEARCH OF MORSELS FOR OUR QUEEN.
    NO SODA SPILL OR PICNIC LUNCH
    OR GARBAGE GOES UNSEEN.
    THROUGH PARKING LOT AND KITCHEN FLOOR
    AND OTHER VAST EXPANSE,
    WE'RE THE FEW, WE'RE THE PROUD, WE'RE THE ANTS!

The ANTS see something.

SQUIRT: Cool!

TAYLOR: Gross!

ALEX: One! Two!

STACY, ALEX, TAYLOR & SQUIRT:
    ON BATHROOM SINK AND BEDROOM WALL,
    WE SING OUR MARCHING SONG.
    WE LEAVE A TRAIL OF PHEROMONES
    THAT NEVER STEERS US WRONG.
    AS LONG AS WE'RE IN LINE,
    WE'LL NEVER SLOW OUR BOLD ADVANCE.
    WE'RE THE FEW, WE'RE THE PROUD, WE'RE THE ANTS!

SQUIRT: Cars and people and rubber! Man, this is buggin'!

ALEX (*without looking behind*): You're bugging me! The life of us male worker ants ain't no field trip.

    THE LIFE OF AN ANT'S FILLED WITH HONOR AND DUTY,

TAYLOR:
    SWEATING AND SLAVING FOR SUGARY BOOTY.

STACY:
    IT'S NOBLE AND BLAMELESS,

TAYLOR:
    BUT STILL SUCH A CHORE.

STACY:
    WE LIVE SIXTY DAYS, MAYBE NINETY IF LUCKY.

SQUIRT:
    I'M TWO WEEKS OF AGE,
    SO I'M STILL YOUNG AND PLUCKY.
    AND YET THIS SEEMS AIMLESS.
    I'M SURE THAT THERE'S MORE.

    A LIFE FILLED WITH MARCHING'S A LIFE THAT'S A LOSS.
    I'VE HEARD THAT THIS WORLD'S MORE THAN FIVE MILES ACROSS.
    THERE'S TUNNELS SO THRILLING AND FLAVORS SO SWEET.
    SO MUCH TO EXPLORE IF I MOVE MY SIX FEET.
    I KNOW THERE'S A PLACE WHERE THE SOIL'S SOFT AND HOMEY,
    AND DUMPSTERS WITH WASTE THAT'S LIKE WINE.
    SO MUCH I COULD SEE, IF I STEPPED OUT OF LINE.

STACY turns and sees SQUIRT lagging behind with one leg out of line.

STACY: Company, HALT!

ANTS crash into each other. SQUIRT looks guilty and returns to the group.

STACY: Squirt, were you thinking of getting Out of Line? Taylor, what is the first rule of the Line?

TAYLOR: The first rule is we don't talk about the Line.

STACY: Wrong! Alex, please remind everyone what the first rule of the Line is?

ALEX: A.N.T., Sir! A, always. N, never. T, transcend. Always never transcend.

STACY: And what does that mean?

TAYLOR: I know this one! Worker ants must stay On the Line at all times. And because 99 percent of ants who get Out of Line die.

STACY: Got it, Squirt?

SQUIRT: But... all the rubber...

TAYLOR: That rubber is the wheel of a car. It will squish you. That rubber there is a shoe of a human. It will squash you. And that rubber there is a piece of gum, where you think it smells like a banana or a strawberry or icy cool bubblemint... but you'll get stuck in it and die!

SQUIRT: Okay, I'll stay in Line.

STACY is waiting to hear SQUIRT say, "Sir!"

Sir!

STACY: Good.

Song begins - "The Few, The Proud, The Ants (reprise)"

Move out!

EVERYONE resumes marching on "Move out!". SQUIRT follows reluctantly.

STACY, ALEX, TAYLOR & SQUIRT:
IN RIGID RANKS WE'RE MARCHING TOWARD
THE TASK THAT WE'RE ASSIGNED.
WITH UNITY AND LOYALTY, WE LEAVE NO ANT
BEHIND.

ALEX, TAYLOR & SQUIRT:
   WE MAY BE SMALL AND BRAINLESS—

STACY stops and sniffs aggressively. EVERYONE collides.

STACY: Wait!

Song begins - "Legendary Stuff"

I never thought I'd smell this!

STACY's face lights up with excitement.

TAYLOR: What? What do you smell?

STACY: A Twinkie!

   IT'S YELLOW FIVE AND XANTHAN GUM,
   AND EV'RY TYPE OF SODIUM.
   WITH CREAMY CELLULOSE AND WHEY,
   AN ARTIFICIAL TASTE BUFFET.
   IT'S NEARLY ALL PRESERVATIVES.
   IT NEVER ROTS, FOREVER LIVES.
   CAKE OF CAKES, ARE WE BRAVE ENOUGH
   TO SAMPLE THY LEGENDARY STUFF?

SQUIRT: Yeah, I smell it too!

ALEX *(to Squirt)*: You do not! I heard the Twinkie was a wild aphid chase, a story they tell gullible pupa to keep them In Line.

STACY: Not at all!

   THE ANCIENT ANTS OF MONTHS AGO
   DID TELL A TEARFUL TALE OF WOE.
   THE TWINKIE GONE FROM EV'RY STORE,
   THE TWINKIE GOD DID TWINK NO MORE.
   AND YET IT'S SAID THE DEAD SHALL RISE.
   THE ADVENT OF OUR SWEETENED PRIZE.

THEN SOME ANTS INTREPID AND TOUGH
SHALL TASTE OF ITS LEGENDARY STUFF.

In the time of my great-great-great-great-grand-Ant-cestor, Promethe-Ant, the parking lots of Seven-Elevens were filled with Twinkies. He knew there would be Twinkie crumbs when he heard the siren of the blue and red flashing car approaching. But then one day, Twinkies vanished. See, the Twinkie God punished us, because Promethe-Ant stepped out of Line. But the Gods promised one day, when all ants stayed In Line, they would smile on us again with the Second Coming of the Twinkie.

STACY turns to them as if a choral director.

The Ant-them with pride!

STACY, ALEX, TAYLOR & SQUIRT:
WE SHALL BRAVE THE DARK UNKNOWN,
AND FOLLOW YONDER PHEROMONE.
DRONE AND QUEEN ALIKE SHALL QUAKE,
WHEN THEY BEHOLD THIS HOLY CAKE.
WE'LL TAKE OUR PLACE IN ANT-ISH LORE.
NO ARTHROPOD COULD ASK FOR MORE.
EVEN IF THE GOING IS ROUGH,
WE'LL TASTE OF ITS LEGENDARY STUFF!

STACY: We're off to see the Twinkie!

Music begins - "Marching (Underscore)"

THEY march forth and arrive at a large fork. They collide, again.

STACY (*crushed*): The Line ends here. The special pheromone disappeared.

TAYLOR: I don't see a Twinkie.

ALEX: That's not a Twinkie, is it?

STACY: But there must be a Twinkie. I smelled it!

ALEX: You sure? You are fifty-nine days old.

TAYLOR: What is that thing anyway?

STACY: It's a fork.

TAYLOR: In Ant-lish please.

STACY: Humans use forks to stab their food dead.

SQUIRT: Buggin'!

TAYLOR: Stab? Dead? Does this mean we're going to die?

STACY: No. It just means that we're at a fork in the road.

TAYLOR: Hail Queen Ant, full of grace...

    TAYLOR crosses herself like a 6-legged ant crucifix.

ALEX: Sir, protocol says we return to the Colony.

STACY: No! I smelled the Twinkie! I'm going to find it even if it's the last thing I...

    STACY steps out of Line and falls.

    Song begins - "Make Your Own Fate"

SQUIRT: Stacy!

    SQUIRT tries to get to STACY but doesn't want to get Out of Line.

STACY:
    KEEP YOUR ANTENNAE ATTUNED TO THE SMELL,
    OF DEXTROSE AND POLYSORBATE.
    ALL ANTS MUST DIE—ONLY SOME WILL LIVE WELL.
    NOW GO, SONS, AND MAKE YOUR OWN FATE.

    Your new mission is to find the Twinkie.

STACY lies motionless.

SQUIRT: Stacy?

Beat.

ALEX: He's dead.

TAYLOR: Are you sure?

ALEX: He was pushing sixty.

TAYLOR: I don't think he died of old age. He stepped out of Line, and the Gods did smite him! Oh Queen, be merciful. Hail Queen Ant!

ALEX: After Stacy, I'm next in line. As your new superior officer, I order you to go back to the Colony. Move out!

Song begins - "Ant-pocalypse Now/Step Out Of Line (reprise)"

SQUIRT, still in the back of the Line, refuses to budge.

SQUIRT: No, Stacy told us to find the Twinkie.

ALEX: That was before he died getting out of Line.

SQUIRT: I'm not leaving this mission!

ALEX:
>RESISTANCE IS FUTILE—WE LIVE FOR THE HIVE.
>AN ANT BY HIS LONESOME CAN NEVER SURVIVE.
>SO FALL INTO LINE OR THIS PARKING LOT WILL BE YOUR TOMB.

SQUIRT:
>THAT'S JUST WHAT YOU ASSUME.

ALEX:
>YOUR HIGH-FRUCTOSE FANTASY'S ALL WELL AND GOOD,
>BUT DEFIANCE I JUST CAN'T ALLOW.

'CAUSE THAT WAY WILL BRING THE ANT-POCALYPSE NOW!

SQUIRT: No, it won't cause the Ant-pocalypse!

>HERE LIES AN ANT WHO GAVE ALL FOR HIS DREAM
>TO REACH THE UNREACHABLE SNACK.
>I SMELL THE SCENT OF THAT CHEMICAL CREAM.
>AND DAMN IT, I'M NOT TURNING BACK.
>
>HERE LIES AN ANT WHO WOULD NEVER SAY "CAN'T."
>NO SILVERWARE STOOD IN HIS WAY.
>WE'LL BE THE HEROES OF TALES THAT ENCHANT.
>THE LARVAE OF SOME DISTANT DAY!

TAYLOR claws at the floor ineffectively.

ALEX: What are you doing?

TAYLOR: I'm burrowing.

ALEX: Why?

TAYLOR:
>I WISH I WAS BORN AS AN ANT WHO CAN MATE.
>INSTEAD I'M A WORKER AND DOOMED TO THIS FATE.
>I NEVER WILL PLEASURE THE QUEEN IN HER UNDER GROUND BED.

SQUIRT:
>I DON'T GET WHAT YOU JUST SAID.

SQUIRT pushes past TAYLOR and tries to move up to the front of the Line while ALEX tries to stop him, unsuccessfully.

TAYLOR:
>I'VE GOT NO CONTROL OVER WHEN I WILL DIE.
>I'LL STILL HAVE A SAY IN THE HOW.

ALEX: Squirt, halt!

TAYLOR:
> I'LL BE UNDERGROUND,
> FOR ANT-POCALYPSE NOW!

SQUIRT climbs the fork.

ALEX: Squirt, get off that thing! You are Out of Line! Get back In Line!

SQUIRT: Listen! Some of you want to head home. Some of you want to burrow down. That might be the right thing to do in ninety-nine percent of all situations. But this, THIS is not a ninety-nine percent kind of day. And even if I die, at least I know the end of the line for me was for the noblest of causes—a Twinkie!

> A LIFE FILLED WITH MARCHING'S A LIFE THAT'S A LOSS.
> THERE'S DAYS WHEN AN ANT MUST BECOME HIS OWN BOSS.
> AND WHEN YOU FIND TREATS FOR WHICH MOST ANTS JUST PRAY,
> NOW THAT DAY I THINK IS A ONE-PERCENT DAY!
>
> AT LEAST I ASPIRED TO AN ANT-TASTIC DREAM.
> A QUEST FOR DESSERT THAT'S DIVINE.
> AT LEAST I'LL BE FREE,
> WHEN I STEP OUT OF LINE.

SQUIRT goes over the fork. ALEX and TAYLOR wait.

SQUIRT: OOOOO!

ALEX and TAYLOR grimace at SQUIRT'S cry.

Music begins - "The Ants Transcend Underscore"

TAYLOR: Is something killing you?

SQUIRT: I found the Line again! Come on over!

ALEX and TAYLOR sniff the Line and follow SQUIRT over the fork.

TAYLOR: I smell it! Oh the Queen's going to be so turned on!

ALEX: Squirt, I'm sorry I doubted you. I just wanted what was best for the team.

SQUIRT: Alex, since our mission is back on track now, would you care to lead the way?

ALEX: As your superior officer, I shall do so with pleasure. Move out!

THEY march.

Song begins - "The Few, The Proud, The Ants (Final reprise)"

TAYLOR: Buggin'!

ALEX, TAYLOR & SQUIRT:
    ALTHOUGH WE'RE SMALL, WE GIVE OUR ALL,
    AND CONQUER ANY TEST.
    AND SOON OUR SACRED SNACK WILL BE A TROPHY FOR OUR NEST.
    WE'LL WIN A HEROES' WELCOME—

TAYLOR:
    MAYBE EVEN SOME ROMANCE?

ALEX and SQUIRT look at TAYLOR skeptically, but continue.

ALEX, TAYLOR & SQUIRT:
    WE'RE THE FEW, WE'RE THE PROUD,
    WE'RE OFF TO TASTE THY LEGENDARY STUFF!

THEY see the TWINKIE and stare reverently. STACY is resurrected.

END

FINDING THE WORDS

Book & Lyrics by *Andy Roninson & Chris Critelli*
Music by *Andy Roninson*

The cast & creatives of *Finding The Words* rehearsing at Ripley Grier Studios for Theatre Now's SOUND BITES. *(Left to right around the circle):* Ron Bopst, Katie Whetsell, Trent Mills, Jennifer Piacenti, Alan Winner, Andy Roninson, and Andrew Garret Karl.

SYNOPSIS

As Opening Night looms over a regional theater's production of the overblown operetta, *"WORDS OF LOVE"*, a tense rehearsal breaks down when dashing lead actor Tony can't remember his lines. The overbearing director Morty Duke charges his bright-yet-klutzy assistant/grand-daughter Fanny with fixing the situation. Fanny psyches herself up to approach Tony, to act on her feelings and *"TALK TO HIM"*.

While the two bond, Tony reveals to Fanny that the reason he keeps forgetting his lines is because of a secret crush on someone in the company... someone who probably doesn't even notice him. Fanny, nervous and hopeful, asks Tony who his crush is, and Tony confesses that it's *"STEVE"* the sound guy.

Fanny encourages Tony to *"TALK TO HIM (reprise)"*, and drags Tony around the whole theater, knocking on doors, looking for Steve. Finally, once Tony accepts that "rejection is better than regret," he finds Steve and asks him out - and Steve says yes!

Each feeling relieved and vindicated, Tony returns to the stage, and Fanny strides to the back of house. As rehearsal strikes back up, Tony remembers his lines in the *"WORDS OF LOVE (reprise)"* and the show goes on!

PRODUCTION HISTORY

Finding the Words, written by Andy Roninson and Chris Critelli, was first presented as a staged reading in 2013 at New London Barn Playhouse in New London, NH. It was directed by Andrew Garret Karl and starred George Merrick.

On November 1st, 2013, it was produced as the inaugural episode of the podcast TAKE A TEN, the first podcast to feature complete original musicals. The cast was as follows:

FANNY	*Eliza Hayes Maher*
TONY	*Chris Critelli*
MORTY	*Stephen Berger*
DESIREE	*Jennifer Piacenti*
STEVE	*Alan Winner*
STAGEHAND	*Santino Lo*

Later that year it had its first stage production in Theatre Now's first annual SOUND BITES festival on December 9, 2013. The production was directed by Andrew Garret Karl, with musical direction by Andy Roninson. It was produced by Thomas Morrissey and Stephen Bishop Seely. The cast was as follows:

FANNY	Katie Whetsell
TONY	Trent Mills
MORTY	Ron Bopst
DESIREE	Jennifer Piacenti
STEVE	Alan Winner
STAGEHAND	Andrew Garret Karl

Katie Whetsell was awarded Best Actress for her role of FANNY at that year's festival.

It was then presented in 2015 at Manhattan Musical Theater Lab as part of a reading of seven TAKE A TEN musicals, which was directed by Emmy-winner Matt Cowart.

SETTING
In the final rehearsal of an operetta at a small regional theater, present day.

MUSICAL NUMBERS

"Words of Love"	Tony, Desiree
"Talk to Him"	Fanny
"Steve"	Tony
"Talk to Him (reprise)"	Fanny, Tony
"Words of Love (reprise)"	Tony, Desiree

CHARACTERS

FANNY   20s to 30s, female-identifying, sharp, kind, and spirited. Quick with a self-deprecating joke and a word of encouragement.

TONY   20s to 30s, male-identifying, young leading man, a "Prince Charming" type, as handsome as he is insecure.

MORTY	60s to 80s, male-identifying, an elder statesman of the New York theatre scene, a bullish, wise-cracking, "Borscht Belt" type.
DESIREE	20s to 40s, female-identifying, self-involved and surrounded by amateurs, a classic "Diva" type.
STEVE	20s to 40s, male-identifying, a soft-spoken, cool techie.
STAGEHAND	Any age and gender. A stagehand.

AUTHOR'S NOTE

In 2013, the 'Take a Ten' podcast was launched. It was an ambitious mission; to write, produce, and record all-original, self-contained, ten-minute musicals, then release them, every month. Easy!

At the time, I remember its creator Andy Roninson and I chatting about what we wanted our inaugural episode to be. We were interested in something that could serve as a love-letter to the theatre and theatre people, while still poking fun at the personalities, preciousness, and cliches of that world.

Those ideas eventually coalesced into *Finding the Words*, a heartwarming tale set in what, for every theatre person, will be a familiar situation; the inevitable tech-week crisis. It's a story that, at its core, is about stepping outside of ourselves, outside of our insecurities, and choosing to make a connection with someone.

- Chris Critelli

Lights up on FANNY DUKE hanging up a sign that reads, "The Ft. Myers Playhouse Presents: WORDS OF LOVE." Under the title, the words "Directed by Morty Duke" are enclosed in a big box.

MORTY (*offstage*): Fanny! Get in here, we're rehearsing!

FANNY: Ah! Coming, Grandpa!

> *The scene shifts to the inside of the theater. The two lead actors, DESIREE and TONY, rehearse the love theme from this operetta. MORTY, the Borscht Belt-era director, watches from the "house." FANNY rushes in.*

MORTY: Where were you? I called you ten minutes ago!

FANNY: Sorry, Grandpa, I was painting the sign, and—

MORTY: Shah! What, you don't hear we're rehearsing? Are your ears slow too?

Song begins - "Words Of Love"

DESIREE:
    I HEAR YOU CALL MY NAME
    AND IT FEELS LIKE A HAND IN A GLOVE

TONY:
    SO SMOOTH, SO WARM,

TONY & DESIREE:
    SO GRAND
    WHEN YOU FILL MY EARS WITH WORDS OF LOVE

DESIREE:
    EVERY SOUND YOUR LIPS DO MAKE

TONY:
    MAKE THE GROUND BENEATH ME QUAKE

DESIREE:
　　　IT'S YOU FOR ME, AND ME FOR YOU,

　　　TONY stumbles on his the lyrics

　　　NO.... DO, BA, DE, BA, DO.. BA DO.....

　　　Song ends.

DESIREE (*cutting off the song*): Ergh!! I can't take it anymore!

MORTY: What? Desiree, what's going on?

DESIREE (*fuming*): Morty, I can't deal with this unprofessionalism! I have played Off-Broadway!

TONY: I'm really sorry, Mr. Duke, I just blanked.

DESIREE: Blanked? Blanked?!? That's the fifth time in the last ten minutes!

MORTY: Tony, boychick, what's happening? You're dropping more lines than my aunt Sadie around New Year's!

　　　The sound of a rimshot is heard, followed by crickets.

　　　Eh? Eh? Anyone? Oy...

DESIREE: Morty, I. Am. Done. I quit!

　　　SHE storms out of the room, muttering angrily.

MORTY: Quit? Desi, no, you can't quit, we open tomorrow! Think of the headline in the paper: "LEADING LADY A NO SHOW: HANDSOME DIRECTOR IN RUINS." Fanny!

FANNY: Yes, grandpa?

MORTY: I need to go talk some sense into Marie Antoinette. You need to get up on that stage and get that boy to sing the right words!

FANNY: What, me? Oh, I would, but I have to... uh, wash my hair.

MORTY: Ptu! What, are you shy? I see how you look at him.

FANNY: What? Tony? No, I never look at him. Never seen him in my life. I don't even know how his eyes crinkle when he smiles.

MORTY: Big, handsome guy like that? Even I can't stop looking at him, and I've got cataracts! Listen, girlie: you'll never know if you don't try. Now, go!

HE pushes her and starts off.

Oy, these kids. They're harder to get going than my first wife!

The sound of a rimshot is heard again, followed by crickets.

I said, "my first wife!" Eh? Eh? Anyone? Ehhh...

HE leaves.

Songs begins - "Talk To Him"

FANNY *(to herself)*: All right, Fanny... No big deal...

SHE sings:

TALK TO HIM, TALK TO HIM
SOUNDS SO EASY WHEN YOU SAY IT
SIMPLE GAME, SO GO AND PLAY IT
THERE'S THE DRAGON, TIME TO SLAY—"SHIT!"

He totally just caught you staring at him. Jesus, Fanny, what does your hair even resemble right now?

She opens a compact mirror.

Ugh, look at you. You look like Tim Burton's armpit.

Beat. SHE continues, optimistically.

Well who knows, maybe he's into that.

She shuts the compact and takes a deep breath.

TALK TO HIM, TALK TO HIM
SHOW HIM THAT YOU'RE FUN & WITTY
AND IN THE RIGHT LIGHT CAN BE QUITE PRETTY
TIME TO HIT THE NITTY GRITTY AND
START THE SHOW, SAY HELLO
LET HIM KNOW YOU'RE NOT SOME SQUARE
RUN YOUR FINGERS THROUGH HIS HAIR
HE'S A STALLION, BE HIS MARE AND—

Whoa, Fanny. Reel it in.

SO WHAT IF HE'S SO HOT
SO WHAT IF YOU'RE, WELL, NOT
SO WHAT IF YOU CAN'T LAST A MINUTE
WITH AN OPEN MOUTH WITHOUT BOTH FEET IN IT
SO WHAT IF YOU DIE OF SHAME
'CAUSE HE THINKS YOU'RE LAME
BUT IF YOU DON'T TRY,
THEN THERE'S NO ONE ELSE TO BLAME
SO WIPE YOUR SWEATY HANDS AND

TALK TO HIM, TALK TO HIM
DON'T PRETEND YOU'RE ON YOUR PHONE
GO! HE'S STANDING ALL ALONE
DON'T ADD THIS TO THE LIST
OF OPPORTUNITIES YOU'VE MISSED
AND ALL THE LIPS YOU HAVEN'T KISSED
TIME TO GIVE THIS PLOT A TWIST
MAKE HIM SEE THAT YOU EXIST!
JUST WALK AND TALK TO—

Song ends.

FANNY (*awkwardly*): Heeey!

TONY: Hey, aren't you supposed to talk to me? Fanny, right?

FANNY (*brimming*): Bingo! I mean, yes, Fanny. I'm Fanny. My name's not Bingo. I'm not a farmer's dog.

TONY (*chuckling*): I can see that.

FANNY: It's after Fanny Brice. The comedienne.

TONY (*happily*): Like in Funny Girl?

FANNY: Exactly! She was the one who pulled my grandpa into show business when he was a boy. Literally, yanked him onstage one night. And he never left.

TONY: I think your grandpa hates me.

FANNY: What? Negative. He doesn't hate you. He's just... difficult around opening nights.

TONY: We open tomorrow. And I keep screwing up all my scenes. I can't focus.

FANNY: Maybe I can help. Talk to me. What's going on in that big, handsome brain of yours?

TONY: It's... complicated.

FANNY: Well, I am fluent in complicated. It's like my second language. Yo hablo... complicado. Sorry, continue.

TONY: Okay. (*pause*) You ever been head-over-heels for someone you see everyday, and they don't even know it?

FANNY (*sweetly*): Yeah.

TONY: Like, there's something there. Something electric. And all it would take is for you to say hi, but—

FANNY: You can't find the right words.

TONY: Yeah.

FANNY: So? Who is it?

TONY: I can't.

FANNY: Tony, you can tell me. It might help to get it off your chest. Who's the mystery lady?

TONY (*this isn't easy*): Steve.

FANNY: Steve?

TONY: The sound guy.

FANNY: The—(*realizing what this means*) OH. You're...?

TONY: Because I turn into a school girl everytime he walks by.

FANNY (*incredulous*): Really? I'm sorry, I don't want to sound insensitive. It's just...you're like the handsomest, most attractive guy I've ever seen. And I watch a lot of "The Bachelorette."

TONY: Thanks. You're sweet. But, what good are looks if I can't formulate a sentence when he's around?

Song begins - "Steve"

TONY: It's ridiculous. I mean, even saying his name is so... just... so...

He sings:

STEVE, STEVE
SETS MY LEVELS RIGHT

MAKES SURE MY PACK IS ON NICE AND TIGHT

STEVE, STEVE
MAKES MY VOICE SO LOUD
AND I FEEL HIM SMILING FROM UP IN HIS CLOUD

STEVE, STEVE
HEARS MY EVERY WORD,
BUT ALL THAT MATTERS IS STILL UNHEARD

STEVE, STEVE
MAKES ME FEEL SO SMALL
LIKE I'M EVERYTHING AND NOTHING AT ALL

WHEN HIS HANDS SCRAPE THE TAPE OFF MY SKIN,
AND HE LINGERS WITH HIS FINGERS, STRONG AND WARM,
I JUST STAND DUMB AND SOMEHOW CAN'T WIN
AND HE'S GOING, NEVER KNOWING THAT WHY I CAN'T PERFORM IS

STEVE, STEVE
DOESN'T SEE
WHAT HE DOES TO ME

OH, STEVE
TAKES MY MIC AWAY
AND THAT'S ONE MORE ALMOST PERFECT DAY
WITH STEVE.

FANNY (*sincerely impressed*): Wow.

TONY: Whatever. It doesn't matter. Can we just run these lines?

FANNY (*getting an idea*): No.

TONY: No?

FANNY: No, because you are clearly too hung up on this guy.

TONY: Well, now I'm really glad I told you—

FANNY: Which is why you're going to find Steve right now.

Song begins - "Talk to Him (reprise)"

TONY: Excuse me?!

FANNY:
    IT'S TIME FOR YOU TO QUIT YOUR MOPING

TONY: Fanny...

FANNY:
    IT'S TIME FOR YOU TO GET OFF YOUR ASS
    NO MORE SITTING, WAITING, HOPING
    HE MIGHT WAKE UP AND MAKE A PASS

TONY:
    THEN WHAT DO YOU SUGGEST I DO?

FANNY:
    GO AND TALK TO HIM
    SAY ANYTHING AT ALL
    MENTION THE WEATHER, SPARK A DEBATE,
    OR MAYBE—OH I DON'T KNOW—MAKE A DATE
    ANYTHING WOULD BE GREAT
    GO TALK TO HIM

FANNY: Come on!

TONY: Where are you taking me?

FANNY: You can't talk to Steve if you're not in the same room.

TONY: Oh, no, no, no, no—

FANNY:
    JUST OPEN YOUR MOUTH, AND SAY, "HELLO!"

TONY:
> THAT'S EASY FOR YOU TO—

FANNY:
> OH, IS THAT SO?
> THEN WHO WAS THE GIRL THAT WAS
> WRINGING HER HANDS,
> SWEATING BULLETS,
> CATCHING HER BREATH,
> JUST TO TALK TO YOU?

TONY: Really?

FANNY:
> YEAH, AND YOU KNOW WHAT?
> I'M STILL ALIVE, AND I'M DOING FINE,
> AND YOU'RE GONNA BE FINE TOO
> GO AND TALK TO HIM
> DON'T SIT AROUND AND STALL
> YOU'VE GOT ALL YOU NEED TO GET THROUGH YOUR FEARS
> YOU'VE GOT A MOUTH, AND HE'S GOT SOME EARS
> SAY, "HEY LET'S GO GRAB SOME BEERS!"
> GO TALK TO HIM

FANNY opens a door.

FANNY: Hey, is Steve in here?

STAGEHAND: Nah, he's grabbing some XLR's from the supply closet.

FANNY: Thanks!

She closes the door.

C'mon, Tony, that's right nearby, let's go!

TONY: Fanny, wait!

He sings:

>   PEOPLE LOOK AT ME AND SEE JAMES DEAN,
>   BUT INSIDE, I'M STILL FOURTEEN.
>   I'M NOT YOU,
>   WORDS DON'T COME EASY

FANNY:
>   THEN FORGIVE ME
>   'CAUSE I'M 'BOUT TO GET REAL CHEESY—
>   DON'T EVER, EVER FORGET:
>   REJECTION IS ALWAYS BETTER THAN REGRET

>   Well. He's inside.

TONY (*sighs*):
>   AND ALL I HAVE TO DO IS

TONY & FANNY:
>   TALK TO HIM...

The supply closet door opens.

STEVE: Oh, hey, Fanny, what's up?

TONY: Actually, Steve, I'm the one who came to bug you.

FANNY: Get in there!

She pushes him.

TONY: Oof! (*to STEVE*) Yeah... so... um...

STEVE: Haha, what is it, Tony?

TONY: Well, I was wondering if you... would want to get some coffee sometime?

STEVE: Coffee?

TONY: Yeah, or lunch. I mean, if you want to or whatever—

STEVE (*laughing*): No, I'd love to! I've been waiting for you to say something. But, let's talk when I'm not knee deep in wires and cables.

TONY: Hahaha, cables... Abso– absolutely.

MORTY (*offstage*): Fanny! Tony! Where are you? I talked Queen Sheba into gracing us with her presence again.

FANNY (*to TONY*): You gotta go.

TONY: I know. (*to STEVE*) See ya later, Steve!

STEVE (*smiling, knowingly*): Haha, bye, Tony...

The door shuts.

TONY: And Fanny?

FANNY: Yeah?

TONY: Thank you. Really.

FANNY: All in a day's work for a... Whatever I do here!

MORTY (*to the offstage "conductor"*): All right, Maestro, strike up the band!

TONY joins DESIREE onstage.

Song begins - "Words Of Love (reprise)"

MORTY: Ah, there's our boy!

FANNY approaches Morty's side in the house.

DESIREE:
EVERY SOUND YOUR LIPS DO MAKE

TONY:
>	MAKES THE GROUND BENEATH ME QUAKE

DESIREE:
>	IT'S YOU FOR ME, AND ME FOR YOU

TONY:
>	NO TRUER TWO COULD EVER DO

FANNY (*happy that Tony remembered his words*): Yes!

MORTY: Shh!

DESIREE & TONY:
>	AND SO,
>	SPEAK OUT MY NAME ONCE MORE
>	WITH A CRY TO THE HEAVENS ABOVE
>	AND FILL MY EARS
>	WITH YOUR WORDS OF LOVE!

DESIREE and TONY kiss onstage. MORTY turns to FANNY and says something funny, maybe, "See? Told you he was straight!" This line was improvised during recording in 2013, so feel free to come up with your own version.

END

FRANKLIN PIERCE: DRAGON SLAYER

The Untold Story of America's Debatably Least Effective President

Book & Lyrics by *Preston Max Allen*
Music by *Will Buck*

Anna Marr and Brad Standley in *Franklin Pierce: Dragon Slayer* at Theatre Now's SOUND BITES 4.0.

SYNOPSIS

Jennifer, an incredibly average eighth grader, is in the midst of struggling to complete a class assignment on tragically boring president Franklin Pierce *"FRANKLIN PIERCE DID NOT"*. Disappointed that everyone in class will have a more interesting president to show off in their presentations, Jennifer puts her project away for the night. But as soon as she goes to sleep, Jennifer is awakened by a mysterious visitor: Franklin Pierce himself!

That's right, former president Franklin Pierce has come to Jennifer to inform her that once a year a student is assigned a report on his presidency, and once a year he pleads with them to set the record straight. It wasn't that he was a boring and disappointing president - he was actually distracted from his White House duties by a secret magical dragon war threatening mankind *"TELL THEM ALL"*. Franklin's world-saving adventure stayed a secret after his death, and now he's determined to finally convince someone to present the truth.

However, Jennifer isn't swayed by his fantastical story and insists he just get used to his real, boring life where he's simply not cool. Franklin sees Jennifer's really talking about herself and tries to get her to see the unique person she is, even if she's not that popular *"THE YOU YOU ARE"*. Jennifer realizes he's right and is ready to embrace her special brand understanding that Franklin was using the dragons as a metaphor to show her how silly it looks when you try to be more exciting than you are. But as Jennifer champions her new positive attitude, Franklin tries to insist that no, it wasn't a metaphor, he really did slay a clan of dragons.

Just then, Jennifer wakes up from what she believes was a wild dream. But when Franklin Pierce appears at the foot of her bed with one last plea, no one can be sure!

PRODUCTION HISTORY

Franklin Pierce: Dragon Slayer (The Untold Story of America's Debatably Least Effective President), written by Preston Max Allen and Will Buck, was first presented as a staged reading as part of the BMI Lehman Engel Musical Theatre Workshop in 2016. The cast was as follows:

JENNIFER_____Anna Marr
FRANKLIN PIERCE_____Brandon Andrus

It's first production premiered at The Irene Diamond Stage at The Pershing Square Signature Center for Theatre Now's SOUND BITES 4.0 on May 28, 2017. The production was directed by Blayze Teicher with musical direction by Danny K. Bernstein. It was produced by Thomas Morrissey, Stephen Bishop Seely, and Chris Giordano. It was stage managed by Abi Rowe. The cast was as follows:

JENNIFER_____Anna Marr
FRANKLIN PIERCE_____Brad Standley

In 2018 it was a finalist for City Theatre's National Award for Short Playwriting Contest and the following year had its regional premiere May 30-June 23 in 2019 at Adrienne Arsht Center for the Performing Arts in Miami, FL as part of City Theatre's Summer Shorts series. It was produced by Margaret M. Ledford and Susan Westfall. The production was directed by Michael Yawney with musical direction by Caryl Fantel. The cast was as follows:

JENNIFER_____Hannah Richter
FRANKLIN PIERCE_____Brian Reiff

CHARACTERS

JENNIFER   A jaded eighth grader. Practical and subdued which reflects in her style.

FRANKLIN PIERCE   Literally the former president.

SETTING
Jennifer's Bedroom. Modern day.

MUSICAL NUMBERS

"Franklin Pierce Did Not"	Jennifer
"Tell Them All"	Franklin Pierce
"The You You Are"	Jennifer, Franklin Pierce

AUTHORS' NOTE

Is *Franklin Pierce: Dragon Slayer* a tale of self-love and acceptance when people don't see you as you wish you could be seen? Or is it really just the story of a US president facing a secret but very real dragon attack in the 1800s? Why choose! The world of the show is a magical mystery, and we hope you have as much fun as we did bringing this story (and Franklin) to life. Part silliness, part a little bit serious, and part actually kind of educational, please take good care of these characters - even if Jennifer will never be as interesting as, say, Cassie Smith.

- Preston Max Allen

Eighth grader JENNIFER, is in her slightly decorated but not too colorful bedroom. She is working on her poster board for a class assignment on President Franklin Pierce. It's barely half done and she seems completely unenthused.

Song begins - "Franklin Pierce Did Not"

JENNIFER:
>EVERY YEAR ON PRESIDENT'S DAY TEACHERS WILL ASSIGN
>A PRESIDENT TO STUDY TO EACH KID, BUT I HATE MINE
>HE DID NOTHING COOL AND DIED ALONE
>AND EVERYONE FORGOT
>LOTS OF PRESIDENTS DID SOMETHING
>BUT FRANKLIN PIERCE DID NOT
>
>WHO IS HE? NO ONE CARES
>OR REMEMBERS HIM AT ALL
>EVEN WHILE IN OFFICE HE DROPPED EVERY SINGLE BALL
>NIXON HAD HIS SCANDALS AND JFK WAS HOT
>EVERY PRESIDENT DID SOMETHING
>BUT FRANKLIN PIERCE DID NOT

SHE starts to get ready for bed.

>EVERY KID IN SCHOOL HAS BETTER LUCK THAN ME, I SWEAR
>LIKE STUPID CASSIE SMITH GOT ANDREW JACKSON, IT'S NOT FAIR
>I'M STUCK HERE WITH A TOTAL DUD
>WHO FAINTED WHEN HE FOUGHT
>EVERY PRESIDENT DID SOMETHING
>BUT FRANKLIN PIERCE DID NOT
>
>WHO IS HE? NO ONE CARES
>HE'S SO DULL THAT IT'S OBSCENE
>WHEN WE LISTED OUT THE PRESIDENTS
>WE ALL FORGOT 14
>CLINTON HAD RELATIONS, AND JFK GOT SHOT
>EVERY PRESIDENT DID SOMETHING
>BUT FRANKLIN PIERCE DID NOT

JENNIFER turns off the light and goes to sleep. After a few moments, in an ominous cloud of smoke, FRANKLIN PIERCE appears.

FRANKLIN: Hey, Jennifer.

SHE wakes up and looks around. It takes her a moment to notice FRANKLIN. SHE'S terrified.

JENNIFER: Jesus Christ!

FRANKLIN: I think you mean 'Franklin Pierce.'

JENNIFER: This is a dream.

FRANKLIN: No, Jennifer, it's a revelation. Once a year, a single child in the entire world is assigned a report on my presidency.

JENNIFER: I mean, that can't be—

FRANKLIN: It is 100% true. And once a year I rise from the grave to try and set the record straight.

JENNIFER: What's there to set straight? The part where you didn't even really care about running for president?

FRANKLIN: No, not that-

JENNIFER: The part where you're described by history.com as "powerfully pro-slavery?"

FRANKLIN: That's out of context.

JENNIFER: Or maybe the part where you are literally considered one of the least effective presidents in history—

FRANKLIN: Okay, shut up, Jennifer.

Song begins - "Tell Them All"

YES, IT'S WIDELY RECOGNIZED MY TIME IN OFFICE STANK
SOME WOULD CALL MY POLICIES A CRIME
SURE, MY FRIENDS IN BATTLE CAME TO CALL ME
"FAINTING FRANK"
BUT THAT JUST HAPPENED, LIKE, ONE TIME
BUT NOW THAT I AM LONG SINCE DEAD
MY REAL STORY'S GONE UNSAID
THE TRUTH BEHIND MY RISE AND MOSTLY FALL
JENNIFER, IT'S TIME TO TELL THEM ALL

I STARTED AS AN ARMY HERO,
WAY BACK IN MY YOUTH
I THOUGHT I KNEW THE ENEMY
BUT THEN I LEARNED THE TRUTH
IT WASN'T MEN WITH MUSKETS
WHO WERE BRINGING OUR DEMISE
BUT DRAGONS ON THE RISE

JENNIFER: I'm sorry, can you repeat that?

FRANKLIN:
    DRAGONS ON THE RISE

JENNIFER: Ahh, great.

FRANKLIN:
    THERE LIVED A MONSTER MENACE
    ONLY I HAD SEEN BEFORE
    A CLAN OF EVIL DRAGONS
    WHO HAD CRAWLED FROM THE EARTH'S CORE
    AND ONLY I COULD SEE THEM
    AS THEY CAME TO DO THEIR WORST
    I PLANNED TO GET TO SLAVERY
    BUT HAD TO DO THIS FIRST

    TELL THEM ALL MY REAL STORY
    TELL THEM WHAT I HAD TO DO
    TELL THEM I WAS A GREAT PRESIDENT
    EXCEPT THEY NEVER KNEW

JENNIFER: Hey, by that point hadn't your children all died tragically, and you turned to alcoholism? So you were probably just dealing with severe depression and alcoholic hallucinations?

FRANKLIN: No, it was dragons.

JENNIFER: And then on top of all that your vice president and wife died of Tuberculosis?

FRANKLIN: Nope, dragons.

JENNIFER: I'm pretty sure it was Tuberculosis—

FRANKLIN: Dragons!

He sings:

I THOUGHT I KILLED THEIR CLAN,
BUT ONE STILL MADE IT THROUGH
SNUCK IN MY HOUSE ONE NIGHT TO MAKE ME PAY
I'D KILLED HIS RACE, SO HE HAD COME FOR ME NOW
BUT WORSE THAN HARMING ME, HE TOOK MY LOVE AWAY
I FRANKLIN PIERCED HIS HEART
AND WATCHED THE DEMON DIE
BUT MY POOR WIFE STILL ANSWERED HEAVEN'S CALL
I LOST MY JANE IN BATTLES NO ONE EVER KNEW I FOUGHT
SO JENNIFER, IT'S TIME TO TELL THEM ALL

TELL THEM ALL ABOUT MY VICTORY
TELL THEM ALL ABOUT MY FIGHT
WAKE UP, JENNIFER, AND TELL THEM,
SET HISTORY STRAIGHT TONIGHT

Triumphant finish! JENNIFER studies him.

JENNIFER: Okay, so you want me to scrap everything I have here, get up in front of my class tomorrow, and tell them the story of how you discovered a secret dragon army that rose from the earth's core to defeat the human race, but only you could see them?

FRANKLIN: ...Yes. (*points out*) You also don't have on here that I was the first president to put up a Christmas tree in the White House.

JENNIFER is fed up.

JENNIFER: Shut up! I'm sick of these stupid, poorly crafted theatrics and your stupid, fake stories about dragons. Why couldn't I have just gotten an interesting president like Andrew Jackson? Cassie Smith got Andrew Jackson and she already has everything! Jackson and homecoming court and class president, and I have you. No one cares about you.

FRANKLIN: Ah.

JENNIFER: What?

FRANKLIN: Jennifer, Jennifer, Jennifer.

JENNIFER: Don't do that.

FRANKLIN: It seems we've found what's really going on here. You're not afraid of a boring presentation, you're afraid of a boring existence.

JENNIFER (*pause*): I just don't understand how you're supposed to get through high school if you're not popular or extraordinary.

FRANKLIN: Well, Jennifer, I know a couple things about being extraordinarily unpopular, and let me tell you, it's not easy, but it is worth it. Because you are special, even if you're not as special as Cassie Smith.

JENNIFER: What?

Song begins - "The You You Are"

FRANKLIN: Because, really, what it all comes down to, is that you're the perfect version of you.

YOU ARE YOUNG

JENNIFER: Stop.

FRANKLIN:
    AND YOU ARE JEALOUS

JENNIFER: I said enough theatrics.

FRANKLIN:
    YOU'RE PROJECTING YOUR SORROW ON ME

JENNIFER: Please stop.

FRANKLIN:
    I KNOW WHAT YOU'RE DOING
    AND I'LL TELL YOU WHAT EL-OUS
    I KNOW THE FEELING OF JEALOUSY
    DON'T LET THE COOL KIDS SCARE YOU
    CAUSE YOU'RE A SHINING STAR
    YOU'VE GOT TO LOVE YOURSELF COMPLETELY
    YOU'VE GOT TO LOVE THE YOU YOU ARE

JENNIFER starts to understand the message.

    YOU DON'T HAVE TO BE TOO SPECIAL

JENNIFER:
    YOU DON'T HAVE TO BE ONE THEY ADORE

FRANKLIN:
    BUT KNOW YOU'RE CAPABLE OF GREATNESS

JENNIFER:
    AND THAT DRAGON THING WAS JUST A METAPHOR

    I get it now, Franklin! I get what you've been trying to teach me this whole time!

SHE'S epically swept up while FRANKLIN realizes she totally misunderstood him.

JENNIFER:
    YOU ARE DEAD

FRANKLIN: Um, wait, Jennifer—

JENNIFER:
    AND SUPER BORING

FRANKLIN: The dragons were real.

JENNIFER:
    BUT I KNOW NOW IT'S BEST NOT TO LIE

FRANKLIN: Don't not tell them about the dragons.

JENNIFER
    SO I'LL SKIP YOUR BULLSHIT
    EVEN IF KIDS ARE SNORING
    WHEN I TELL THEM YOU WERE ONE DULL GUY
    YOU'VE GO TO WRAP YOURSELF IN COMFORT
    YOU'VE GOT TO RAISE YOUR OWN PERSONAL BAR

FRANKLIN: Why don't you fix the poster and then do this song?

JENNIFER:
    YOU'VE GOT TO LEARN TO BE QUITE HONEST

FRANKLIN:
    BUT ALSO NOT HIDE THAT YOU DID SAVE THE PLANET

JENNIFER:
    DRIVE YOUR AMBITION LIKE A CAR

FRANKLIN:
    SURE BUT ALSO FIX YOUR POSTER

JENNIFER:
>YOU'VE GOT TO LEARN TO LOVE THE HERE AND NOW

FRANKLIN:
>YOU'VE GOT TO FIX THIS GODDAMN POSTER NOW

JENNIFER:
>YOU'VE GOT TO LOVE THE YOU YOU ARE!
>YOU'VE GOT TO LOVE THE YOU

An alarm goes off, JENNIFER wakes up from her dream (nightmare?) alone.

Huh. I had the weirdest dream.

Suddenly, FRANKLIN PIERCE is at the foot of the bed.

FRANKLIN: Uh-huh, but also fix your poster.

JENNIFER shrieks.

Blackout.

END

ON YOUR MARK!

Book & Lyrics by *Danny K. Bernstein*
Music by *Aaron Kenny*
Based on the Aesop Fable *The Tortoise and the Hare*

The cast of *On Your Mark!* at Theatre Now's SOUND BITES 3.0.
(Left to right): Bianca Di Cocco, Evan Zimmerman, Kieron Cindric, and AnnMarie Powers.

The 10-Minute Musical: an anthology from the SOUND BITES festival

SYNOPSIS

It's race day as all of the woodland critters race through the forest. Unsurprisingly the humble favorite, the Hare, finishes first and collects the cash prize as her winnings *"WHO WILL FINISH FIRST"*. The hare gives her cash winnings to her parents, to help them afford the rent on their burrow. However, matters get complicated when their landlord, a badger, badgers them for the rent, informing them that their rent will be considerably higher next month. *"RAISE YOUR RENT"*. The new rent is higher than the Hare's winnings can accommodate, so she seeks out a loan from a shady tortoise. *"PAPA TORTOISE"*. However, the tortoise hatches a scheme - to fix the race, and rig all of the bets that will be placed on it. The hare will throw the race, thereby making all those who placed bets on her to win lose, and instead the tortoise will fool everyone into thinking he finished first. *"FAST"*. Just before the race is about to win, the Hare considers whether she is really doing the right thing, and if there's any moral to be learned at all. *"WHO WILL FINISH FIRST (REPRISE)"*.

PRODUCTION HISTORY

On Your Mark!, written by Danny K. Bernstein and Aaron Kenny, had its first production during Theatre Now's SOUND BITES 3.0 at The 47th Street Theater in New York on January 18th, 2016. It was directed by Juliana Kleist-Mendez with musical direction by Josh Kight. It was produced by Thomas Morrissey and Stephen Bishop Seely with associate producer, Zan Vailento. The cast was as follows:

HARE	AnnMarie Powers
TORTOISE	T.J. Wagner
BADGER	Evan Zimmerman
ENSEMBLE 1	Bianca Di Cocco
ENSEMBLE 2	Kieron Cindric

AUTHOR'S NOTE

We loved the idea of telling the "real story" of the Tortoise and the Hare. Fun fact: I was living in Williamsburg at the time, and my rent went up at the end of my first lease in NYC. I wasn't aware that was even a thing that could happen; I was very young. Anyway, we recommend this musical be performed with several sets of animal ears, minimal set, a quick pace, and lots of fun. Enjoy!

– *Danny K. Bernstein*

CHARACTERS

HARE — Sharp, spritely, determined and practical. Our heroine.

TORTOISE — A large, shadowy figure. Mysterious, full of ulterior motives. Holds all the power in the forest.

BADGER — Sneaky and conniving. A financial vulture. Raises the rent on the hare family because he can.

ENSEMBLE 1 — Plays Mrs. Fox, a sportscaster, Mother Hare, a kindly old mother, and one of the Tortoise's lackeys.

ENSEMBLE 2 — Plays Jamie The Fox, a sportscaster, Father Hare, a kindly old father, and one of the Tortoise's lackeys.

NOTE: ENSEMBLE 1 and ENSEMBLE 2 tracks can be divided up to create more roles.

SETTING

Woodland Critters Race, the forest.

MUSICAL NUMBERS

"Who Will Finish First"	Ensemble 1, Ensemble 2, Hare
"Raise Your Rent"	Badger, Hare, Ensemble 1, Ensemble 2
"Papa Tortoise"	Tortoise
"Fast"	Tortoise, Hare
"Who Will Finish First (reprise)"	Full Company

Scene 1 – Music starts and lights come up on two FOXES holding microphones.

JAMIE THE FOX: Good afternoon, and welcome back to Fox Sports!

MRS. FOX: I'm Mrs. Fox!

JAMIE THE FOX: I'm Jamie the Fox!

BOTH: And we're the foxes!

JAMIE THE FOX: For those of you just joining us now, we are live covering the weekly race across the forest!

MRS. FOX: That's right Jamie, woodland animals of all shapes and sizes trying to make it from one side of the forest to the other!

JAMIE THE FOX: And what a race it has been so far!

Song begins - "Who Will Finish First"

He sings:

WATCH THEM RUN LIKE LIGHTNING,
FEEL THE TENSION TIGHTENING,
EARS ARE PERKED,
AND BEAKS ARE PURSED.

MRS. FOX:
THE FINISH LINE IS WAITING,
WE'RE ANTICIPATING
WHO WILL FINISH FIRST?

BOTH:
OH, TO SEE THEM RACING PAST YOU,
RIGHT BEFORE YOUR EYES!
SPECULATING WHO WILL WIN
THE BIG CASH PRIZE!

JAMIE THE FOX (*putting his hand to his earpiece*): We're getting word that Barry the Beaver has exited the race to build a dam.

MRS. FOX (*also with her hand to her earpiece*): Sloane the Sloth has also exited the race because she stopped giving a damn.

JAMIE THE FOX: Penelope Porcupine is still stuck beneath a fallen tree branch.

MRS. FOX: And Marvin the Mouse is still stuck to Penelope Porcupine. Any word on whose in the lead?

JAMIE THE FOX: No surprise, here, folks: it's the returning champion, and everyone's favorite competitor,

BOTH:
> THE HARE!

> *The music shifts. The HARE appears running in slow motion, elsewhere onstage.*

MRS. FOX: There she goes now, dashing ahead of the rest of the pack, and quickly approaching the finish line!

> *The lights shift to the HARE.*

HARE:
> YOU LET THEM TAKE THE LEAD,
> AND THEN YOU PICK UP SPEED:
> IT'S JUST HOW YOU'VE REHEARSED.
> EXCITING RACES QUELL THEM;
> STILL YOU GET TO TELL THEM
> WHO WILL FINISH FIRST.
>
> EVERY WEEK THEY ALL APPLAUD
> THE MOST ATHLETIC BUNNY.
> LITTLE DO THEY KNOW I WIN
> BECAUSE I NEED THE MONEY,
> FOR EVERY CENT,

                IS ALWAYS SPENT
                TO HELP MY FAMILY
                PAY OUR RENT ON TIME...
                AND THAT'S WHY I'M...

BOTH FOXES:
                SHE'S...

ALL:
                RACING TO THE FINISH,
                NOTHING CAN DIMINISH
                MY/HER UNDYING, CONSTANT THIRST:

JAMIE THE FOX: She's thirsty!

ALL:
                BUSHES MAY BE PRICKLY,
                SHE MOVES THROUGH THEM QUICKLY,
                WITH A SWIFT AND MIGHTY BURST. (*BURST*)

She bursts through a bush.

                Wow!

                SHE SURE PUTS ON A SHOW,
                BUT IN THE END, WE KNOW
                JUST WHO
                WHO WILL FINISH
                WHO WILL FINISH
                WHO WILL FINISH...

The HARE crosses the finish line.

MRS. FOX: She's won!

ALL:
                SHE'S WHO WILL FINISH FIRST!

> *The HARE begins to congratulate the other animals on their participation, the scene begins to shift as the lights come up again on just the FOXES.*

JAMIE THE FOX: Well, Mrs. Fox, it sure was quite a race.

MRS. FOX: It certainly was, Jamie. To all you viewers at home, don't forget to tune in next week for the big forest marathon, where racers will run a much more complicated route.

JAMIE THE FOX: That's right, Mrs. Fox—it runs through all parts of the forest! Through the Turtle Bay, the Hunter's Point, over the Murray Hill...

MRS. FOX : They even have to cross the East River, don't they Jamie?

JAMIE THE FOX: That's right, Mrs. Fox; it's sure to be quite a race; so don't forget to tune in and find out...

> *They sing:*

BOTH FOXES:
WHO WILL FINISH FIRST!

> *Scene 2 – The scene shifts to the interior of the HARE'S BURROW. MOTHER HARE and FATHER HARE sit in their bed, looking sickly and clearly very old, and the HARE enters.*

HARE: Mother? Father? I'm home!

MOTHER HARE: Harriet? Come in, dear!

HARE: I won my race!

MOTHER HARE (*to FATHER HARE*): Did you hear that? She won another race!

FATHER HARE : How much did you win?

MOTHER HARE : Dear!

HARE : It's okay; it's something. If I win the marathon next week, it should be just enough to make this month's rent, right on time.

FATHER HARE: Thank goodness for that. I hate being badgered to pay the rent.

Song begins - "Raise Your Rent"

Suddenly, we hear a chord, and the BADGER enters.

BADGER:
    DID SOMEBODY SAY 'RENT?'

MOTHER HARE: Oh, no! It's the badger!

BADGER: That's right!

FATHER HARE: What are you doing here? The rent isn't due until next week!

BADGER: I'm here today to deliver some important news about your rent.

HARE: What sort of news?

BADGER: You see...

    THE WORLD OF FOREST REAL ESTATE—
    IT CALLS FOR BEING WISE,
    LIKE RECOGNIZING ECONOMIC TRENDS
    BEFORE YOUR EYES,
    AND KNOWING WHEN THE VALUE
    OF A HOME BEGINS TO RISE,
    THE MARKET IS A CRIME,
    BUT, IN SHORT, THIS MEANS IT'S TIME FOR ME TO
    RAISE YOUR RENT!

> THAT IS WHY I'M HERE TODAY:
> TO RAISE YOUR RENT!
> SO BEFORE YOU TRY TO PAY,
> I'LL RAISE YOUR RENT!
> TWENTY-FIVE PERCENT THIS COMING JUNE!

MOTHER HARE:
> BUT THAT'S SO SOON!

FATHER HARE:
> WHY MUST YOU...

HARES/BADGER:
> RAISE YOUR (OUR) RENT?

MOTHER HARE:
> CAN HE REALLY DO THAT? SIMPLY...

HARES/BADGER:
> RAISE YOUR (OUR) RENT?

FATHER HARE:
> NO, I NEVER KNEW THAT HE COULD

HARES/BADGER:
> RAISE YOUR (OUR) RENT...
> RAISE IT TWENTY-FIVE PERCENT.

HARE: But how could this happen?!

BADGER: This area of the forest is quickly becoming one of the hottest spots for young woodland creatures to move to!

MOTHER HARE: But how? We live in but a modest burrow alongside a brook, beneath the large Linden tree!

BADGER: I'm afraid the Brook-Linden Tree Burrow has become the most up-and-coming part of the forest!

ALL:
> SO I (HE) MUST RAISE YOUR (OUR) RENT!

MOTHER HARE:
> HONEY, THIS IS TERRIFYING!

ALL:
> RAISE YOUR (OUR) RENT,

BADGER:
> FOR THE WOODS ARE GENTRIFYING!

ALL:
> RAISE YOUR (OUR) RENT!
> RAISE IT TWENTY-FIVE PERCENT!

BADGER:
> HEY! NO WAY TO CIRCUMVENT, I'VE

ALL:
> RAISED YOUR (OUR) RENT!

HARE:
> HOW CAN I HELP THEM NOW, HE'S

ALL:
> RAISED YOUR (OUR) RENT?

HARE:
> THERE MUST BE SOMEWAY HOW...

ALL:
> I (HE) RAISED YOUR (OUR) RENT...

BADGER:
> IT'S A COMMON REAL ESTATE TECHNIQUE...
> I RAISE YOUR RENT, AND EVERY CENT,
> IS WHAT I WILL COLLECT THIS TIME NEXT WEEK!

Raise your rent!

The BADGER exits. MOTHER HARE bursts into tears.

Scene 3 – The scene shifts to a darker, murkier part of the forest. The HARE disguises herself with a headscarf and a mustache, and treads very carefully. The TORTOISE faces upstage. HARE treads carefully, and tries to remain disguised.

HARE: Hello? Is anyone there? I'm looking for...

TORTOISE (*speaking with a heavy, old Italian dialect*): You're looking for money.

HARE: Yes... how did you know?

TORTOISE: How do I know?

Song begins - "Papa Tortoise"

He sings:
    THE ONLY THING I KNOW IS THAT
    NO MATTER THE SEASON:
    THE CREATURES IN THIS FOREST ONLY
    SEEK ME FOR ONE REASON:
    TO TELL ME THAT THEIR FUNDS ARE SHORT,
    WHATEVER THEY THINK "SHORT" IS,
    AND THAT THEY NEED MY HELP;
    THAT'S WHY THEY CALL ME "PAPA TORTOISE"

Tell me, what's the occasion for such a visit?

HARE: Well you see, they've raised the rent on my burrow.

TORTOISE: Ah, don't tell me... you live alongside the brook beneath...

HARE: Yes, yes, the Brook-Linden Tree Burrow.

TORTOISE: What a shame; used to be such a modest part of the forest.

He glances at her more closely.

Forgive me miss, but you look familiar; would I know you from somewhere?

HARE shields her face a bit more.

HARE: No, I don't think so...

She gets flustered and her headscarf and mustache fall off, revealing her tall bunny ears.

TORTOISE: Well, well, well! If it isn't the fastest of the forest fauna? (*announcing loudly, as if over a loudspeaker*) The racing rabbit, herself!

HARE: Shhh, quiet, please! Yes, it's me, but no one can know I've come here; if I'm caught, I'll be barred from the marathon.

TORTOISE: Ah, the marathon! That's a big day for Tortoise Business; lots of animals want to make wagers on who will win... many of them are betting on you.

HARE: Yes, well I am the crowd favorite to win.

TORTOISE: Ah, yes, but some have placed bets on others. The reward would be much greater for calling an upset.

A chord. The TORTOISE hatches an idea.

Much greater for calling an upset... And that's exactly what we're gonna give them.

HARE: What!?

TORTOISE: You're gonna lose the marathon, but your family's going to win the pool.

HARE: How?

TORTOISE: By placing a bet on the one contestant no one else in their right mind ever would...

HARE: The sloth?

TORTOISE: The tortoise!

HARE: You?

TORTOISE: Me!

Song begins - "Fast"

TORTOISE:
I'M GONNA BE FAST!
NO MORE COMING IN LAST...
WATCHING OTHERS FLY PAST...

HARE:
You're going to enter the race?
You're going to enter the race, and... win?
I'm not totally sure I follow.

TORTOISE:
   I'M IMAGINING THE LOOKS ON THEIR FACES,
   WHEN THE ONE IN FIRST PLACE IS
   THE TORTOISE, AND HIS SPORT IS
   FINALLY RUNNING RACES, AND FAST!

HARE: How exactly do you plan on winning?

TORTOISE: We're gonna fix the race, plant tortoises that look just like me throughout the course, plant me at the finish line, and just as you approach you'll slow down just enough for me to claim victory, and I'll finally be fast!

HARE: But you won't really be fast, though... you'll just be cheating to make it look like you are.

TORTOISE: Ah, yes...

He sings:

BUT EVERYONE WILL THINK THAT I'M FAST.

BACK-UP TORTOISES:
EVERYONE WILL THINK HE'S FAST.

TORTOISE:
NO LONGER SEEN AS "OUT-CLASSED."

BACK-UP TORTOISES:
HE'S IN YOUR CLASS!

TORTOISE:
ONCE THE ROLES HAVE BEEN RECAST

BACK-UP TORTOISES:
EVERYTHING WILL BE RECAST.

ALL TORTOISES:
CREATURES WAIT AROUND FOR YOU TO DECEIVE THEM,
SO YOUR DREAMS CAN ACHIEVE THEMSELVES
'CAUSE YOU CAN MAKE 'EM TRUE
BY MAKING OTHERS BELIEVE THEM, AND FAST!

HARE: But just because everyone believes something, doesn't make it true!

TORTOISE : Silly, rabbit...

He sings:
IF THERE'S ONE THING I'VE LEARNED
FROM LIVING YEAR AFTER YEAR,
ANIMALS BELIEVE WHATEVER TALES THEY HEAR,
THEY MIGHT BE UNTRUE, AND THEY MIGHT BE BIZARRE,
BUT ONCE THEY'RE TOLD
THEY'RE BASICALLY THE WAY THINGS ARE.

HARE: I don't know...

TORTOISE: Come on, kid! It's the perfect arrangement; I finally get mine, and your family finally gets theirs!

HARE: You think the pool will be enough to pay the rent?

TORTOISE: The rent? HA! With this kind of money, you and your family could buy a new home! Maybe a lofty nest by the Southern Honeysuckles!

HARE (*dreamily*): Soho...

TORTOISE: What do you say, hare? Do we have a deal?!

He sings:

WILL YOU LET ME BE FAST?

HARE:
    I WON'T HAVE TO BE FAST...

TORTOISE:
    'CAUSE IT LOOKS LIKE A BLAST!

HARE:
    NO MORE BEING HARASSED.

TORTOISE:
    WHY, THEY'LL ALL BE AGHAST?

HARE:
    I'LL HAVE FREEDOM, AT LAST.

BOTH:
    ALL WE NEED IS TO MAINTAIN AN ILLUSION,
    AND CAUSE SOME CONFUSION,
    AND WE CAN FIND A DIFFERENT KINDA SORTA CONCLUSION:

TORTOISE:
    ME WITH THE FAME, AND THE FEELING OF SPEED...

HARE:
>   ME AND MY FAMILY HAVING MORE THAN WE NEED!

BOTH:
>   AND EVERYBODY ELSE REMAINING QUITE UNAWARE
>   OF THE TRUTH BEHIND THE RACE BETWEEN
>   THE TORTOISE AND THE HARE
>   THE RACE BETWEEN THE TORTOISE AND THE HARE

Scene 4 – The music shifts again and the FOXES re-enter.

JAMIE THE FOX: Good afternoon, and welcome back to Fox Sports!

MRS. FOX: I'm Mrs. Fox

JAMIE THE FOX: And I'm Jamie the Fox.

BOTH: And we're the foxes!

JAMIE THE FOX: Well folks, today is the day of the big marathon!

MRS. FOX: And as I understand it, we have a last minute entry: a tortoise!

Song begins - "Who Will Finish First (reprise)"

TORTOISE:
>   I GET TO BE FAST...

JAMIE THE FOX: That's right, but I doubt it will be a problem for our returning champion, the Hare!

HARE:
>   I'LL BE FREE, AT LAST...

MRS. FOX: It's sure to be quite a race, Jamie.

JAMIE THE FOX: One for the books!

The SKUNK enters, holding his tail like a checkerboard flag.

The skunk is in place; it looks like we're about to begin!

HARE (*perhaps having second thoughts*):
    IT'S A NEW BEGINNING,
    ONE WITHOUT THE WINNING,
    ONCE OUR ROLES HAVE BEEN REVERSED.
    SHOULD I TAKE A BEATING...

SKUNK: On your mark!

HARE:
    EVEN THOUGH HE'S CHEATING?

SKUNK: Get set!

HARE: What's the moral, here!?

SKUNK:
    GO!

ALL:
    WHO WILL FINISH
    WHO WILL FINISH
    WHO WILL FINISH FIRST?

Blackout.

END

PELLETS, CHERRIES, AND LIES: THE PAC MAN STORY

Book, Music, & Lyrics by *Erik Przytulski*

Danette Holden, Eddie Andrews, and Darryl Winslow in *Pellets, Cherries, and Lies: The Pac Man Story* at Theatre Now's SOUND BITES 2014.

SYNOPSIS

In the Pac Family House in Mazeland, Ms. Pac Man paces in the living room of her house, worried about her husband, Pac Man's whereabouts at such a late hour *"PROLOGUE"*. When he tries to sneak in, she confronts him and learns he's been out in the maze eating pellets again. Ms. Pac Man pleads with him to stop and get help with his addiction. Pac Man is appalled at such an accusation and attempts to convince his wife that he is *"IN CONTROL"*. He pulls a power pellet out from his pocket to prove he can resist eating, but realizes he does have a problem when he nearly gives in to his urges. Ms. Pac Man informs her husband that they have another problem. She shows Pac Man a box filled with power pellets that she found hidden in their son's room. Pac Man calls his son, Junior Pac Man, and asks where he learned to eat such things. Junior tries to deny it, but after his father presses him for an answer, he finally breaks down and admits that he learned in watching him. Junior expresses how he just wants to be cool and popular like his father, but even he is realizing that his dad has a problem and is a loser *"LIKE YOU"*. This revelation is too much for Pac Man to handle and runs out of the room. Junior is soon comforted by his mother who confesses to a secret of her own: That she, too, once had a pellet addiction. But after years of nearly falling into the same habits as Pac Man, she found her reason to kick her habit with the birth of her son *"OUT OF THE GAME"*. Later, as Pac Man is flushing power pellets down their toilet, Sue the Ghost appears along with her cohorts, Inky, Blinky, and Pinky. She calls out to Pac Man, trying to seduce him back into the maze and indulge in his pellet addiction *"TASTE"*. In the *"FINALE"*, Ms. Pac Man and Junior plead to Pac Man not to go back into the maze. Sue entices Pac Man by telling him this next board has a Kiwi. After his family begs him to stay, Pac Man refuses, promising that he's going out into the maze just one last time. Ms. Pac Man and Junior hold each other close as Pac Man disappears into the maze with Sue and the Ghosts.

PRODUCTION HISTORY

Pellets, Cherries, and Lies: The Pac Man Story, written by Erik Przytulski, had its world premiere production at The 47th Street Theater in New York, NY for Theatre Now's SOUND BITES 2014 on December 8, 2014. The production was directed & choreographed by Allison Bibicoff, with musical direction by Doub Oberhamer. It was produced by Thomas Morrissey, Rebecca Nell Robertson, and Stephen Bishop Seely, with associate producer, Charles Quittner. The cast was as follows:

MS. PAC MAN	Danette Holden
PAC MAN	Darryl Winslow
JR. PAC MAN	Eddie Andrews
SUE THE GHOST	Jenny Ashman
INKY	Ali Axelrad
BLINKY	Eileen McHugh
PINKY	Kellie Pailet

It later went on to have its west coast premiere at The Hudson Theatres in Los Angeles, CA, as part of After Hours Theatre Company's Strip Show: *One Act Stories...Stripped Down* on March 1, 2019. The production was again directed & choreographed by Allison Bibicoff, with musical direction by Erik Przytulski.

MS. PAC MAN	Jessica Joy
PAC MAN	Ted Barton
JR. PAC MAN	Jonny Lee Jr.
SUE THE GHOST	Katherine Washington
INKY	Ali Axelrad
BLINKY	Josie Adams McCoy
PINKY	Corrine Glazer

CHARACTERS

MS. PAC MAN — Female, caring wife and mother with a past.

PAC MAN — Male, strung-out pellet addict in denial.

JUNIOR PAC MAN — Male, emo kid with a secret.

SUE THE GHOST — Female, ghostly seductress of Pac Man.

INKY, BLINKY, PINKY — Female, a trio of ghosts and Sue's back-up singers.

OFF-STAGE VOICES and MARIO, Q-BERT, TAPPER, & FROGGER

Note: INKY, BLINKY, and PINKY are optional cast members and can be omitted if necessary. Actors playing SUE THE GHOST, INKY, BLINKY, and PINKY can double the roles of OFF-STAGE VOICES, MARIO, Q-BERT, TAPPER, and FROGGER.

SETTING

A late evening at the Pac family house in Mazeland.

MUSICAL NUMBERS

"Prologue"	Ms. Pac Man
"In Control"	Pac Man
"Like You"	Junior Pac Man
"Out of the Game"	Ms. Pac Man
"Taste"	Sue, The Ghost Man
"Finale"	Company

AUTHOR'S NOTE

This musical almost never happened! While taking part in a musical theatre writing program, we were presented with the task of writing a show involving the theme of addiction. I pitched the idea of Pac Man confronted with his addiction to eating pellets through an intervention with his wife, Ms. Pac Man, and son, Junior Pac Man. Even though the team I was working with decided on another premise, I felt this was a project worth pursuing. Several months later, I completed and submitted the musical to the Theatre Now's SOUND BITES in 2014 and the rest is history!

The tone of this show is a cross between *Spring Awakening* / *Next To Normal* and a Lifetime Made-for-TV Movie-of-the-Week. The humor comes from presenting the material very seriously, almost over-dramatically. It can be played up to the point of melodrama, but never take it to the point of farce. Have faith that the absurdity of the setting and characters will drive the comedy and allow the actors to find the heart within the story.

This show pays loving tribute to the world of classic arcade video games and there are subtle and obvious references throughout. For those unfamiliar with circa-1980s video games, take time to look up (and even play) the following games: *Pac Man, Ms. Pac Man, Mario Brothers, Frogger, Q-Bert, Tapper, Burgertime, Breakout*.

In the song *LIKE YOU*, the dialogue between Pac Man and Junior references a classic 1980s television commercial about the war on drugs: "PSA—I learned it by watching you!" It is very helpful to watch this classic ad to get a sense of the parody being referenced in this scene. To watch it, look up "I learned it by watching you" on YouTube and it should be one of the top videos!

Finally, a few production suggestions: Minimal sets and props work well for this show. Costumes can be made to look exactly like the video game characters, but even regular clothing and accessories can evoke the look of the characters (ex. Ms. Pac Man: Yellow sweater with a red bow in her hair). The show can be performed with a minimum of 4 cast members in the lead roles. However, the 3 additional ensemble/ghost roles enhance the production considerably.

I hope you enjoy performing this quirky mini-musical as much as I had writing it. Thank you for making *Pellets, Cherries, and Lies: The Pac Man Story* a part of your production and have a great show!

- Erik Przytulski

Lights Up. Late Evening At The Pac Family House In Mazeland. Ms. Pac Man Paces Back And Forth In Her Living Room.

Song begins - "Prologue"

MS. PAC MAN:
    NIGHT AFTER NIGHT
    WONDERING WHY I STAY
    I DON'T WANT TO FIGHT
    SO ALL I CAN DO IS PRAY
    I KNOW HE'S OUT THERE RUNNING 'ROUND
    PLEASE LET HIM COME HOME SAFE AND SOUND

PAC MAN enters through the front door, trying to sneak in without being noticed.

MS. PAC MAN: Where have you been?

PAC MAN: Uh... I'm having an affair.

MS. PAC MAN: Liar! You've been out in the maze, eating pellets again.

PAC MAN: Don't be ridiculous.

MS. PAC MAN: Please. I can smell the fruit on your breath. And what's this? You've been bitten by a ghost... again!

PAC MAN: So what? I had an extra life.

MS. PAC MAN: How many do you have left? *(no response)* How many? *(still no response)* I can't believe this. You're down to your last life, aren't you?

PAC MAN: I'm so close to getting that bonus, dear.

MS. PAC MAN: I've had all I can take of this, Pac. You have a family now... responsibilities! You need to get help.

Song begins - "In Control"

PAC MAN: Get help? You're acting like I'm some kind of addict.

>I'M IN CONTROL!
>NOTHING THAT I CANNOT HANDLE
>I'M IN CONTROL
>I CAN AVOID ANY SCANDAL
>I'VE GOT THIS WRAPPED UP GOOD AND TIGHT
>NO ONE CAN BRING ME DOWN OR LEFT OR UP OR
>DOWN OR LEFT OR RIGHT
>
>I'M IN CONTROL
>I CAN JUST TELL WHAT YOU'RE THINKING
>PLEASE DON'T FREAK OUT

PAC MAN pulls a power pellet out of his pocket.

>JUST 'CAUSE THIS PELLET IS BLINKING
>I BARELY NOTICE IT AT ALL
>I'LL SIMPLY THROW AWAY THIS TEMPTING, SWEET,
>AND GORGEOUS GLOWING BALL
>OFFSTAGE VOICES:
>AHHHH!

PAC MAN/OFFSTAGE VOICES:
>I THINK I LOVE YOU, POWER PELLET
>(OOO, HE LOVES YOU, POWER PELLET!)
>I'D MARRY YOU IF IT WAS NOT A CRIME
>(OOO, THAT'S KIND OF CREEPY, HONEY!)
>I'VE GOTTA HAVE YOU, POWER PELLET
>(OOO, HE'S GOTTA HAVE YOU!)
>BUT I WON'T, 'CAUSE I CAN STOP THIS ANYTIME
>(HE CAN STOP, HE CAN STOP, HE CAN STOP, HE CAN
>STOP IT ANY...)

PAC MAN:
>I'M IN CONTROL
>I'M NOT THE ONE WITH THE PROBLEM

>   I'M IN CONTROL
>   NO, YOU ARE THE ONE WITH THE PROBLEM

PAC MAN/OFFSTAGE VOICES:
>   I CAN STOP WHEN I WANT! (EAT IT!)
>   I CAN STOP WHEN I WANT! (EAT IT!)
>   I CAN STOP! I CAN STOP! (EAT IT! EAT IT! EAT IT!)

MS. PAC MAN: Honey? Honey...

PAC MAN:
>   I CAN'T STOP! I CAN'T STOP! I CAN'T...

MS. PAC MAN: Stop!

> *PAC MAN hands the power pellet to Ms. Pac Man.*

PAC MAN:
>   I'M IN CONTROL

> Maybe I do need a little help.

MS. PAC MAN: Well, turns out we have another problem.

> *MS. PAC MAN picks up a box and gives it to Pac Man.*

> Look what I found in your son's room.

> *PAC MAN opens the box.*

PAC MAN (*shocked*): Power pellets? Junior! Get in here right now!

> *JUNIOR enters.*

JUNIOR: Take a chill pill, Dad.

PAC MAN: Are you wearing an earring? How is that even possible?

JUNIOR: You're noticing now? I've had it for nearly a year.

PAC MAN shows the open box of power pellets to Junior.

PAC MAN: Is this yours?

JUNIOR: You went through my stuff? How could you?

MS. PAC MAN: Sweetie, I was worried...

PAC MAN: Your mother said she found this in your room.

JUNIOR: Look, Dad, it's not mine.

PAC MAN: Where did you get it?

JUNIOR: Dad, I...

PAC MAN: Answer me! Who taught you to eat these things?

JUNIOR: You, all right? I learned it by watching you!

Song begins - "Like You"

I learned it by watching you, Dad!

    IS IT HARD TO BELIEVE
    THAT I'M NOT SO NAÏVE
    ARE YOU OVER YOUR GUILT AND YOUR DOUBT
    YES, I KNEW IT WAS WRONG
    I'VE BEEN HIDING SO LONG
    NOW IT LOOKS LIKE MY SECRET IS OUT
    I WANNA BE JUST LIKE YOU
    I WANNA BE JUST LIKE YOU

    YOU'VE GOT FANS, YOU'VE GOT FAME
    PEOPLE SCREAMING YOUR NAME
    I'M JUST ANOTHER ROUND FACE IN THE CROWD
    THE KIDS IGNORE ME AT SCHOOL
    BUT THEY THINK THAT YOU'RE COOL
    I ASSUMED YOU WOULD BE SO PROUD

>   IF I COULD BE JUST LIKE YOU
>   IF I COULD BE JUST LIKE YOU
>
>   I WOULD EAT IT ALL
>   I'D DEFEAT THEM ALL
>   GONNA HAVE THE WHOLE WORLD ON MY PLATE

JUNIOR:	MS. PAC MAN:
IS IT HARD TO BELIEVE	FOR ONCE SHUT YOUR
THAT I'M NOT SO NAÏVE	MOUTH
ARE YOU OVER YOUR GUILT	
AND YOUR DOUBT	AND OPEN YOUR EYES
YES, I KNEW IT WAS WRONG,	
I'VE BEEN HIDING SO LONG	YOUR SON'S HEADING SOUTH
NOW IT LOOKS LIKE MY	
SECRET IS OUT	IT'S NO BIG SURPRISE

JUNIOR:
> I WANNA BE JUST LIKE YOU

MS. PAC MAN:
> HE WANTS TO BE JUST LIKE YOU

JUNIOR:
> I'LL DO EVERYTHING YOU DO

MS. PAC MAN:
> HE WANTS TO BE JUST LIKE YOU

JUNIOR:
> I FIGURED YOU ALWAYS KNEW
> I WANNA BE JUST LIKE YOU, DAD!

PAC MAN: Junior... I... I'm sorry.

> *PAC MAN exits.*

Song begins - "Out of the Game"

JUNIOR: Man, I can't believe I looked up to that loser.

MS. PAC MAN: Hey, don't be so hard on him. It's true, your father has a problem. But trippin' on dots, riding the ghost… It could happen to anyone. Even your mother.

JUNIOR: You Mom?

MS. PAC MAN: Oh yes.

She sings:

I WAS A PLAYER,
I KNEW HOW TO SCORE
MY BINGES WERE EPIC,
BUT SOON I WOULD HUNGER FOR MORE
SPENT EVERY QUARTER, LOST EVERY DIME
WHEN PELLETS RAN DRY, I HIT BURGERTIME
THE PAST I'LL FORGIVE
BUT IT'S STILL HARD TO LIVE WITH THE SHAME
I TRIED TO BREAK OUT
BUT I COULDN'T GET OUT OF THE GAME

As MS. PAC MAN continues her story, the following video game characters appear on stage: MARIO from "Mario Bros.", Q-BERT from "Q-BERT", TAPPER from "Root Beer Tapper", and FROGGER from "FROGGER".

THEN MY FRIEND MARIO, OBSESSED WITH HIS COINS,
TOOK ONE TOO MANY BRICKS TO HIS HEAD
WHEN Q-BERT JUMPED, IT WAS A CRY FOR HELP
BUT WE COULDN'T UNDERSTAND WHAT HE SAID
TAPPER'S LIFE WAS SHATTERED,
FROGGER'S DREAMS WERE SQUASHED
NOBODY KNEW WHO TO BLAME
I KNEW IT WAS TIME, TIME TO GET OUT OF THE GAME

MS. PAC MAN (MARIO/Q-BERT/TAPPER/FROGGER):
    (OOO... AH!) MONTHS OF REHAB (REHAB! AH...)
    SO MUCH JENNY CRAIG (JENNY CRAIG!)
    COACH AFTER LIFE COACH (AH...)
    I FELT SHATTERED AND TORN (OOO...)
    BUT EVERYTHING CHANGED THE DAY YOU WERE BORN

    I GOT OUT OF THE GAME (AH...)
    AND INTO THE LIGHT
    OUT OF MY WAY (AH...)
    AS I STRUGGLED TO FIGHT FOR ME (FOR ME!)
    AND YOU (AND YOU!)
    THERE'S NOTHING I WOULDN'T DO (I WOULDN'T DO!)

    I GOT OUT OF THE GAME (AH! OUT OF THE GAME!)
    AND INTO THE SUN (INTO THE SUN!)
    THAT'S WHEN I FELT LIKE MY LIFE
    HAD FINALLY BEGUN! BEGUN! (AH...!)
    ONCE I WAS OUT OF THE GAME, I WON!
    (I GOT OUT! I GOT OUT! I GOT OUT OF THE GAME!)

Lights fade on Junior and Ms. Pac Man. Lights up on PAC MAN in the bathroom, dumping the power pellets into the toilet. At the window, SUE THE GHOST appears. With her are her ghost cohorts, INKY, BLINKY, and PINKY.

Song begins - "Taste"

SUE:
    HEY THERE, BIG AND YELLOW.
    CAN YOU COME OUT AND PLAY?

PAC MAN: Leave me alone.

SUE:
    WE GOT A BRAND NEW LEVEL HERE.
    WHAT DO YOU SAY?

PAC MAN: I... I'm giving it up. All of it.

SUE:
>ROWS OF PELLET GOODNESS,
>SO DELICIOUS THROUGH AND THROUGH

PAC MAN: Go find another glutton to punish.

SUE:
>NOW YOU KNOW I ONLY HAVE EYES FOR YOU!
>
>HOW ABOUT A LITTLE TASTE?
>OOO, IT'S GONNA FEEL SO RIGHT
>JUST TAKE MY HAND, HONEY
>I DON'T BITE
>PEOPLE CALL IT ADDICTION
>I SAY YOU'RE MISUNDERSTOOD
>IF PELLETS ARE SO BAD
>WHY DO THEY TASTE SO GOOD?
>
>COME GRAB MY CHERRY, YOU KNOW YOU NEED IT
>OPEN UP THAT FLAPPING JAW WIDE AND FEED IT!
>YOU ON A DIET? ARE YOU LOSING YOUR COOL?
>'CAUSE I CAN SEE YOU STARTING TO DROOL

SUE (INKY/BLINKY/PINKY):
>WHY DON'T YOU TAKE A LITTLE TASTE? (TASTE!)
>A LITTLE NIBBLE WON'T HURT (JUST A NIBBLE, BABY!)
>TRY A POWER PELLET ENTREE
>AND THEN ME FOR DESSERT (MM-MM-MM!)
>YOU'RE BELLY'S RUNNIN' EMPTY
>SO LET'S POP THAT HOOD (OOO...)
>'CAUSE ONCE IT HITS YOUR LIPS
>IT'S GONNA TASTE SO GOOD (TASTE SO GOOD!)
>
>(AHH...) YOU'RE THE GREATEST ADVERSARY WE'VE EVER FACED
>(YOU'RE THE GREATEST, YOU'RE THE GREATEST! YEAH, YEAH, YEAH!)
>BOARD AFTER BOARD (BOARD AFTER BOARD)
>IT'S TIME TO CLAIM YOUR REWARD

(CLAIM YOUR REWARD)
YOU WANNA LET THOSE JUICY DOTS GO TO WASTE?

NO, NO, NO! YOU GOTTA TAKE A LITTLE TASTE (TASTE!)
JUST GIVE IT ONE MORE TRY (ONE MORE TRY!)
DON'T DWELL ON THE FACT
THAT IF WE CATCH YOU—YOU'LL DIE! (AWW!)
IT'S USELESS TO RESIST (OOO...)
HA! YOU WOULDN'T IF YOU COULD (AH!)
YOUR FINAL MEAL IS WAITING
AND IT TASTES—SO—GOOD!

SUE:	INKY/BLINKY/PINKY:
OH YEAH!	COME AND GET IT
IT'S GONNA TASTE SO GOOD!	COME AND GET IT!
SO GOOD!	COME AND GET IT
YOU'RE GONNA TASTE SO GOOD!	COME AND GET IT!
	COME AND GET IT
YOU'RE GONNA TASTE SO...	COME AND GET IT!
I KNOW YOU WILL!	TASTE SO GOOD.
YOU'RE GONNA TASTE,	OOO...
YOU'RE GONNA TASTE SO...	OOO...

Song begins - "Finale"

GHOSTS:
    COME AND GET IT, COME AND GET IT!
    COME AND GET IT, COME AND GET IT!

MS. PAC MAN and JUNIOR enter.

JUNIOR: Dad! Don't do it!

MS. PAC MAN: We can help you, just stay inside!

SUE:
    IT'S GONNA TASTE SO GOOD!

GHOSTS:	PAC MAN:	MS. PAC MAN:	JUNIOR:
COME AND GET IT, COME AND GET IT! COME AND GET IT, COME AND GET IT!	I'M IN CONTROL! I'M IN CONTROL!	GET OUT OF THE GAME!	I WANNA BE LIKE YOU!

SUE:		MS. PAC MAN:	
IT'S GONNA TASTE SO...		GET OUT OF THE...	

MS. PAC MAN:
    ... GAME!

SUE:
    ... GOOD!

JUNIOR:
    DAD!

PAC MAN:
    SON!

SUE: Did I mention that this level has a kiwi?

PAC MAN: Wait... Kiwi? I've never made it as far as "kiwi" before!

MS. PAC MAN: It's a trick! There's no kiwi!

PAC MAN: I... I... Just one last time, I promise!

    PAC MAN runs out and joins the ghosts as they chase him around.

JUNIOR: Dad, please! Come back!

MS. PAC MAN: Let him go, son. Just let him go.

MS. PAC MAN and JUNIOR hold each other close.

PAC MAN, SUE, GHOSTS:
    IT'S GONNA TASTE SO GOOD!

Blackout.

END

RUN THIS TOWN

Book & Lyrics by *Cindy Sideris*
Music by *Assaf Gleizner*

The cast of *Run This Town* at Theatre Now's SOUND BITES 5.0.
(Left to right): Taylor Coriell, Jordan Wolfe, Patricia Sabulis, Matt Giroveanu, and Alan Trinca.

SYNOPSIS

Run This Town is a jazzy comedy about a 1920's gangster named Big Al who is frustrated with his friends and accomplices, and wants to work with and learn from a pro. He laments his current friends and their botched crimes *"RUN THIS TOWN"*. He soon meets a mysterious stranger who promises him he can learn from his friend, a real pro *"NOWHERE TO HIDE"*. He is taken to a jazz club where the Hairdo Sisters greet him *"THERE'S NOTHING SHADY GOING ON IN THIS JOINT"*. He meets One-Eyed Pete, who isn't as he seems *"THE CONFESSION"*. Al soon realizes that the people he idolized aren't all they've portrayed to be- and sometimes you need to stick with your friends to make an honest living out of a life of crime *"RUN THIS TOWN (REPRISE)"*.

PRODUCTION HISTORY

Run This Town, written by Assaf Gleizner and Cindy Sideris, was developed at The BMI Lehman Engel Musical Theatre Workshop, where it was first presented as a final class presentation in June of 2017. The cast was as follows:

BIG AL	Jordan Wolfe
GANGSTER #1	Charlie Oh
GANGSTER #2	Amanda D'Archangelis
SHADY MAN	Landon Zwick
HAIRDO SISTER	Taylor Coriell
HAIRDO SISTER	Tegan Miller
HAIRDO SISTER	Madeline Fansler
ONE-EYED PETE	Bobby Underwood

Its first professional production premiered at The Irene Diamond Stage at The Pershing Square Signature Center for Theatre Now's SOUND BITES 5.0 on May 28, 2018. The production was directed by Angelique Ilo, with musical direction by Assaf Gleizner. It was produced by Thomas Morrissey, Chris Giordano, and Stephen Bishop Seely. The cast was as follows:

BIG AL	Jordan Wolfe
GANGSTER #1/HAIRDO SISTER	Taylor Coriell
GANGSTER #2/HAIRDO SISTER	Patricia Sabulis
SHADY MAN	Alan Trinca
HAIRDO SISTER	Tegan Miller
ONE-EYED PETE	Matt Giroveanu

The show was awarded Best Direction (Angelique Ilo) in that year's festival.

CHARACTERS

BIG AL	Male identifying, a gangster modeled after a young Al Capone, who is the protagonist of the piece, but is definitely more goofy than threatening.
HAIRDO SISTERS	Three, Female identifying/non-binary "Andrews Sisters" type singers in a 1920's jazz club.
ONE-EYED PETE	Male identifying, a burly, over-confident gangster who is not who he appears to be. Donald Trump, but a 1920's gangster character version.
GANGSTERS #1 AND #2	Any gender, goofy gangsters who are terrible at committing crimes.
SHADY MAN	Male identifying, accomplice to One-Eyed Pete, slightly mysterious, but never very threatening.

Note: The roles of HAIRDO SISTERS and GANGSTERS #1 AND #2 can be played by the same actors.

SETTING
Chicago, 1925.

MUSICAL NUMBERS

"Run This Town"	Big Al
"Nowhere to Hide"	Shady Man
"There's Nothing Shady Going on in this Joint"	Hairdo Sisters
"The Confession"	One-Eyed Pete
"Run This Town (reprise)"	Big Al, Company

AUTHORS' NOTE

Run This Town was born out of the idea of making fun of some villains from the past, but living in a world where they actually weren't scary or good at their respective jobs. During the writing and rehearsal process, we ended up realizing there were a lot of parallels to people in power in the present day. We feel this show encapsulates themes of comedy and the power of friendship and loyalty above all else, while also hopefully shedding light on the masks people wear and the tricks they can easily play on us all.

- Cindy Sideris & Assaf Gleizner

Early 1920's, Chicago. We hear a police siren as a group of GANGSTERS run out into the street after a failed bank robbing job. They are led by a very frustrated BIG AL.

BIG AL: Shh!

>*BIG AL looks around to see if the coast is clear.*
>
>Guys, guys, how many times I gotta tell ya? If we're robbing a bank, we don't need to fill out no deposit slips!

GANGSTER #1: Come on now, that's an easy mistake!

GANGSTER #2: I'm just so used to it!

BIG AL: This is the second big job this week you've messed up.

GANGSTER #1: Don't worry boss, next time we'll get 'em!

BIG AL: There shouldn't have to be a next time!

GANGSTER #2: Look Al, we can't all have as many scars as you. We'll see you tomorrow.

GANGSTER #1: Bye Al, see you tomorrow!

The other gangsters leave, and Al is alone on an empty street.

BIG AL: Yeah, see you tomorrow. And then the day after that. Is anything ever gonna change? I bet the serious gangsters around here don't have to walk home with holes in their shoes and empty pockets. I should have a house made out of gold by now!

>*Song begins - "Run This Town"*

I'M SICK OF THESE POINTLESS JOBS
AND WORKING WITH BUMS AND SLOBS
I'VE ALREADY PAID MY DUES

I SHOULD RUN THIS TOWN

I'M SICK OF THESE AMATEURS
WE DON'T EVEN HAVE CHAUFFEURS!
I'VE GOT NOTHING LEFT TO LOSE
I COULD RUN THIS TOWN

ONE DAY I WILL FIND WORK THAT DELIGHTS ME
CHEERS AND EXCITES ME TO GET BEHIND

ONE DAY I WILL FIND A MENTOR TO GUIDE ME
AND HE WILL FIGHT BESIDE ME, NOT HIDE BEHIND ME
QUICK! I'M LOSING MY MIND

A SHADY MAN in a pinstripe suit enters.

HEY, YOU THERE, PASSING BY
YOUR SNAPPY OL' SUIT AND TIE
IT LOOKS LIKE YOU KNOW A GUY
WHO RUNS THIS TOWN

SO WHAT ABOUT HELPING ME?
I'M READY TO WORK, YOU'LL SEE
I'M READY TO LEARN
HOW I CAN RUN THIS TOWN

SHADY MAN:
    I'LL SHOW YOU A MAN I KNOW WHO RUNS THIS TOWN

SHADY MAN:	BIG AL:
YEAH KID, ONE DAY YOU MIGHT JUST RUN THIS TOWN	ALRIGHT! ONE DAY I MIGHT JUST RUN THIS TOWN

Song ends.

SHADY MAN: But first, I gotta ask—who's asking?

BIG AL: The name's Alphonse, or Big Al as my friends call me, and I'm looking for a real boss to show me the ropes. You know, meet some new partners, collect a few new scars here and there. I'm ready to be a serious gangster; no more playing around.

SHADY MAN: Yeah? I think I know just the guy for you.

BIG AL: Is it ol' Slippery Fingers Frank?

SHADY MAN: Uh, no.

BIG AL: Ol' Sugar-Lips Adams? Bad-Shot Beckford?

SHADY MAN: Wow, no. You really do need my help. They call him One-Eyed Pete.

We hear mystery music and BIG AL looks out to the audience and freezes.

BIG AL: I know him! I heard that after he lost his eye, he just kept on fighting!

SHADY MAN: Of course he did! Now, there's a few things you should know before meeting him.

Song begins - "Nowhere To Hide"

HE'S BIG, QUITE A HORRIBLE GUY.
HE'S SMART, BUT EV'RY WORD IS A LIE.
HE'S KNOWN AMONG MANY PLACES AS AN "HONEST" GUY.

HE'S FAST, QUITE A THREAT WITH A KNIFE.
HE'S COLD, NO REMORSE FOR A LIFE.

HE KNOWS JUST HOW TO PLAY THE GAME.
THERE'S NOWHERE THAT YOU CAN HIDE.

SO COME ON DOWN TO OLD SIDE STREET.
HE'LL TAKE YOU UNDER HIS CARE.
COME WITH ME TO OLD SIDE STREET.

>   WE'LL GET YOU A DRIVER AND NEW SHOES TO WEAR!

BIG AL: Oh my God, I can't wait!

>   *SHADY MAN hushes BIG AL. They can't be heard.*

SHADY MAN:
>   REMEMBER HE'S HARSH.
>   IF HE HEARS US WE'LL DIE.
>   BUT, HEY! HE'S A POPULAR GUY.
>
>   HE'S ALWAYS GONNA PLAY THE GAME,
>   BEND THE RULES IT'S ALL THE SAME.
>   THERE'S NOWHERE YOU CAN GO.
>   NOWHERE YOU CAN HIDE.

BIG AL:
>   WHY WOULD I NEED TO RUN AND HIDE?

SHADY MAN:
>   WE'RE HERE.
>   YOU BETTER COME INSIDE.

>   *Song transition - "There's Nothing Shady Going on in this Joint"*
>
>   *The two of them enter an unmarked door into a lavish speakeasy. THE HAIRDO SISTERS come on stage to perform.*

HAIRDO SISTER 1:
>   WELCOME SIRS, COME SIT DOWN,
>   AT THE CLASSIEST CLUB IN TOWN.
>   I BOUGHT THESE JEWELS AND SEWED THIS GOWN.
>   THERE'S NOTHING SHADY GOING ON IN THIS JOINT.

HAIRDO SISTER 2:
>   YES, NOTHING HERE IS OUT OF PLACE.
>   COPS AND ROBBERS MIGHT JUST EMBRACE.
>   GET ALCOHOL HERE BY THE CASE.
>   THERE'S NOTHING SHADY GOING ON IN THIS JOINT.

ALL SISTERS:
    EV'RY SINGLE EVENING,
    DRINK YOUR CARES AWAY.
    EV'RY SINGLE EVENING,
    FORGET WHAT YOU SAW OR ELSE WE'LL MAKE YOU PAY.

HAIRDO SISTER 3:
    JUST RELAX, HAVE A SMOKE.
    SEE THAT GUY? WE MADE HIM CROAK!
    SETTLE DOWN, THAT WAS A JOKE!

THE HAIRDO SISTERS all smile and laugh for two beats, then stare menacingly out at the audience for two beats.

    THERE'S NOTHING SHADY GOING ON IN THIS JOINT.

ALL:
    ONE-EYED PETE RUNS THE SHOW.
    HE DECIDES IF YOU STAY OR GO.
    WHEN THEY GO HIGH, THEN HE GOES LOW.
    HE'LL TELL YOU ALL YOU NEED TO KNOW.
    YES ALL HE DOES IS ROLL IN DOUGH.

    BUT THAT'S NOT CRAZY, HAZY
    NOTHING THAT IS SHADY,
    IS GOING ON IN THIS...

    (*spoken in rhythm*) Tiny little bar, where the whiskey is the star, stick with us and you'll go far...

    JOINT!

Song ends. BIG AL applauds as the HAIRDO SISTERS run offstage giggling. SHADY MAN enters with ONE-EYED PETE. He exits, leaving ONE-EYED PETE alone with BIG AL to discuss business.

BIG AL: Wow, what a show!

ONE-EYED PETE: Please, let's take a seat somewhere more quiet.

They move a few steps to the left or the right and sit.

Song begins - "The Confession"

BIG AL:
>IT SURE IS AN HONOR TO MEET YOU
>I CAN SEE THAT YOU RUN QUITE A SHOW
>BUT BEFORE WE BEGIN THIS BRIEF MEETING
>THERE IS SOMETHING I'M DYING TO KNOW
>
>THEY SAY THAT YOUR AIM IS QUITE DEADLY
>THAT YOUR SOUL IS AS DARK AS THIS PLACE
>SO, TELL ME SIR, IF YOU WOULD BE SO KIND
>HOW YOU GOT THAT BIG SCAR ON YOUR FACE?

One-Eyed Pete removes his eye patch to reveal a healthy-looking eye.

ONE-EYED PETE (*mouthing/whispering*):
>IT'S A FAKE, YOU SEE

BIG AL: What?!

ONE-EYED PETE (*whispering louder*):
>IT'S A FAKE, YOU SEE
>BUT IT SURE MAKES PEOPLE CARE
>
>IT'S A FAKE, YOU SEE
>IT'S A FAKE, YOU SEE
>HOW I LOVE IT WHEN THEY STARE
>
>THEY KNOW ME ALL AROUND
>FROM MY BUSINESS AND MY NAME
>I KNOW IT'S NOT PROFOUND
>BUT I LIVE FOR ALL OF THIS FAME
>
>IF YOU'RE FAKE LIKE ME
>IF YOU'RE FAKE LIKE ME
>YOU CAN PULL OFF ANYTHING

COME ALONG WITH ME
COME ALONG WITH ME
I CAN HELP YOU BE A KING

SO GRAB YOUR SUIT AND TIE
AND I'LL SHOW YOU HOW IT COULD BE
YES, WITH MY NAME AND WITH YOUR BRAIN
I CAN TEACH YOU TO BE FAKE LIKE ME

BIG AL:
    THE STORIES?

ONE-EYED PETE:
    FAKE!

BIG AL:
    THE WOMEN?

ONE-EYED PETE:
    FAKE!

BIG AL:
    THE PAPERS?

ONE-EYED PETE:
    FAKE FAKE FAKE!

BIG AL:
    THE VENUE?

ONE-EYED PETE:
    FAKE!

BIG AL:
    THE MONEY?

ONE-EYED PETE:
    FAKE!

BIG AL:
>   THE MURDERS?

> *Silence.*

ONE-EYED PETE (*ad-libs*): So my lawyer said I can't talk about that... etc..

>   LIFE'S BETTER WHEN YOU LIE
>   IF YOU'RE SMART THEN YOU WILL AGREE

> *ONE-EYED PETE pulls a knife out of this pocket and waves it.*

>   SO SAY GOODBYE TO YOUR OLD LIFE
>   I CAN TEACH YOU TO BE FAKE LIKE ME

> *ONE-EYED PETE stabs BIG AL. He screams (a lot), but then realizes it was a fake knife.*

BIG AL: Wait a minute... "fake like you"? I don't want to be a fake! I thought I was going to learn from a great businessman how to build an honest business of stealing and and selling and murdering.

ONE-EYED PETE: Yeah, well whatever your name is buddy.

BIG AL: Alphonse Gabriel Capone, sir.

> *BIG AL goes to shake his hand but ONE-EYED PETE stabs his hand with the knife. ONE-EYED PETE slowly exits the stage while threatening BIG AL with the knife.*

ONE-EYED PETE: Well, Mister Alphonse, whatever your name is. If you tell a word or a soul of anything that we talked about today... I swear on my mother's lasagna that I will do something that no one's seen before.... no one will ever know your name, no one will ever know your face...

> *ONE-EYED PETE is gone.*

BIG AL: I need to get out of here!

BIG AL runs out of the speakeasy and into the empty street.

BIG AL: What have I gotten myself into? How can someone so incompetent be running everything? You know, I never thought I'd say this, but...

Song begins - "Run This Town (reprise)"

I MISS MY AMATEURS
WHATEVER FIGHT OCCURS
THEY ALWAYS STOOD BY ME
HAVE I LET THEM DOWN?

The GANGSTERS enter excitedly.

GANGSTER #1: Hey Al! AL! We got the bank money after all!

GANGSTER #2: Don't you see? That deposit slip worked!

BIG AL: Oh my God, we did it!

GANGSTERS & BIG AL:
    WE'LL GIVE 'EM HELL, YOU'LL SEE

BIG AL:
    WITH MY CREW AND ME

GANGSTERS & BIG AL:
    YES OUR TEAM IS KEY
    AND WE'LL RUN THIS TOWN

The rest of the cast enters.

EVERYONE ENTERING:
    WE WILL SEE HOW THEY WILL
    RUN THIS TOWN

ALL:
        YES ONE DAY I KNOW WE'LL
        RUN THIS TOWN

Blackout.

END

SUPERHOTS!

Book & Lyrics by *Blair Bodine*
Book & Music by *Joel Esher*

The cast of *Superhots!* at Theatre Now's SOUND BITES 4.0.
(Left to right): Feathers Wise, Anna Stefanic, Chris Ignacio, Nicolette Stephanie Templier, and Sarah Haines.

SYNOPSIS

In this culinary comedy, we first meet the organic farmer Taylor as he drives around the spicy little town of Cayenne, Texas. He delivers vegetables to restaurants and farmers markets and sings about his favorite day of the week "TUESDAY". At Carlotta's Cantina, we meet Carlotta, chef and owner of this beloved local restaurant. Carlotta is distracted. She's had a rough day. She shares with Taylor that Pepper Pete, the villainous Texas businessman, is planning on opening a competing restaurant nearby. Pepper Pete developed the recipe for Kablammo! Hot Sauce (a local favorite).

As if on cue, Carlotta turns on the radio to hear an announcement "SUPERHOT JINGLE". Pepper Pete enters, loudly and obnoxiously, telling Carlotta that she can no longer serve his Kablammo! Hot Sauce (due to their non-compete clause). He and The Superhots sing a fire and brimstone comedy song "KABLAMMO!". The song ends and Pepper Pete exits, taking all of his coveted hot sauce.

Taylor, knowing that Carlotta is desperate, offers to help. They go to his greenhouse where he's been working on growing a superhot pepper, hotter than Pepper Pete's. The music begins to swell. They sing "THE HEAT OF A PEPPER" as they taste-test the different peppers in Taylor's greenhouse. The song ends with a kiss. Taylor and Carlotta decide to challenge Pepper Pete.

The characters transition to the grand opening of Pepper Pete's Kablammo! Casa. Armed with hot peppers and a renewed sense of confidence, Carlotta challenges Pepper Pete to a "pepper-off" to prove who has the hottest pepper in town. The Superhots reluctantly agree to taste-test. Taylor's pepper is SO HOT that The Superhots run off stage and dunk their heads in donkey troughs. Pepper Pete, in disbelief, also tries Taylor's pepper. He runs offstage screaming...and literally explodes from the heat!

Taylor and Carlotta cannot believe they defeated Pepper Pete. Excited, Taylor finally builds up the nerve and asks Carlotta out on a date. When? How about next "TUESDAY (REPRISE)"? Carlotta, Taylor and The Superhots all sing together as the sun sets over Cayenne, Texas.

PRODUCTION HISTORY

Superhots!, written by Blair Bodine and Joel Esher, was created as a final presentation for the First Year BMI Lehman Engel Musical Theatre Workshop. It was presented as reading at BMI in New York City on June 13th, 2016. It was directed by Blair Bodine & Joel Esher, with musical direction by Joel Esher and accompaniment by Matti Kovler. The cast was as follows:

NARRATOR	Brandon Lambert
TAYLOR	Joel Esher
CARLOTTA	Blair Bodine
THE SUPERHOTS	Joanna Burns, Danielle Good, Natalie Storrs
PEPPER PETE	Sam Reiff-Pasarew
CUSTOMER	Gil Varod

Superhots! premiered as a fully staged production at The Irene Diamond Stage at The Pershing Square Signature Center for Theatre Now's SOUND BITES 4.0 on May 28, 2017. The production was directed by Charles Quittner with musical direction by Andy Bell. It was produced by Thomas Morrissey, Stephen Bishop Seely, and Chris Giordano. The cast was as follows:

TAYLOR	Chris Ignacio
CARLOTTA	Nicolette Stephanie Templier
THE SUPERHOTS	Feathers Wise, Sarah Haines, Anna Stefanic
PEPPER PETE	Sam Reiff-Pasarew

CHARACTERS

TAYLOR	Late 20s, an earnest organic farmer.
CARLOTTA	Late 20s, chef and proprietor of "Carlotta's Cantina," a beloved local restaurant.
PEPPER PETE	Mid 50s, insists on being referred to as a successful Texan businessman, because "an entrepreneur" sounds "too French."
SUPERHOT FRIEND	Super friendly, member of "The Superhots" singing troupe
SUPERHOT VILLAGER	Super local, loves supporting farm-to-table industry, member of "The Superhots"
SUPERHOT SINGER	Super confused, not into spicy food, but still a proud member of "The Superhots"

SETTING

Harvest season in Cayenne, Texas, a spicy little town where the sun is hot, but the peppers are hotter. Present day.

MUSICAL NUMBERS

"Tuesday"	Taylor & Carlotta
"Superhots Jingle"	The Superhots
"KABLAMMO!"	Pepper Pete & The Superhots
"The Heat of a Pepper"	Taylor, Carlotta & The Superhots
"Tuesday (reprise)"	Taylor, Carlotta & The Superhots

AUTHORS' NOTE

The title "*Superhots!*" is derived from a variety of chili peppers with the same name. Superhots are defined as extremely fiery peppers that surpass 350,000 Scoville Heat Units. To put that in perspective, it's more than one hundred and fifty times hotter than a jalapeño pepper! People have become fascinated with the "near-death experience" of eating superhots, and there are world-wide competitions to see who can grow the hottest peppers. The show's creators became fascinated by this competitive and hilarious subculture, where pepper growers engage in one-upmanship, trash-talk the competition, and shroud their own growing techniques in secrecy. But within the community, there is also deep reverence for the farmers who study the seeds, experiment with varietals and try to bring the hottest pepper into existence.

We imagined a fictional town, called Cayenne Texas, where these two worldviews come face-to-face. Will an organic farmer, who has spent years tinkering in his greenhouse, be able to defeat a big-time Texan businessman? What if love is on the line? These are the questions that helped shape Superhots!

For additional research, we suggest reading the New Yorker article "Fire-Eaters" by journalist Lauren Collins about superhots and competitive chili pepper growing. We would also like to give our heartfelt thanks to the brave souls who film themselves eating superhots on YouTube: THANK YOU for taking the heat so we didn't have to!

- Blair Bodine & Joel Esher

Lights up on a small town in Texas. We see TAYLOR, a very happy organic farmer maneuvering a cardboard cut-out car around the stage. The car can also be mimed. THE SUPERHOTS walk around the stage. In his car, TAYLOR passes by SUPERHOT FRIEND and waves.

SUPERHOT FRIEND: Morning, Taylor.

TAYLOR: Good Morning, Friend! My oh my, what beautiful weather we're having here in Cayenne, Texas.

SUPERHOT FRIEND: Wow. You sure are chipper!

TAYLOR: Well, it just so happens to be my favorite day!

Song begins - "Tuesday"

TAYLOR:
> TUESDAY!
> WHEN I GET TO MAKE DELIVERIES DOWN AT THE VILLAGE SQUARE
> TUESDAY
> SEEING FRIENDS AND NEIGHBORS EVERYWHERE
> THE SUN IS SHINING
> THE BIRDS ARE CHIRPING
> I'M SMILING FROM CHEEK TO CHEEK
> TALKIN' BOUT TUESDAY
> TUESDAY
> THE BEST DAY OF THE WEEK

Speaking.

> Hope you like the cucumbers today!

SUPERHOT VILLAGER: Thanks, Taylor!

TAYLOR: You bet!

TAYLOR continues singing.

TUESDAY
WHEN I GET TO SEE THE FRUITS THAT FLOURISHED
FROM THE SEEDS I'VE SOWN
TUESDAY
DROPPING OFF THE VEGETABLES I'VE GROWN

FRESH TOMATOES
SQUASH AND POTATOES
I'VE HARVESTED MY CROP

TALKIN' BOUT TUESDAY
TUESDAY
WHEN I MAKE MY FAVORITE STOP

Spoken, smiling.

Carlotta's Cantina!

Interior of Carlotta's Cantina, we see CARLOTTA moving around to her restaurant, setting tables, arranging salt & pepper shakers, etc.

CARLOTTA: Oh, hey Taylor.

TAYLOR: Hey Carlotta!

CARLOTTA (*shakes her head in disbelief*): I swear I could set my clock by you—10:30 am every Tuesday. What do you have for me today?

TAYLOR: Some vine ripened tomatoes for your salsa, an assortment of summer squash for your enchiladas, and some wildflowers... for you.

CARLOTTA: For me?

TAYLOR (*stammering*): I mean, for your tables. For centerpieces.

CARLOTTA: Thanks Taylor. I really could use some cheering up today.

TAYLOR: Why, what's wrong?

CARLOTTA: Didn't you hear? Pepper Pete is opening up his own restaurant right down the street!

TAYLOR: Pepper Pete! The hot sauce guy?

CARLOTTA: Yeah.

> *She sings:*
>
> TUESDAY
> I THOUGHT I HAD THE HOTTEST RESTAURANT
> IN THIS LITTLE TOWN.
> TUESDAY
> BUT PEPPER PETE'S GONNA SHUT ME DOWN
> I'LL HAVE TO FIGURE IT OUT SOMEHOW.

TAYLOR (*sung as an aside*):
    SHE SEEMS REALLY STRESSED OUT RIGHT NOW,

CARLOTTA:
    I CAN'T BELIEVE THIS IS HAPPENING TODAY...

TAYLOR & CARLOTTA:
    TUESDAY

CARLOTTA (*sung as an aside*):
    MORE LIKE AWFUL NEWS DAY!

CARLOTTA turns away from TAYLOR to go about her tasks setting up the restaurant.

TAYLOR (*continues singing*):
    TUESDAY
    EVERY WEEK I WANNA ASK HER OUT,
    BUT THE CHANCES PASS ME BY
    TUESDAY
    LOOKS LIKE THERE ARE BIGGER FISH TO FRY

I LOVE THIS RESTAURANT
I WANNA HELP HER
I'M GONNA FIND A WAY
TALKIN' BOUT TUESDAY

TAYLOR:
    TUESDAY...

CARLOTTA:
    TUESDAY...

TAYLOR:
    TUESDAY...

CARLOTTA:
    TUESDAY...

SUPERHOTS, TAYLOR and CARLOTTA:
    TUESDAY

TAYLOR:
    THE BEST DAY OF THE WEEK!

The restaurant is officially open, the customer SUPERHOT VILLAGER walks in.

SUPERHOT VILLAGER: Miss, do you serve "Pepper Pete's Kablammo Hot Sauce" here?

CARLOTTA hands SUPERHOT VILLAGER a menu.

CARLOTTA *(defeated)*: Yeah, yeah. There's a bottle on every table.

CARLOTTA walks over to the radio and turns on. It's a commercial.

ALL THE SUPERHOTS: And now, a word from our sponsor...

Song begins - "Superhots Jingle"

SUPERHOTS:
>   PEPPER PETE
>   AS HOT AS IT COMES
>   PLACE ONE DROP ON THE TIP OF YOUR TONGUE...
>   AHHH!

SUPERHOT SINGER: It feels like the roof of my mouth is trying to make me pay for all of my mistakes!

SUPERHOTS:
>   SOON TO BE EXCLUSIVE
>   AT HIS BRAND NEW RESTAURANT...
>   PEPPER PETE!

CARLOTTA: Soon to be exclusive at his brand-new restaurant!? Wait, I can't even serve Pepper Pete's hot sauce here? This will close me down for sure! UGH! I can't stand that bible-thumpin' cowboy.

PEPPER PETE enters wearing a comically large cowboy hat.

PEPPER PETE: Did somebody say "bible-thumpin' cowboy"?

CARLOTTA and TAYLOR: Pepper Pete!

PEPPER PETE: Praise Jesus! Carlotta, you are looking absolutely scrumptious today if I do say so myself.

CARLOTTA: Gross. What are you even doing here?

PEPPER PETE: Following through on my non-compete clause.

TAYLOR: What?

PEPPER PETE: I'm taking back every bottle of my hot sauce you got!

CARLOTTA: Right now? But I've got customers!

PEPPER PETE: Lord almighty, you're like a helpless little kitten stuck in a tree. And by tree, I mean your failing family restaurant!

CARLOTTA: This can't be true.

PEPPER PETE: Well, Carlotta, some people say the truth hurts... I say it burns. Like fire and brimstone. Kablammo!

Song begins - "KABLAMMO!"

I THINK WE ALL RECALL
THE PREHISTORIC AGE
T-REXES HERE IN TEXAS ROAMING FREE
BUT DINOSAURS ARE DUMB
WITH LITTLE TINY BRAINS
AND DON'T KNOW JESUS DIED FOR YOU AND ME

PEPPER PETE:	SUPERHOTS:
SO OUR FATHER,	AH
HALLOWED BE HIS NAME	
SOLVED THE PROBLEM WITH	AH
A BALL OF FLAME	
KABLAMMO!	KABLAMMO!
THOSE DINOS FELT	
THE HEAT	
KABLAMMO!	KABLAMMO!
EXTINCTION WAS	
COMPLETE	
KABLAMMO!	KABLAMMO!
TRADEMARK	
PEPPER PETE	

PEPPER PETE (*spoken*): A Monsanto subsidiary!

SUPERHOTS:
    THEY OWN ALL OUR VEGETABLES!

PEPPER PETE:
>   I'LL TELL ANOTHER TALE
>   FROM OUR SACRED BOOK
>   WHEN MOSES WANDERED IN THE DESERT SAND
>   HE'D BEEN LED OFF TRACK
>   BY EVIL DEMOCRATS
>   AND JESUS HAD TO MAKE HIM UNDERSTAND

PEPPER PETE:	SUPERHOTS:
THEN OUR FATHER,	AH
HALLOWED BE HIS NAME	AH
SOLVED THE PROBLEM WITH	
A BALL OF FLAME	
KABLAMMO!	KABLAMMO!
THOSE SINNERS FELT THE HEAT	
KABLAMMO!	KABLAMMO!
THE MESSAGE WAS COMPLETE	
KABLAMMO!	KABLAMMO!
TRADEMARK PEPPER PETE	

PEPPER PETE (*spoken*): Not a fair-trade company!

SUPERHOTS:
>   WE USE AGROCHEMICALS!

PEPPER PETE:
>   I'LL FINISH UP MY TALE
>   WITH STORIES FROM OUR TIME
>   IN WORLD WAR II, IN 1945
>   WHEN TEXAS WAS ATTACKED
>   BY HEATHENS FROM JAPAN
>   GOD MADE A BOMB THAT NO ONE COULD SURVIVE...
>   KAMBLAMMO!

SUPERHOTS *(shocked, overlapping ad-libs)*: "Dude!" "Oh no!" "That's just not right." "I did not realize that's where this song was headed," "Not at all factually accurate..." etc.

PEPPER PETE: You don't have to like it, but it's the way of the world, y'all.

PEPPER PETE and SUPERHOTS *(singing)*:
KABLAMMO!

PEPPER PETE shakes the hot sauce at Carlotta.

PEPPER PETE: I'm taking this!

PEPPER PETE exits. The SUPERHOTS follow.

CARLOTTA: Oh my goodness, what am I gonna do?! There's no way I can make a hot sauce as hot as Pepper Pete's.

TAYLOR: Well, you happen to know an organic farmer who would love to help you. Come with me to the greenhouse?

CARLOTTA: Okay...

CARLOTTA and TAYLOR both spin in a circle, signifying a change in location. We hear a melodica glissando.

CARLOTTA and TAYLOR: The Greenhouse!

CARLOTTA: Wow, I've never been here before; it's so... beautiful.

TAYLOR: Here, let me show you something I've been tinkering with.

Song begins - "The Heat of The Pepper"

TAYLOR *(speaking over the musical intro)*: Here are Pepper Pete's peppers.

CARLOTTA: The kind he uses in his hot sauce?

TAYLOR: Yep, should we try it? Size up the competition?

CARLOTTA: Alright...
    TAYLOR and CARLOTTA eat the pepper.

TAYLOR and CARLOTTA (*screaming, frantically*): Ahhhhhhhhh!

TAYLOR: It's like being skewered by angry villagers with red-hot pitchforks!

CARLOTTA: It's like being tongue-pierced... by Satan!

    The music stops.

    ...it's gone. Hm, I wonder why it didn't last that long?

    She sings:

    HOW DO YOU MEASURE THE HEAT OF A PEPPER
    THE PLEASURE THAT COMES FROM THE PAIN
    IS IT A FLASH ON THE TIP OF YOUR TONGUE

TAYLOR:
    OR DOES IT BUILD AND SUSTAIN
    INTO A FIRE
    THAT WE CANNOT DENY
    HOW WILL WE KNOW?
    IF WE DON'T GIVE IT A TRY?

    TAYLOR and CARLOTTA look at each other deeply. Beat.

    HERE IS ONE OF MY HOME-GROWN PEPPERS
    LOOKS A LITTLE BUMPY AND

CARLOTTA (*bluntly*):
    SMALL

TAYLOR: Hey! I was gonna say cute! Anyway...

He sings:

YOU'RE THE FIRST TO TRY MY CREATION
I'M NOT SURE IF IT'S HOT AT ALL
BUT HOW DO YOU MEASURE THE HEAT OF A PEPPER
THE PLEASURE THAT COMES FROM THE PAIN
IS IT A FLASH ON THE TIP OF YOUR TONGUE

CARLOTTA:
OR DOES IT BUILD AND SUSTAIN

CARLOTTA and TAYLOR:
INTO A FIRE
THAT WE CANNOT DENY
HOW WILL WE KNOW?
IF WE DON'T GIVE IT A TRY?

TAYLOR hands a pepper to CARLOTTA.

TAYLOR: Shall we?

TAYLOR and CARLOTTA: Cheers!

TAYLOR and CARLOTTA clink peppers, as if they're glasses, and take a bite. The SUPERHOTS begin singing in a round in the background.

SUPERHOTS:
HOW DO YOU MEASURE THE HEAT OF A PEPPER
THE PLEASURE THAT COMES FROM THE PAIN
IS IT A FLASH ON THE TIP OF YOUR TONGUE
OR DOES IT BUILD AND SUSTAIN
HOW DO YOU MEASURE THE HEAT OF A PEPPER
THE PLEASURE THAT COMES FROM THE PAIN
IS IT A FLASH ON THE TIP OF YOUR TONGUE
OR DOES IT BUILD AND SUSTAIN...

CARLOTTA (*apologetically, spoken over the SUPERHOTS singing*): Well, it tastes good... but, I'm not really feeling the heat yet.

TAYLOR: Really? My other versions ranked pretty high on the Scoville scale...

TAYLOR and CARLOTTA (*screaming, frantically, together*): Ahhhh!

TAYLOR: It feels like I'm on the surface of the SUN!

CARLOTTA: It feels like a rocket blasting off in my mouth!

TAYLOR (*ad-lib*): I can't...

CARLOTTA (*ad-lib*): I can't... It's too hot...

> *The song builds. SUPERHOTS sing the final line holding out the word "sustain." CARLOTTA and TAYLOR kiss.*

CARLOTTA: That was so...

TAYLOR: That was so...

CARLOTTA and TAYLOR (*together*): ... Hot.

CARLOTTA: You know what we have to do...

TAYLOR: Get married?!

CARLOTTA: What?

TAYLOR: Huh?

CARLOTTA: No, we've got to get your spicy peppers into my new Superhot Sauce.

TAYLOR: What?

CARLOTTA: Huh??

TAYLOR: We gotta go to Pepper Pete's new restaurant and show him that he's no longer the only game in town!

We hear a melodica glissando again as CARLOTTA and TAYLOR spin to a new location. They look around in disbelief.

CARLOTTA and TAYLOR: The Kablammo Casa!

CARLOTTA: It's so... tacky! I can't stand this dime-store cowboy!

PEPPER PETE *(loudly)*: Did somebody say tacky dime-store cowboy!? Welcome everyone to the Grand Opening of the Kablammo Casa! We're here to celebrate me! Pepper Pete! And my patented hot sauce that knocks your socks off: Kablammo! *(quieter, as an aside)* Registered trademark.

CARLOTTA: Not so fast, Pepper Pete! I have an announcement to make. Taylor and I made a Superhot Hot Sauce hotter than yours.

PEPPER PETE *(gasp)*: Impossible!

CARLOTTA: Possible! I challenge anyone here to try both and see for yourself!

PEPPER PETE: You're on!

CARLOTTA motions to the SUPERHOTS, seeking to engage them in the competition.

CARLOTTA: Girls, get over here.

SUPERHOT SINGER: Oh, yeah, uh...I don't really like hot sauce... I'm actually from Connecticut.

PEPPER PETE *(cutting her off)*: Shut up and try this.

PEPPER PETE force-feeds all the SUPERHOTS hot sauce, or depending on the number of SUPERHOTS, hands them each a bottle of Kablammo! We hear the music plunk notes, building after each line representing the "hotness" affecting their mouths.

Plunk.

SUPERHOTS: Ahhh! (*Plunk.*) Hoo!

Plunk. Plunk.

SUPERHOT FRIEND: ... Oh, it's fading. Thank God.

SUPERHOT VILLAGER: I'll never do that again.

CARLOTTA: Wait, try ours!

SUPERHOT SINGER: This really wasn't in our contract...

CARLOTTA: Please? For my Cantina?

SUPERHOTS look at one another, determination on their face.

SUPERHOT FRIEND: We got you, Carlotta.

SUPERHOT SINGER (*still hesitant about the situation*): But, like, how bad is it going to be?

TAYLOR (*ignoring protestations*): Here you go!!!

TAYLOR pops the peppers into their mouths before they can question any further. We hear the music plunk notes, building after each line again.

SUPERHOTS: Huh. (*Plunk.*) Not too bad. (*Plunk.*) Oh my God... (*Plunk.*) Oh. My. God. (*Plunk.*) Oh my God!

Each of the SUPERHOTS heads emit steam. They run offstage. We hear the sound of their heads dunking into a donkey trough, a splash, and the sound of steam, like when cold water hits a hot pan.

PEPPER PETE: Aww, they're in cahoots! Your sauce can't be that hot. Give it to me.

> *PEPPER PETE tries CARLOTTA's hot sauce. As before, again we hear the music plunk notes, building after each line.*
>
> *Plunk.*

PEPPER PETE: Huh. (*Plunk.*) Not too bad. (*Plunk.*) Oh my God... (*Plunk.*) Oh. My. God. (*Plunk.*) Oh my God!

> *PEPPER PETE runs offstage screaming to the donkey trough, same as the SUPERHOTS. Sound cue: and explosion as if PEPPER PETE has combusted from the heat. PEPPER PETE's hat is tossed back on stage, badly charred.*

SUPERHOTS VILLAGER: Whoa... that pepper changed my LIFE. Where can I get my hands on that hot sauce?

> *TAYLOR looks at CARLOTTA meaningfully.*

TAYLOR: At Carlotta's Cantina! Featuring fresh, fiery, fair-trade peppers delivered weekly!

SUPERHOT VILLAGER: We'll see you there!

> *SUPERHOTS move to the side and mime talking excitedly about the hot sauce.*

CARLOTTA: Taylor! We did it! I think we just saved the restaurant.

TAYLOR: Yes! We need to celebrate! Can I take you out sometime?

CARLOTTA: Sure! When?

TAYLOR: How about next...

> *Song begins - "Tuesday (reprise)"*
>
> *He sings:*

TUESDAY...

Hearing the music, the SUPERHOTS come over and join in singing.

SUPERHOTS:
    TUESDAY...

TAYLOR and CARLOTTA:
    TUESDAY

ALL:
    TUESDAY, THE BEST DAY OF THE WEEK!

Blackout.

END

THE ALMOST IN-LAWS

Book & Lyrics by *Greg Edwards*
Music by *Andy Roninson*

Rebecca Odorisio, Kyle Olsen, Nicholas Alexiy Moran, and Adrien Swenson in *The Almost In-Laws* at Theatre Now's SOUND BITES 5.0.

SYNOPSIS

Soon-to-be-married couple Des and Jennifer step out of the car so Jennifer can finally meet his parents for the first time. When Jennifer asks why they're in the middle of a forest, Des explains that his parents... are elves. Yes, elves. They celebrate Christmas every day, bake far too many cookies, and wear hats that jingle nonstop, and Des claims he couldn't be more different *"I AM NOT LIKE MY PARENTS"*.

The couple approaches the family's home (in a tree) and are greeted by Des's parents, two overly sweet elves who are so excited to reminisce about Des's favorite lullaby *"HAPPY HAPPY ELF ELF"* and find out more about his human fiancée. When they are perplexed by her human ways and suggest she find a real job like cobbling, Des points out that they are being "species-ist." His parents are shocked by the accusation and claim it can't possibly be true because *"SOME OF OUR BEST FRIENDS"* are people.

Des immediately pulls Jennifer outside and apologizes for his parents. But Jennifer wants Des to go back in and make things better *"PARENTS ARE DUMB"*. He knocks on the tree door, but his parents are too upset to let him back in. He resorts to singing through the door *"HAPPY HAPPY ELF ELF (REPRISE)"* until his parents join in, won over by the sweet gesture. They embrace Jennifer too, accepting that even though she's human, "at least you're not a hobbit."

PRODUCTION HISTORY

The Almost In-Laws, written by Greg Edwards and Andy Roninson, was developed at Manhattan Musical Theatre Lab in July 2015, and it then debuted on the Take a Ten Musicals podcast on August 1, 2015. It was produced, directed, and music directed by Andy Roninson. The cast was as follows:

DES	Aaron Phillips
JENNIFER	Christiana Cole
MOTHER	Tiffany Topol
FATHER	Bruce Sabath

Its first professional production premiered at The Irene Diamond Stage at The Pershing Square Signature Center for Theatre Now's SOUND BITES 5.0 on May 28, 2018. The production was directed by Erin Thompson with music direction by Andy Roninson. It was produced by Thomas Morrissey, Chris Giordano, and Stephen Bishop Seely. The cast was as follows:

DES	Kyle Olsen
JENNIFER	Rebecca Odorisio
MOTHER	Adrien Swenson
FATHER	Nicholas Alexiy Moran

At that year's festival, the show was awarded Best Musical, and Kyle Olsen was awarded Best Actor.

There was subsequently a production from May 31 through July 1, 2018, at the Adrienne Arsht Center for the Performing Arts in Miami, FL as part of City Theatre's Summer Shorts series. It was produced by Margaret M. Ledford and Susan Westfall.

The following year it was produced at Bennington Community Theatre in Bennington, VT from November 15 through 17, 2019

CHARACTERS

DES — Late 20s, an average city-dwelling man, Jennifer's fiancé.

JENNIFER — Late 20s, a smart city-dwelling woman, Des' fiancée.

MOTHER — Looks 50s, Des' mother, matronly.

FATHER — Looks 50s, Des' father, patronly.

SETTING

Des' childhood home in the woods of Delaware. The present.

MUSICAL NUMBERS

"I Am Not Like My Parents"	Des
"Happy Happy Elf Elf"	Mother, Father
"Some Of Our Best Friends"	Mother, Father
"Parents Are Dumb"	Jennifer
"Happy Happy Elf Elf (reprise)"	Des, Mother, Father

AUTHOR'S NOTE

Originally, the show was about an elf who was afraid to tell his parents he was getting his ears surgically modified. Then we realized the emotional core of the show was the relationship between the protagonist and his parents, and the current version was born. They're still elves, though. In terms of performance tips, we'd suggest playing the truth of the scenes and songs. Yes, there are a lot of elf jokes, but at its heart, the show is about a kid's relationship with their parents and how it changes over time. Playing the show honestly will best communicate that message.

- Greg Edwards and Andy Roninson

DES and JENNIFER walk down a wooded road. JENNIFER talks on her phone.

DES: We're here. And right on time. How... lucky.

JENNIFER: Okay, Mom, I'll talk to you later. Okay, bye. Bye. Bye.

> *She hangs up.*
>
> Um, honey, why are we in the middle of an old growth forest? Where's your parents' house?

DES: Well, uh—We really don't have to do this, I promise, they won't mind!

JENNIFER: Des, we're getting married in two weeks, and you've never introduced me to your parents. Why are you so scared for me to meet them?

DES: Well...

> *Song begins - "I Am Not Like My Parents"*

He sings:

> SOME PARENTS ARE OUTGOING;
> SOME KEEP TO THEMSELVES.
> SOME PARENTS ARE ALL-KNOWING.
> MINE... ARE ELVES.

JENNIFER: Elves? Like elf-ish? Jolly demeanor, twinkle in the eye?

DES: No, elves. Like fresh off the sleigh, first-generation North Pole expats. Like they're always talking about how things were in the cold country.

JENNIFER: But elves aren't real.

DES: Sure they are.

JENNIFER: Then why haven't I ever seen one?

DES: Cause elves live in places where humans never go. Like Middle Earth, and Delaware.

He sings:

> IN TWO-POINT-FOUR MINUTES,
> THERE'S NO WAY TO HIDE IT.
> YOU'LL MEET MY PARENTS,
> AND I'LL SHUDDER WITH DREAD.
> YOU SEE THAT BIG TREE?
> WELL, THEY LIVE INSIDE IT.
> MY MOM AND DAD
> AND THEIR REINDEER FRED.
>
> BUT I AM NOT LIKE MY PARENTS.
> I HAVE A HOUSE AND A CAR.
> I AM NOT LIKE MY PARENTS.
> I'LL NEVER BE THE WAY THEY ARE.

JENNIFER: Baby, you're making a big deal out of nothing. I'm sure I'll love your parents.

DES: Really?

> THEY'LL ASK US TO JOIN THEM
> IN DECKING THEIR HALLWAYS.
> THEY'LL LIGHT A YULE LOG,
> CAUSE, YEAH, THAT'S A THING.
> IMAGINE A HELL
> WHERE CHRISTMAS IS ALWAYS,
> WHERE HATS HAVE BELLS
> AND THEY RING-RING-RING.
>
> BUT I AM NOT LIKE MY PARENTS.
> I MAKE CHRISTMAS ONE DAY.
> I BELIEVE IN A WORLD
> WHERE HATS ARE QUIET.

> I AM NOT LIKE MY PARENTS.
> NO! NO, NOT IN ONE WAY.
> IT'S JUST A CRUEL TRICK OF DNA.

JENNIFER: Des—

DES:
> YES, I KNOW THEY'RE WELL-INTENTIONED.
> YES, I NEED A LONGER FUSE.
> BUT THEY'RE ALWAYS MAKING SMALL TALK
> AND COOKIES
> AND SHOES.
>
> AND I AM NOT LIKE MY PARENTS.
> I WEAR KHAKIS, NOT TIGHTS.
> I HAVE RATIONAL HOBBIES:
> MICROBREWING,
> PAY-PER-VIEWING.
> I AM NOT LIKE MY PARENTS.
> I'M SERIOUS THROUGH AND THROUGH.
> FOR ELVES FLIT,
> BUT I COMMIT
> AND I COMMIT TO LOVING YOU.

Song ends.

JENNIFER: Des, you have nothing to worry about. Now, come on, ring the doorbell.

Des rings the doorbell, which plays a lick of "Jingle Bells." They exchange looks. The door bursts open, revealing:

MOTHER: Baby!

FATHER: Son!

DES: Parents.

MOTHER: It's lovely to see you.

FATHER: And you, you must be Joonifer.

JENNIFER: Jennifer.

FATHER: Sorry, we're terrible with foreign names.

MOTHER: Come in, make yourself at tree.

FATHER: Sweetheart, can we offer you a cookie, a candy, a ring to rule them all? Kidding, that's for the wedding.

MOTHER: And we can't wait for you two to be married, now can we?

FATHER: Our little boy is all grown up. It seems just yesterday we were singing him his favorite lullaby.

MOTHER (*warming up*): La, la, la, la...

DES: Don't do it.

Song begins - "Happy Happy Elf Elf"

MOTHER and FATHER sing:

MOTHER & FATHER:
    HAPPY HAPPY ELF ELF
    JUMP FOR JOY.

DES: Stop singing.

MOTHER & FATHER:
    YOU'RE MY HEALTHY ELF-LY BOY.

DES: We have company, and this is really...

MOTHER & FATHER:
    HAPPY HAPPY ELF ELF
    SING ALONG
    TO MY HAPPY ELF ELF SONG.

Song ends.

DES: Okay, enough! Sorry, they sang that to me when I was five.

MOTHER: Until he was twenty-four.

FATHER: Then his roommate complained.

JENNIFER: Well, I think it's sweet.

FATHER: Thank you, Jeenifer. Now tell us, what do you do?

JENNIFER: Well, I majored in chemistry, interned in pharma, and now I'm a project manager for an HMO.

The parents stare blankly.

DES: Those are people things.

MOTHER & FATHER (*half-heartedly*): Oh, wow, neat...

MOTHER: Maybe someday you'll find a real job, like cobbling.

DES: Mom!

MOTHER: What?

DES: You're being species-ist!

MOTHER: What, no! Absolutely not!

FATHER: Son, your mother and I are definitely not species-ist. I don't see how you could even think that.

Song begins - "Some of Our Best Friends"

He sings:

SOME OF OUR BEST FRIENDS ARE PEOPLE.

>
> WE HONESTLY CONSIDER THEM OUR PEERS.
> WE LOVE THEIR PEOPLE HAIR,
> THE PANTALOONS THEY WEAR,
> THEIR MUSIC,
> THEIR GRAMMAR,
> THEIR EARS!
> (HOW ADORABLE.)
>
> IT'S TOTALLY FINE SHE'S A PERSON,
> THOUGH THIRTY-MILLION ELVES MAY DISAGREE.
> SHE COULDN'T BE MORE GREAT,
> SO PLEASE MISCEGENATE.
>
> YOU'RE MARRYING A PERSON.
> WHOOPEE!

DES: Dad, she's right here, you know.

MOTHER: Of course she is. How thoughtless of us! Jawnifer, dear—

> *(to Jennifer)*
> SOME OF OUR BEST FRIENDS ARE PEOPLE.
> IF YOU WALKED BY, I'D NEVER CROSS THE STREET.

DES: Mom!

MOTHER: I wouldn't.

> *She sings:*
>
> I'D NOTICE FROM AFAR
> HOW ELOQUENT YOU ARE:
> WELL-SPOKEN,
> WELL-SHAVEN,
> AND SWEET.
> (YOU'RE ONE OF THE GOOD ONES.)
>
> TRULY, I HAVE NO OBJECTION.
> BROAD-MINDEDNESS IS ROOTED IN MY SOUL.

> SO GO AHEAD AND MATE
> CAUSE WHEN YOU PROPAGATE,
> YOUR HALF-AN-ELF WILL ROUND UP
> TO WHOLE.
>
> There's just so much we want to ask you...
>
> YOUR DIMPLES
> ARE LOVELY. ARE THEY REAL?

DES: Mom!

MOTHER:
> NO BIG DEAL.

FATHER:
> YOUR SHOES...
> ARE THOSE STORE-BOUGHT?

JENNIFER: I—

FATHER:
> SO I THOUGHT.

MOTHER:
> WHEN YOU DON YOUR GAY APPAREL,
> HOW POINTY IS YOUR HAT?

FATHER:
> AT CHRISTMAS, DO YOU CAROL?

JENNIFER: I'm a Jew.

MOTHER: Cool.

Beat, then sings:

> WHAT'S THAT?

MOTHER & FATHER:
>SOME OF OUR BEST FRIENDS ARE PEOPLE.
>FOR INSTANCE, WE ADORE ELIJAH WOOD.

MOTHER:
>HE KIND OF LOOKS LIKE YOU,

FATHER:
>BUT THEN ALL PEOPLE DO.

MOTHER & FATHER:
>CAN YOU TELL
>THE DIFFERENCE?
>DON'T THINK I COULD.
>
>BUT
>WE'RE REALLY FRIENDS WITH A PERSON.
>THERE'S PHOTOGRAPHIC PROOF UPON OUR SHELVES.

MOTHER: Somewhere.

MOTHER & FATHER:
>AND, HONEY, WE CAN TELL
>THAT YOU'RE OUR FRIEND AS WELL,
>SO TWO OF OUR BEST FRIENDS ARE PEOPLE,
>AND ALL OF OUR BETTER FRIENDS ARE ELVES.

Song ends.

DES: You know what, we have to go.

MOTHER: But you just got here.

DES: Yeah, but there's traffic, we're tired, and this—this was plenty.

FATHER: Can we walk you to your car?

DES: We'll be fine. Thank you.

He leads Jennifer away. As they exit:

JENNIFER It was lovely meeting both of—

DES: Goodbye.

He slams the door.

JENNIFER: Des, what the hell was that?

DES: I'm sorry. They're old. They're from a generation that's into being really polite and really offensive all at the same time.

JENNIFER: No, what did you do to your parents? That was incredibly uncool.

DES: You wouldn't understand. You have a great relationship with your parents. Today, you called your mom, voluntarily.

JENNIFER: That doesn't mean she doesn't drive me crazy. All parents do.

Song begins - "Parents Are Dumb"

It's a universal condition.

She sings:

PARENTS ARE DUMB.
I GET IT, I DO.
THEY RAISE US, AND THEN THEY'RE INEPT.
YES, PARENTS ARE DUMB,
BUT CHILDREN ARE TOO,
SO WHAT'S THERE TO DO BUT ACCEPT?
OH, YOU CAN WALK IN THERE
AND PUT YOUR FOLKS AT EASE,
OR YOU CAN DRIVE AWAY,
BUT NO, YOU CAN'T, I'VE GOT THE KEYS.
PARENTS PRETEND

>   WE NEED THEIR ADVICE.
>   HONOR THEIR DELUSION.
>   GO BE NICE.
>
>   OH, HALF OF LOVE IS EASY:
>   YOU LAUGH AND YOU KISS.
>   THE OTHER HALF,
>   WELL,
>   IS THIS
>   AND STRANGULATION.
>
>   PARENTS ARE DUMB,
>   BUT GIVE THEM A SHOT
>   AND TEACH THEM WRONG FROM RIGHT.
>   AT EVERY TURN,
>   THEY'LL NEVER LEARN,
>   BUT SOMEDAY,
>   HEY,
>   YOU MIGHT.
>
>   *Song ends.*

DES (*smiling*): You know, you're great at making people feel terrible.

JENNIFER: I work in medicine.

> *They kiss. He knocks on the door.*

DES: Mom, Dad?

MOTHER: Still here? We thought you'd left.

DES: Would you please open the door?

FATHER: I'm not sure that's a good idea.

DES: But...

FATHER: Honestly, son, the way you treated us... we haven't been this betrayed since we bought the store-brand rice krispies.

MOTHER: The only sound they made was snarf, crookle, and thud.

FATHER: You'd better go.

DES: Dad...

FATHER: Your fiancée seems...nice. We hope you treat her the way she deserves.

MOTHER (*through tears*): And give her many flavors of nog.

DES (*"What should I do?"*): Jennifer?

JENNIFER: Keep trying.

>*Song begins - "Happy Happy Elf Elf (reprise)"*

>*He sings:*

DES:
> HAPPY HAPPY ELF ELF
> JUMP FOR JOY
> I'M YOUR HEALTHY ELF-LY BOY.

MOTHER: I don't know.

FATHER: We're not feeling very jump-y.

DES:
> HAPPY HAPPY ELF ELF
> SING ALONG
> TO MY HAPPY ELF ELF SONG.

>*The door cracks open, as the parents join in:*

DES, MOTHER & FATHER:
> YOU COULD TRAVEL CROSS THE WORLD,

        CLEAR TO TIMBUKTU,
        BUT I'LL STILL BE THERE THERE
        IN YOUR HEART,
        HAPPY ELF, I LOVE LOVE YOU.

MOTHER & FATHER: Elf hug!

FATHER: You too, Jennifer. You know, our parents didn't want us to get married either. They said I was too old for her.

MOTHER: To me, dear, you'll always be 126.

FATHER: But if age didn't stand in the way of love, then neither should an inferior genome.

DES: Um...

JENNIFER (*to DES*): Let it go.

FATHER: So welcome to the family, dear.

MOTHER: And whatever our differences, know that we are so, so happy...you're not a hobbit.

Music ends.

END

THE ANSWERING MACHINE

Book & Lyrics by *Kevin Hammonds*
Music by *Andy Roninson*

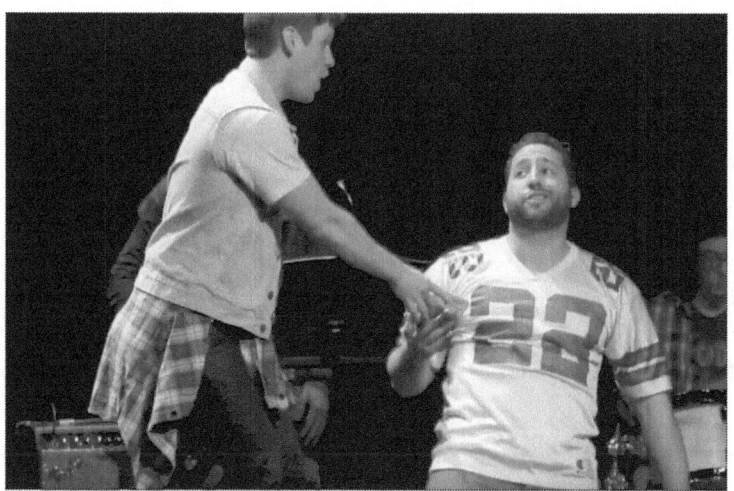

Brennan Caldwell and Gabe Aguilar in *The Answering Machine* at Theatre Now's SOUND BITES 2014.

SYNOPSIS

A Telephone rings. After a few rings, an answering machine clicks on and we hear Ben and Stafford's outgoing message. Ben and Stafford are two college roommates whose outgoing message reveals that it's a new year, and although a new semester has begun, they have no plans to stop partying anytime soon. *"OUTGOING MESSAGE #1"*. When the answering machine beeps, Lauren, another college student, leaves a message for Ben who stole her lucky hoodie while they were both at the same party. He has even gone so far as to leave a ransom note with his telephone number. Lauren makes it perfectly clear that she will meet him in order to get her hoodie back, but she has no intention of going on a date with him. *"GET THE MESSAGE"*.

A telephone rings. An answering machine clicks, and we hear from Ben and Stafford's outgoing message that Valentine's Day is around the corner. *"OUTGOING MESSAGE #2"*. After the beep, Ben calls out to Stafford, desperate for him to pick up the phone. He nervously announces that he is out with Lauren and she has agreed to come back to their place for a nightcap. Ben begs for Stafford to clean up the apartment and make it presentable for his new girlfriend. *"SHE'S COMING OVER"*.

Months have passed and now Ben and Stafford's outgoing message is very mature and labored on Stafford's part, a sign that Ben is at least making an attempt to be more responsible. Lauren leaves a message for Ben. The night before, he blacked out and left her at the bar. She reminds him that midterms are around the corner, and she has serious concerns about his partying. *"PICK UP, BEN"*.

In the next outgoing message, Stafford excitedly announces that finals are over, and party-time has begun. Ben leaves a desperate message for his roommate revealing that he has bottomed out. Earlier that morning he was supposed to meet Lauren and her parents for breakfast, before she left for the summer. But he partied the night before and missed breakfast. And now she has gone back to her parents for the summer, and has not left a number to reach her. Ben knows that his partying days are over. He is making this phone call from the airport, and he is about to board a plane and fly to rehab. *"NOWHERE ELSE TO GO BUT UP"*.

A telephone rings. After a few rings, an answering machine clicks and we hear Ben and Lauren's outgoing message. *"OUTGOING MESSAGE #3"*. They suggest that the caller leave a message at the beep, but please do so quietly, because the baby is sleeping. Beep.

PRODUCTION HISTORY

The Answering Machine, written by Kevin Hammonds and Andy Roninson, was first recorded and released on March 1, 2014 as episode #5 of the audio podcast "Take a Ten." The cast was as follows:

BEN _____ Gus Curry
LAUREN _____ Kristin Piacentile
STAFFORD _____ Gabe Aguilar

Later that year, it had its first full production at The 47th Street Theater in New York, NY for Theatre Now's SOUND BITES 2014 on December 8, 2014. The production was directed by Andrew Garret Karl, with music direction by Andy Roninson.. It was produced by Thomas Morrissey, Rebecca Nell Robertson, and Stephen Bishop Seely, with associate producer, Charles Quittner. On guitar was Anthony Rubbo, on bass was Mike Roninson, and on drums was Alex Aitken. The cast was as follows:

BEN _____ Brennan Caldwell
LAUREN _____ Kyra Kennedy
STAFFORD _____ Gabe Aguilar

The show was awarded Best Lyrics (Kevin Hammonds) and Best Musical in that year's festival.

Another production occurred in December 2014 at Baldwin Wallace University's One Act festival with direction by Nicholas Wilders.

It was then presented in the Summer of 2015 at Broadway au Carré, Paris, France with direction by Lisandro Nesis. During the same summer, it also had a reading during the Manhattan Musical Theater Lab as part of a reading of seven TAKE A TEN musicals, which was directed by Emmy-winner Matt Cowart.

CHARACTERS

BEN — 19 years old, a college student. Lovable party boy who is always up for a good time. He is warm hearted, good-natured and always the life of the party, although secretly desperate to find true love.

LAUREN — 19 years old, a college student. She's strong, independent and intelligent. She can let her hair down and have a good time, but is sensible enough to know when to stop. She has a life plan, and good luck to anyone who tries to stop her.

STAFFORD — 19 years old, a college student. He is the party boy who refuses to grow up and has come to college to get away from his strict parents, nothing takes precedence over partying and drinking.

SETTING
A college town, 1992.

MUSICAL NUMBERS

"Outgoing Message #1"	Ben, Stafford
"Get the Message"	Lauren
"Outgoing Message #2"	Ben, Stafford
"She's Coming Over"	Ben
"Pick Up, Ben"	Lauren
"Nowhere Else To Go But Up"	Ben
"Outgoing Message #3"	Ben, Lauren

AUTHORS' NOTE

Writing *The Answering Machine* was great fun, as it took us back to a time that doesn't seem like too long ago, and yet with the technological advances in the past thirty years, it seems like a different world. In fact, actors playing these roles might not even know what an answering machine is! But back in the day, answering machines were as crucial as cell phones are today. You see, before we carried phones in our pockets, they were left at home, attached to the walls. If you weren't home when someone called, you were out of luck. Until the invention of the answering machine, a magical box that would allow the caller to leave a message on a cassette tape. It was also the first opportunity for "screening calls" as the caller's message was playing out loud as they were leaving the message. As the new invention was new and exciting, one of the greatest joys of an answering machine (at least for those of us in college) was the ability to record your outgoing message, so there were no limits as to how inventive and creative one could be. Truth be known, I was probably a little too inventive, much like our characters Ben and Stafford. And that was the inspiration for this musical.

- Kevin Hammonds & Andy Roninson

A telephone rings. After the third ring... CLICK.

     Song begins - "Outgoing Message #1"

BEN:
  THIS IS BEN

STAFFORD:
  THIS IS STAFFORD

BEN & STAFFORD:
  AND WE'RE WICKED FRICKIN' COOL
  WE'RE OUT BALLIN'
  THANKS FOR CALLIN
  SO LEAVE A MESSAGE FOOL

BEN:
  HAPPY NEW YEAR

STAFFORD:
  TIME TO PARTY

BEN:
  'CAUSE THE JAGER SHOTS ARE FREE

BEN & STAFFORD:
  AND TONIGHT WE'RE
  GONNA THROW DOWN
  LIKE IT'S 1993
  SINCE WE CAN'T COME TO THE PHONE
  'CAUSE WE'RE DRUNK OR JUST ASLEEP
  THROW YOUR DOGGIES HERE A BONE
  THIS CONTRAPTION ISN'T CHEAP
  LET YOUR MESSAGES BE KNOWN
  GO AHEAD AND TAKE THE LEAP
  LEAVE YOUR MESSAGE AT THE TONE
  BEEP

  Beep.

LAUREN: Wow, that just happened. Yes, Ben, this is Lauren. I'm the girl you stole the hoodie from, at the Delta Nu party. I'll be brief, as I have to get to class. Class, I'm sure you've heard of it. Anyway, you stole my hoodie, and in its place you left a ransom note with your phone number. I tell you this because no doubt you will have a hard time remembering. So how about you do your first good deed of '93 and you give me back my hoodie?

Song begins - "Get The Message"

I want it back, Ben. You get me?

I HOPE YOU GET THIS MESSAGE
I'M NOT THE TYPE TO MAKE A STINK
IT'S IN FACT MY LUCKY HOODIE
AND YOU'RE FAR TOO PALE FOR PINK
NOW I KNOW YOU MIGHT NOT GIVE A DAMN
BUT NEXT WEEK I'VE GOT A PSYCH EXAM
SO FORGIVE ME IF I DON'T GIVE ANY SLACK
I HOPE YOU GET THE MESSAGE
I NEED MY HOODIE BACK

I assume you thought this would be an adorable ploy to get me to call you, and go out with you, but that's really not how this is going to play out. I'm sure you're a fun guy, and there is no doubt in my mind that some impressionable freshman is going to find heaven on your futon.

I HOPE YOU GET THE MESSAGE
I'LL SPEAK AS CLEARLY AS I CAN
WERE YOU TRYING TO IMPRESS ME
TRY ACTING LIKE A MAN
NOT A BOY WHO PULLS A CHILDISH PRANK
I AM NOT SOME STUCK UP JOYLESS CRANK
PETTY CRIME MIGHT WORK ON SOME GIRLS I'LL AGREE
I HOPE YOU GET THE MESSAGE
IT DIDN'T WORK ON ME

TO BE FAIR
IT'S A SHAME
THAT YOU HAD TO STEAL
YOU WERE THERE
AND I THOUGHT
THAT YOU HAD APPEAL
I FLIPPED MY HAIR
LEANED CLOSER IN
I SMILED AND LAUGHED
I SHOWED SOME SKIN
I GAVE YOU EVERY SIGN
THE MESSAGE WAS LOUD AND CLEAR
BUT IF YOU MISSED THE MESSAGE THEN
WILL YOU MISS THE MESSAGE HERE

I HOPE YOU GET THE MESSAGE
TOMORROW I'LL BE AT THE QUAD
I WILL BE THERE AT TWELVE THIRTY
AND YOU WILL TOO BY GOD
I'LL BE WAITING AT THE PIZZA SHACK
AND YOU'LL GIVE MY LUCKY HOODIE BACK
AN APOLOGY WOULD BE QUITE NICE
AND PERHAPS A PEPPERONI SLICE
PLUS A MEA CULPA JUST FOR KICKS
IN THE FORM OF MOZZARELLA STICKS
THIS IS NOT A DATE SO PLEASE DON'T MISCONSTRUE
I HOPE YOU GET THE MESSAGE
I WANT MY HOODIE
I WANT MY HOODIE
I WANT MY HOODIE
THAT'S ALL I WANT FROM YOU

Dial tone. Telephone ringing. Click.

Song begins - "Outgoing Message #2"

BEN:
    THIS IS BEN

STAFFORD:
>THIS IS STAFFORD

BEN & STAFFORD:
>AND THERE'S NO ONE ON THE LINE
>DON'T BE STUPID
>BE LIKE CUPID
>AND SAY THAT YOU'LL BE MINE

STAFFORD:
>I GOT CANDY

BEN:
>YOU LIKE CHOCOLATE

STAFFORD:
>I WON'T BREAK YOUR HEART IN TWO

BEN & STAFFORD:
>NO WE CAN'T PICK UP THE PHONE NOW
>SO DO WATCHA GOTTA DO

Beep.

BEN: Staff, it's Ben. Why in the hell did I let you talk me into that outgoing message? Please erase that. Are you there? Pick up. I need you to clean the apartment. I'm out with Lauren. Yes, hoodie Lauren. We're at the restaurant and we're coming back to the apartment in half an hour. I invited her over for a nightcap, and she said yes.

Song begins - "She's Coming Over"

Staff, what's a nightcap?

He sings:

I'M SURE SHE WANTS A MAN OF MEANS
TRASH THE NASTY MAGAZINES

TOSS OR EAT MY LEAN CUISINES
SHE'S COMING OVER

SO THROW SOME FLOWERS IN SOME VASE
DO YOUR BEST—SPRUCE UP THE SPACE
OH, I KNOW—TAPE MELROSE PLACE
SHE'S COMING OVER

I KNOW WHAT YOU'RE THINKING
NO
I'M NOT WHIPPED
I'M NOT ABOUT TO LET A GIRL
TELL ME WHO I AM
SO NO
I'M NOT WHIPPED
I'LL LIVE MY LIFE THE WAY I WANT
I DON'T GIVE A DAMN

I TRUST THAT YOU WILL BE DISCREET
CLEAN THE FILTHY TOILET SEAT
HEAR THIS MESSAGE - PRESS DELETE
SHE'S NOT SOMEONE THAT I AM CHANGING FOR
JUST SLIGHTLY RE-ARRANGING FOR
DUDE
I'M SO SCREWED
SHE'S COMING OVER

WHEN THE FOUTON'S A ROCKIN'
DON'T COME A KNOCKIN'

Dial tone. Telephone ringing. Click.

BEN (*voiceover*): Hey, you've reached Ben.

STAFFORD (*voiceover*): And this is Stafford. Please excuse our boring outgoing message.

BEN (*voiceover*): Staff...

STAFFORD (*voiceover*): Ben says we need to be more mature. So, kindly leave a message at the tone. God bless you all.

Beep.

LAUREN: Ben? Are you awake? Ben, pick up. It's Lauren. Are you passed out? Are you dead? I wouldn't know because you left me at the bar last night. Ben? Look, it's college. I get that, I do. But I'm worried. Your partying is getting out of control. Spring Break is next week, and at this rate, I don't think you'll make it out alive. More importantly, I don't know how we're gonna make it out alive.

Song begins - "Pick Up, Ben"

You and me, Ben.

She sings:

YOU MAKE ME LAUGH
I ADMIT THAT
THESE PAST THREE MONTHS HAVE BEEN GREAT
WAIT
PARTLY GREAT
WHEN YOU'RE NOT DRUNKENLY LEAVING THE BAR
WHEN YOU'RE NOT PEEING INSIDE YOUR GUITAR
I KNOW I SHOULD LOVE ALL THE THINGS THAT YOU ARE
BUT BEN
SWEET BEN
IT'S NOT CUTE ANYMORE

PICK UP BEN
SO WE CAN TALK
PICK UP BEN
SO I KNOW YOUR ALIVE
I'M RUNNING OUT OF PATIENCE
OKAY
I'M OFF TO CLASS

Class? I'm sure you've heard of it.

OKAY BEN
I'LL CALL YOU AT FIVE

Dial tone. Telephone ringing. Click.

STAFFORD (*voiceover*): Yo, Stafford and Ben, not in da house. Finals are over! YEAAHHH!! If you need Ben, leave a message. If you need me, I can be found a) at any local bar b) in jail c) dead d) all of the above.

Beep.

BEN: Stafford, it's Ben. Pick up. Jesus, I'm not kidding. Please pick up. PICK UP!! *(silence)* Okay, I don't know what to do. If Lauren calls, I need you to give her a message. She's gone back to Phoenix for the summer. I was supposed to meet her and her parents this morning for breakfast. But I totally screwed up, big time. I went out last night for a few beers, and..Oh, Jesus. I really messed this up. Staff, I missed breakfast. I woke up in jail. And she's gone. I didn't get her parents number. I think I used up all my chances with her. She'll probably never call again. But if she does, if she calls, Staff, you have to tell her. Last night was it.

Song begins - "Nowhere Else to Go But Up"

As soon as my dad bailed me out, I had him drive me to the airport. I'm going to Santa Fe. I'm going to rehab. And I'm gonna do this.

BEN:
I TRIED MY OWN WAY
I MADE MY OWN RULES
THE KING OF ALL FOOLS
WHERE'D IT GET ME
BUT TELL HER I'LL CHANGE
I'M WELL ON MY WAY

I'LL CLEAN UP THE MESS
IF SHE'LL LET ME

CAUSE FOR THE FIRST TIME
I KNOW IT'S ALL UP TO ME
FOR THE FIRST TIME
I CAN FINALLY SEE

THERE'S NOWHERE ELSE TO GO
BUT UP
NOTHING LEFT AT ALL
BUT A WILLINGNESS TO TRY
FINALLY I KNOW
I CAN GET ONLY SO HIGH
AND ONCE YOU'VE BEEN SO LOW
THERE'S NOWHERE ELSE TO GO
BUT UP

I'M SICK AND TIRED
OF FEELING SICK AND TIRED
THOUGH IT'S SCARY AS HELL
THE CHOICES WERE FEW
I WANNA RUN AWAY
AND GET THE HELL OUT
BUT THE ONLY WAY OUT IS THROUGH

THERE'S NOWHERE ELSE TO GO
BUT UP
NOTHING LEFT AT ALL
BUT A WILLINGNESS TO TRY
FINALLY I KNOW
I CAN GET ONLY SO HIGH
AND ONCE YOU'VE BEEN SO LOW
THERE'S NOWHERE ELSE TO GO
BUT UP

Dial tone. Telephone ringing. Click.

Song begins - "Outgoing Message #3"

BEN:
> THIS IS BEN

LAUREN:
> HEY THIS IS LAUREN
> AND WE CAN'T COME TO THE PHONE

BEN:
> IT'S POSSIBLE WE'RE SCREENING
> LEAVE YOUR MESSAGE AT THE TONE

BEN & LAUREN:
> COMING HOME TO NO MESSAGES
> WOULD SURELY MAKE US WEEP
> SO FROM US TO YOU
> YOU KNOW WHAT TO DO
> JUST MAKE IT SHORT AND QUIET
> THE BABY IS ASLEEP

Beep.

END

THE CHARM

Book & Lyrics by *Christiana Cole*
Music by *David Shenton*
Based on *The Talisman* by Hans Christian Andersen

SYNOPSIS

A pair of fairytale newlyweds, He and She, want to find some way to guarantee that they'll always love each other *"WEDDING SONG"*. They hop on a golf cart to seek the advice of the Wizard of the Wood. *"GOLF CART TRIP"*. The Wizard tells them to find a perfectly happy couple, and then ask for a snip of their underwear as a good-luck charm for their marriage. *"SONG OF THE WIZARD"*. The couple sets off on a world-wide tour to find the right couple *"HOT AIR BALLOON RIDE"*. A French couple is mostly happy, but sort of sad that they have no children *"ZEE FRENCH PEOPLE"*. He and She paddle down to Italy *"CANOE SONG"* and meet an Italian couple who are mostly happy, but truly, they have too many children *"THE ITALIANS"*. He and She zip on some scooters *"SEXY VESPAS"* and finally meet a couple that might just fit the bill: an Egyptian couple has two kids, cocktails at 2pm, and are very happy... but they don't wear underwear *"WITH HE AND SHE IN EGYPTLAND"*. She is defeated, but He reassures her—their love won't slip away, even if they don't find the charm *"WEDDING SONG REPRISE"*. The Wizard returns and the couple has an epiphany—it is they themselves that are the world's happiest couple! They snip off pieces of their own underwear and rejoice.

PRODUCTION HISTORY

The Charm, written by Christiana Cole and David Shenton, first premiered as a reading at the BMI Workshop on May 29, 2013 in New York, NY. The cast was as follows:

SHE	Christiana Cole
HE	James Benjamin Rodgers
THE WIZARD	Ryan Kinsella
CHARACTER MAN	John Jeffords
CHARACTER WOMAN	Erin Shields

Later that year, it had its first fully staged production by Theatre Now in their first SOUND BITES festival on December 9, 2013. The production was directed by Donald Garverick, with musical direction by Erik James. It was produced by Thomas Morrissey and Stephen Bishop Seely. It was performed by the same cast.

On June 22, 2015 it was performed at The D Lounge at the New York Theatre Barn, as part of "Thank God We Perceive Time as Linear: An Evening with Christiana Cole". The cast was as follows:

SHE	Christiana Cole
HE	Chris Critelli
THE WIZARD	Aaron Phillips
CHARACTER MAN	Chris Gwynn
CHARACTER WOMAN	Melody Madarasz

On October 29, 2016 it was performed at the People's Improv Theater, as part of their One Act Comedy Fest. It was directed by Adam Chisnall, with music direction by Satoko Mori. The cast was as follows:

SHE	Abby Krenz
HE	Phil Pineno
THE WIZARD	Javan Zapata
CHARACTER MAN	Kevin Necciai
CHARACTER WOMAN	Laura Wilson

CHARACTERS

HE	A newly-married fairy tale prince. A genuine, kind man. Any age.
SHE	A newly-married fairy tale princess. An assertive, confident woman. Any age.
CHARACTER MAN	Track covers the French, Italian, and Egyptian men.
CHARACTER WOMAN	Track covers the French, Italian, and Egyptian women.
THE WIZARD	Stately and wise. Any age.

NOTE: The Character Man and Character Woman tracks can be divided up to create more roles.

SETTING

A series of delightful fairytale kingdoms. The past.

MUSICAL NUMBERS

The Charm is a musical performed as one continuous piece of music. However, the music can be broken down into the following sections:

"Wedding Song"	He, She
"Golf Cart Trip"	He, She
"Song of the Wizard"	The Wizard
"Hot Air Balloon Ride"	He, She
"Zee French People"	French Man, French Woman, He, She
"Canoe Song"	He, She
"The Italians"	Italian Man, Italian Woman, He, She

"Sexy Vespas"	He, She
"With He and She in Egyptland"	Egyptian Man,
	Egyptian Woman,
	He, She
"Wedding Song (reprise)"	Company

AUTHORS' NOTE

When composer David Shenton and I sat down to write a short musical, we knew we wanted it to be colorful, funny, warm-hearted, but with a healthy dose of weirdness. So when I stumbled upon the Hans Christian Andersen tale *The Talisman*, I knew I'd found what we'd adapt: a story about magical underwear.

The Charm is charming when performed by adults or kids/teens. It is never blue or smutty. Its humor is innocent: it makes adults feel like kids and kids feel like adults.

We wanted to be sure that *The Charm* was easy to produce. Because of David's playful and evocative traveling music, you don't need fancy sets—the audience hears the float of the hot air balloon, the splash of the canoe, the buzz of the sexy Vespa. The show can be done with as few as five actors, but the "Character Man" and "Character Woman" roles can also be divided up to accommodate up to four more actors (especially useful in an academic setting). The memorable melodies can be sung by singers comfortable in golden age, pop/contemporary, and everything in between. And the timeless moral of the show—that loving actions are the real way to ensure a life of love—is one that everyone can agree on. *The Charm* is a clever wink with a heart of gold.

One note on casting: We do not care about the color, gender, height, weight, age, disability status, of any actor. IE: All roles can be played by any kind of person, in any kind of body.

Our fondest wish as you put *The Charm* on your audience is that you simply enjoy the ride.

- Christiana Cole and David Shenton

The couple, HE and SHE, rush into their bridal suite, laughing gaily!

Music section begins - "Wedding Song"

HE & SHE:
    HA HA! HA HA!
    HA HAAAA! *Etc.*

SHE: My Prince!

HE: My Princess!

BOTH: The Honeymoon Suite!

They kiss.

BOTH:
    WE DID IT, WE DID IT.
    LOOK AT ME, LOOK AT ME.
    WE DID IT, WE DID IT.
    YOU MARRIED ME, YOU MARRIED ME.

SHE:
    AND OH HOW WE DANCED,
    HOW YOU THREW ME CROSS THE FLOOR

HE:
    AND OH HOW I DRANK,
    I HAD SIX MARTINIS MORE THAN I PLANNED

BOTH:
    WE DID IT, WE DID IT.

SHE:
    YOU'RE MY HUSBAND

HE:
    YOU'RE MY WIFE

BOTH:
    AND NOW ALL WE MUST DO
    IS LIVE OUR LIVES—OUR LIFE.

SHE: You love me?

HE: Isn't it obvious?

    AFTER THE WEDDING IS OVER
    WE'VE BID OUR GUESTS ADIEU
    THE TOASTS HAVE BEEN TOASTED
    THE WEENIES BEEN ROASTED
    AND NOW IT'S JUST ME AND YOU

    AFTER THE WEDDING IS OVER
    THE BELLS HAVE ALL BEEN RUNG
    THE VOWS HAVE BEEN SPOKEN
    AND WINE GLASSES BROKEN
    AND YET THE NIGHT FEELS YOUNG

SHE:
    YOU LOOK SO MUCH LIKE THE MAN
    I KNEW JUST A FEW HOURS AGO
    AND YET SOMEHOW YOU'RE DIFFERENT TOO.

HE:
    I CAN'T SEE HOW.

SHE:
    IN TIME I'LL KNOW.

BOTH:
    AFTER THE WEDDING IS OVER
    IT'S OVER MUCH TOO SOON
    FOR NOW WE MUST START
    ON THE DIFFICULT PART—
    BUT FIRST
    A HONEYMOON.

Music pauses. They gaze at one another, so in love, but suddenly...

SHE: Oh I just can't stand it!

HE: What, aren't you happy?

SHE: Yes, very happy!

HE: Then why are you distressed?

SHE: How do I know that we shall always be this happy, and this in love?

HE: I—I don't know! What are we going to do?

They have a momentary moment of panic, and then SHE gets an idea.

SHE: I know! There is a wizard who lives in a cabin in the heart of the forest. We'll seek his advice. It's just a short trip. The concierge gave me this map, and this golf cart.

HE: You're so cute when you're plotting.

HE tries to kiss her, SHE grabs his face.

SHE: This is serious. We're talking about the certainty of our love, not some silly romantic nonsense. To the golf cart!

Music Transition -"Golf Cart Trip"

SHE:
    RUMBLE RUMBLE RUMBLE

HE:
    BUMP BUMP BUMP

BOTH:
    RUMBLE RUMBLE RUMBLE RUMBLE
    BUMP BUMP BUMP

SHE: Look, there!

HE: The Wizard of the Woods!

> *The WIZARD appears.*

SHE: Oh Wizard! We are a Prince and Princess, just married. We need your help.

WIZARD: Yes?

> *They enter the Wizard's cabin and the Wizard music begins.*

HE: How do we know that we'll always be happy together, that death alone will part us?

WIZARD: Well, if you're still together when one or both of you dies...

SHE: This disturbs me.

WIZARD: You are in a serious situation. You need is a charm: something small to carry in your pocket, to protect you from every possible disappointment in marriage.

HE: Excellent. How much does it cost?

SHE: We're very rich. We will buy several, in case we live a very long time.

WIZARD: I don't have any. You must seek it out yourself.

SHE: But we've just begun our honeymoon!

WIZARD: You'll have to put your honeymoon on hold—this is the certainty of your love we're talking about, not some silly vacation.

> *Music section begins - "Song of The Wizard"*

HE: He's right.

SHE: Fine. So what is this charm? What do we look for?

WIZARD:
>LOOK FOR THE LOVERS
>WHOSE FINGERTIPS BRUSH
>WHEN PASSING A LOAF OF BREAD
>
>LOOK FOR THE LOVERS
>WHOSE BLOOD STARTS TO RUSH
>WHEN EYEING THE SIDE OF THE BED
>
>LOOK FOR THE LOVERS
>WHO STILL TALK IN MUSH
>A GOOGLEY-SWEETIE A GOOGLEY-GOO!
>
>LOOK FOR THE LOVERS
>WITH CHEEKS THAT ARE FLUSH
>FOR FRIENDS, THAT COULD BE YOU.

HE: Yes, we want that forever, guaranteed!

WIZARD: And here is what you must do. You must journey through all the lands of the world, and when you meet a truly contented couple, you must ask them a favor.

He sings:
>LOOK FOR THE LOVERS
>WITH SECRETIVE SMILES
>THAT SEEM TO HIDE ROMANCE
>
>LOOK FOR THE LOVERS
>WITHSTANDING ALL TRIALS,
>AND ASK THEM TO TAKE OFF THEIR PANTS!

SHE: Wait, what?

WIZARD:
>LOOK FOR THE LOVERS
>WITHOUT ANY PANTS

AND THEN WHAT YOU NEED TO DO—

IS ASK FOR A PIECE OF THEIR UNDERWEAR
AND KEEP THAT PIECE OF PANTY FOREVER WITH YOU.

That's the charm.

SHE: The charm is a small piece of underwear?

HE: That we get from a happy couple?

WIZARD: Yes.

HE: That seems a little obscene!

WIZARD: It's an ancient wizarding secret! And it works. Do you want to be happy?

HE and SHE exchange a glance.

SHE: I'll bring the scissors.

The music stops and the WIZARD exits.

HE: Where shall we begin? Where are the world's greatest lovers?

SHE: Let's take my hot air balloon; we'll spot them from above.

They get into their balloon.

Music section begins - "Hot Air Balloon Ride"

BOTH:
FLOAT FLOAT, FLY FLY,
FLOAT FLOAT, FLY FLY

SHE: There! Look at those two! Lower the flame; let's descend.

The balloon lands and they disembark. A FRENCH COUPLE enters and music starts.

HE: They look quite happy; see how they clink their wine glasses!

FRENCH WOMAN:
    OH YOU'RE SO HANDSOME

FRENCH MAN:
    OH HOW YOUR EYES GLEAM

FRENCH WOMAN:
    YOU SMELL LIKE A GARDEN

FRENCH MAN:
    YOU DANCE LIKE A DREAM

FRENCH WOMAN & FRENCH MAN:
    WE'RE HAPPY, SO HAPPY, SO TRES TRES TRES HAPPY
    MY BEAUTY
    MY CHERE
    MON AMOUR

SHE:
    AH BUT THEY'RE HAPPY
    THEIR EYES ALMOST GLOW

HE:
    HE ISN'T THAT HANDSOME
    BUT WHAT DO I KNOW

HE & SHE:
    THEY'RE HAPPY, SO HAPPY, SO TRES TRES TRES HAPPY
    HIS BEAUTY
    HER CHERE
    THEIR AMOUR

SHE: Pardonnez-moi.

HE:
    DO YOU EVER FIGHT?

FRENCH MAN:
    NEVER!

SHE:
    HOW LONG WILL YOU LOVE HIM?

FRENCH WOMAN:
    FOREVER.

HE & SHE:
    AND WOULD YOU SAY,
    IT'S BEEN THIS WAY SINCE YOUR WEDDING DAY?

FRENCH COUPLE:
    OUI OUI.

SHE pulls out the scissors, excited.

FRENCH WOMAN:
    BUT SOMETHING IS MISSING

FRENCH MAN:
    SOMETHING QUITE SMALL

FRENCH WOMAN:
    A SOMEONE TO CARE FOR

FRENCH MAN:
    TO CUDDLE AND CRAWL

FRENCH MAN & FRENCH WOMAN:
    A BABY, A BABY, A BON BON BON BABY
    A BOY
    A GIRL
    UN BEBE

FRENCH MAN: We have all this wine, and no babies to share it with!

FRENCH WOMAN: It is our one sadness.

SHE *(lowering the scissors)*: Oh how sad, they can't help us.

HE: We must move on. Adieu.

FRENCH MAN & FRENCH WOMAN: Au revoir.

The FRENCH couple exit.

SHE: Look, a canoe! Let's continue our search along the river.

HE: Indeed! A lovely paddling trip.

Music section begins - "Canoe Song"

They get into the canoe and paddle.

HE:
    PADDLE PADDLE PADDLE PADDLE

SHE:
    PADDLE DIDDLE DEE!

HE:
    SPLISH SPLASH SPLISH SPLASH

SHE *(delighted)*:
    OH DARLING STOP SPLASHING ME!

BOTH:
    PADDLE PADDLE PADDLE PADDLE
    PADDLE DIDDLE DUM!
    DUM DUM DUM, DUM, DUM, DUM –

HE: What's that, along the banks?

Italian music plays as they get out of the canoe. An ITALIAN COUPLE enter.

Music section begins - "The Italians"

ITALIAN MAN:
    OH CHE BELLA, COME AND SIT A MOMENT ON MY KNEE
    LET ME FEEL YOUR HEART A-BEATING, BEATING NEXT TO ME
    AND SNEAK A KISS, A KISS A TWO OR MAYBE TWO OR THREE OR FOUR AND MAYBE IF WE'RE QUIET, EVEN MORE!

ITALIAN CHILDREN'S VOICES:
    OH MAMMA MIA!

SHE: Scuzi, are you two perfectly in love?

SHE holds up scissors behind her back.

ITALIAN MAN and ITALIAN WOMAN: Si!

ITALIAN WOMAN: But...

ITALIAN WOMAN:
    HOW I DREAM OF BACK WHEN IT WAS ONLY HIM AND I
    ATE AS MUCH AS I COULD EAT OF EVERY PIZZA PIE
    AND SPENT EACH SUMMER EVE'NING RESTING ON HIS HAIRY THIGH BUT NOW I SPEND THE NIGHT
    WITH BABIES;
    HEAR THEM CRY:

ITALIAN CHILDREN:
    OH MAMMA MIA! ETC.

ITALIAN WOMAN: We are very much in love. But we have far too many children.

HE: It's a pity.

SHE: Thank you for your time.

ITALIAN WOMAN: Always Mamma mia! Never "pappa mio!"

    ITALIANS exit.

SHE: I don't understand. If children matter so much to people, then why don't I care about them at all?

HE: You're so funny. Shall we hop these Vespas to continue our quest?

    HE and SHE hop on the Vespas and ride.

BOTH:
    BZZZZZZ DANGEROUS!
    BZZZZZZ POW, POW!
    BZZZZZZ YEAH YEAH YEAH YEAH.
    BZZZZZZ CIAO!

    They park their Vespas.

    Music section begins - "With He and She In Egyptland"

SHE: Wait, listen! Do you hear that?

HE: Phrygian scales!

SHE: We are someplace very foreign. I have a good feeling about this.

    EGYPTIAN COUPLE enter.

EGYPTIAN WOMAN:
    SUN ON MY FACE, GENTLE BREEZES OFF THE NILE

EGYPTIAN MAN:
    DRINKING A COCKTAIL MADE BY A CROCODILE

EGYPTIAN WOMAN:
    AND TWO PERFECT CHILDREN, WHO ALWAYS MAKE ME

SMILE
THANK ALL THE GODS I'M JUST A TOUCH NUBILE.

SHE (*to HE*): This could be it! They have kids, but not too many!

HE: And they're drinking mai tais at 2 in the afternoon by a river! They look absolutely perfectly content!

EGYPTIAN WOMAN:
AND OH MY HANDSOME HUSBAND HOW I LOVE YOU!

EGYPTIAN MAN:
AND OH MY LOVELY WIFE HOW I LOVE YOU!

HE & SHE:
COULD WE PLEASE ASK A STRANGE FAVOR OF YOU?

Scissors come out from behind SHE's back, music rises to a crescendo—the big moment!

SHE: Could we please have a small snip of your underwear, for good luck?

EGYPTIAN COUPLE exchanges a glance, and burst into peals of laughter.

EGYPTIAN MAN & WOMAN (*in unison*): We don't wear underwear!

HE & SHE: No underwear?

EGYPTIAN WOMAN: Sorry! Maybe you could try France?

EGYPTIAN couple continues laughing as they exit.

SHE: That's it; it's hopeless. How can we know that we will always love each other?

HE: Maybe, we just make up our minds about it.

SHE: What, just decide?

HE: Yes, when we got married we promised to always love each other, through sickness, health, all that—and I'm sure it won't always be easy, but I think if we just agree keep that promise—to love each other, love like a verb, love like something you do—we always will.

SHE: And... you'll always love me?

HE: Of course.

SHE: You're sure? I can be difficult.

HE: I knew what I was getting into. But this is the certainty of our love we're talking about. And I'm certain.

Music section begins - "Wedding Song (reprise)"

HE:
NOW THAT THE WEDDING IS OVER
OUR LOVE WON'T SLIP AWAY:
IT'S NOT JUST A FEELING
THAT LEAVES YOUR HEAD REELING,
IT'S ALL THAT YOU DO AND SAY.

SHE:
NOW THAT THE WEDDING IS OVER,
I'LL PUT MY HAND IN YOURS,
AND TRUST IN MY HEART THAT
WE NEVER WILL PART—

The WIZARD pops out of nowhere.

WIZARD:
HEY! DID YOU EVER FIND THOSE MAGICAL DRAWERS?

HE: Wizard! How did you get here!

WIZARD: Some underwear provides marital bliss; other underwear provides hassle-free international travel.

HE: We didn't find the charm, no, but we're on to you, old Wizard, old pal.

SHE: We know now there IS NO charm, just faith and trust in each other.

WIZARD: Wait, no charm? You're wrong, there is a charm.

SHE: You mean the answer wasn't inside us the whole time?

WIZARD: No. But it's been on you the whole time.

Simultaneously, the lightbulb goes off in HE & SHE's heads.

HE & SHE: Oh my God. We are the most perfectly content couple!

SHE: We've been wearing our own underwear this whole time.

HE: The scissor!

Music starts. They take turns cutting pieces of each other's underwear off each other, and trading them.

WIZARD: There you go. You're welcome.

SHE and HE: Oh, I'm so happy!

HE:
    YOU LOOK SO MUCH LIKE THE GAL I KNEW,
    JUST A FEW MINUTES AGO.
    AND YET SOMEHOW, I'M DIFFERENT TOO.
    AND AS WE GO, OUR LOVE WILL GROW!

ALL:
    AFTER THE WEDDING IS OVER,
    AND LIFE AS ONE WILL START
    YOU SHOW EVERY DAY
    THROUGH WHAT YOU DO AND SAY
    THE LOVE THAT'S IN YOUR HEART!

WIZARD:
    AND IN YOUR PANTS!

END

THE FACEBOOK FIGHTER

Book, Music & Lyrics by *Chris Kerrigan*

The cast of *The Facebook Fighter* at Theatre Now's SOUND BITES 4.0.
(Left to right): Nina Gabriela Gross, Eric Stephenson, Darnell Kenney, Chris Kerrigan, Sarah Shear, Aaron Heaps and Natalie Perry

SYNOPSIS

Garon, a thirty-year old line cook with a crappy attitude sits on his bed and posts morosely on his Facebook timeline about his rotten life *"OPINIONS"*. He begins to scroll through his new feed and reads a fiery post from a radical feminist acquaintance named Beth *"MAN ON THE Q TRAIN"*, detailing her interaction on the subway with a man disingenuously claiming to be a feminist ally. Garon is triggered by this and lets loose on her in an aggressive, nonconstructive manner. She fires back at him, informing him that he basically proved her point, and unfriends him.

Elsewhere on Garon's news feed, an acquaintance named Devin enthusiastically informs his friend Jolie that their favorite band will be at the Greek Theatre soon. Garon intervenes with snark and derision, insulting them for being fans of both The Decemberists and Arrested Development. Devin and Jolie, mildly annoyed by this, attempt to give Garon a lesson in social media etiquette *"MEAN AND BITTER"*. Garon hits back even harder, and they both unfriend him.

Jacob, a sweet metrosexual man with lots of friends online and otherwise makes a "vague-post" asking for prayers and good vibes in advance of a big event in his life, which is met with a chorus of likes and positive energy *"GOOD VIBES"*. Disgusted by this, Garon antagonizes Jacob, which prompts all of Jacob's friends to immediately come to his defense. Jacob thanks his friends for their support and proceeds to unfriend Garon.

A man named Richard does a copy-and-paste of a popular post invoking the Code of Intellectual Property to protect his data from new software employed by Facebook. Garon mocks and derides him for being gullible *"COPY AND PASTE"*. Richard silently unfriends him.

Garon continues to burn bridges and turn everybody against him one by one *"FINALE"* until finally he goes too far while commenting on a birth announcement and is reported to Facebook. His account is disabled. In the deafening silence of a lonely Facebookless existence, Garon begins to have regrets.

PRODUCTION HISTORY

The Facebook Fighter written by Chris Kerrigan, was first premiered at The Irene Diamond Stage at The Pershing Square Signature Center for Theatre Now's SOUND BITES 4.0 on May 28, 2017. The production was directed by Amanda Connors with musical direction by Chris Kerrigan. It was produced by Thomas Morrissey, Stephen Bishop Seely, and Chris Giordano. The cast was as follows:

GARON	Chris Kerrigan
BETH/CARLY	Nina Gabriela Gross
JOLIE/SUSAN	Natalie Perry
DEVIN/ROB	Aaron Heaps
JACOB	Eric Stephenson
LINDSEY	Sarah Shear
RICHARD	Darnell Kenney

The musical won multiple awards from that year's festival including, Best Musical, Best Music, Best Lyrics, Best Direction (Amanda Connors), and Best Actor (Chris Kerrigan).

The 10-Minute Musical: an anthology from the SOUND BITES festival

CHARACTERS

GARON	30, antagonistic and opinionated line cook.
BETH	25, radical third wave feminist, no time for bullshit.
DEVIN	28, lover of Arrested Development and The Decemberists.
JOLIE	28, Devin's friend who equally loves these things.
JACOB	30, sensitive sweet man who leans on his friends.
RICHARD	45, paranoid about photos/video being appropriated.
LINDSAY	24, in a relationship with a much older man.
CARLY	32, expectant mother.
ROB	35, expectant father.
SUSAN	30, lover of Pilates.
MIKE	45, alpha Broncos fan.

The following roles are doubled:
BETH/CARLY, DEVIN/ROB, JOLIE/SUSAN, RICHARD/MIKE

SETTING
On Facebook. The present.

MUSICAL NUMBERS
The Facebook Fighter is a musical performed as one continuous piece of music.

AUTHOR'S NOTE

In the spring of 2016, my relationship with social media in general (and Facebook in particular) took a dark turn. We were in the middle of a democratic primary and I had a lot of opinions. Things would get nasty pretty quickly. The same cycle repeated itself on a daily basis; somebody would post something innocuous, stating a cultural or political belief I disagreed with, I would then attempt to write a cogent and respectful response, then somebody else would join the fray and slightly raise the temperature of the argument which was all I needed to immediately get the taste of blood in my mouth and go after them. Nobody's mind was ever changed. I was fighting the good fight badly.

In the fall of that same year, I got in a truly discouraging and ugly argument with somebody I really liked as a person and it made me feel awful. I deactivated my account for a few months, then came back with a solemn promise not to engage in nonconstructive arguments. Some days were better than others, and every time I silently scrolled while keeping my comments to myself, there was an unmistakable itch that was begging to be scratched. So I did the next best thing I could think of to scratch the itch; I wrote a musical about it.

- Chris Kerrigan

GARON sits on an unmade bed in a studio apartment with a smart phone in his hand and a beer between his legs. He begins to pen an overlong, oversharing Facebook status.

GARON:
    I LOST MY GIRLFRIEND WHEN I
    DIDN'T GIVE A FUCK WHEN SHE WOULD TALK
    ABOUT HER DAY AND COULDN'T EVEN JUST PRETEND I DID,
    AND NOW I'M THIRTY AND SHE'S GONE
    AND ALL MY FRIENDS HAVE DISAPPEARED INTO THEIR
    SHITTY BORING LIVES WITH ALL THEIR SHITTY KIDS.
    AND IF WE GO OUT AND GET A DRINK
    THEY ACT SUPERIOR AND SAY THEY HAVE TO GO
    BEFORE RIGHT WHEN I ORDER US THE SECOND PITCHER.
    AND THEY TEXT THE NEXT DAY,
    "DO YOU THINK YOU DRINK TOO MUCH?"

    IT'S A CLICHE TO PINE FOR YOUNGER DAYS AND SAY
    YOU ALWAYS THOUGHT YOU'D HAVE HAD YOUR SHIT
    ALL FIGURED OUT BY NOW.
    BUT IF YOUR LIFE IS A CLICHE THEN MAYBE
    EVERYTHING'S OK BECAUSE IT MEANS NOBODY
    ELSE IS HAPPY ANYHOW.
    I HATE MY FUCKING JOB SO BAD I WANT TO SHATTER
    MY OWN SKULL AGAINST A SAUTÉ PAN,
    I'M TIRED OF BEING A MINION.
    AND WHEN I SCROLL DOWN FACEBOOK ALL I SEE,
    IS OTHER ASSHOLES JUST LIKE ME.
    TALKING SHIT AND GIVING THEIR OPINION.

BETH enters in a huff and addresses the audience with the contents of an angry Facebook post.

BETH:
    DEAR MAN ON THE Q TRAIN,
    YOU SAY YOU HAVE RESPECT FOR WOMEN,
    YOU EXPLAIN THE GENDER GAP
    IF YOU TRULY WANT TO HELP,
    YOU SHOULD REALLY SHUT YOUR TRAP

YOUR OPINIONS COME OFF ARROGANT AND SNARKY
WE DON'T NEED THE GLIB SUGGESTIONS
OF THE MIGHTY PATRIARCHY
BE AN ALLY, BE A LISTENER,
BE SUPPORTIVE AND KIND
DON'T BE SCARED OF A WOMAN
WHO'S SPEAKING HER MIND
SINCERELY, THE FEMINIST BITCHES.

GARON grumbles and types away at a response.

GARON:
I DON'T KNOW WHO THIS SORRY BASTARD WAS
WHO DARED TO CONDESCEND
TO YOU BY VOICING HIS SUPPORT
AND TRYING TO ADVOCATE.
BUT WOULDN'T YOUR BIG ANGRY DIATRIBE
BE MORE PRODUCTIVE AIMED AT ALL
THE XENOPHOBIC PEOPLE IN THE SOUTHERN STATES?
AND THAT PATRIARCHY SHIT IS GETTING BORING.
LOOK AT ALL THE SYMPATHETIC
MEN THAT YOU'RE IGNORING.
SO IF YOU REALLY WANT TO BE A FEMINIST, I SUGGEST
MAYBE DON'T EXPECT YOU'RE GOING TO BE
OPPRESSED. THEN WE ALL WON'T BE SUCH A BOTHER.
YOU BETTER LEARN PRETTY QUICK,
NOT EVERYBODY WITH A DICK IS YOUR FATHER.

AND YOU'RE A HYPOCRITE FOR SAYING THAT SHIT,
BECAUSE LET'S CALL A SPADE A SPADE: IT'S REVERSE
SEXISM.

By the end of his rant, a small crowd of people have gathered around GARON. They all groan at his last line. They sing his Facebook notification.

DEVIN/JOLIE/RICHARD/JACOB/LINDSEY:
BETH COLLINS REPLIED TO YOUR COMMENT ON HER POST.

BETH:
DID YOU REALLY JUST SAY,
QUOTE—"REVERSE SEXISM"—UNQUOTE?
MY HEART FUCKING BLEEDS FOR YOU.
YOU AMERICAN MALES HAVE NEVER
HAD A SINGLE OPPORTUNITY.
AND PLEASE TELL ME MORE ABOUT
WHAT IT TAKES TO BE A FEMINIST,
WISE AND POWERFUL WHITE MAN.
AND WHILE YOU'RE AT IT, CAN YOU
SHOW ME HOW TO FEED MYSELF?
BUT SERIOUSLY THOUGH,
I PROBABLY SHOULD THANK YOU.
YOU BASICALLY PROVED MY POINT.

RICHARD/DEVIN:
UNFRIEND.

BETH has deleted him from her Facebook friends.

DEVIN and JOLIE enter and run to opposite ends of the stage in very high spirits. They address each other via Facebook after he tags her in a post. He is holding up a big poster advertising The Decemberists at The Greek Theatre.

DEVIN:
OH MY GOD, JOLIE REEVES!
MY HEART IS GOING TO BURST!
THE DECEMBERISTS ARE AT THE GREEK THEATER,
AUGUST 31ST!

DEVIN & JOLIE:
HOLY CRAP!

JOLIE:
THIS IS JUST WHAT I NEEDED TO FILL THE VOID
AFTER FINALLY FINISHING ARRESTED DEVELOPMENT!

DEVIN AND JOLIE:
>	I'M GLAD THAT YOU AND I LOVE BANDS
>	AND SHOWS THAT ARE SO QUIRKY AND INTELLIGENT!

>	*GARON cannot let this go. He responds.*

GARON:
>	NO OFFENSE, I DON'T WANT TO BE CONTENTIOUS,
>	BUT CAN WE AGREE THE DECEMBERISTS
>	ARE BORING AND PRETENTIOUS?
>	THEY THINK THEY'RE SO PROFOUND AND LITERATE,
>	ALL THEY REALLY DO IS PLUCK STRINGS
>	LIKE A BUNCH OF FUCKING IDIOTS

>	AND LET'S BE HONEST,
>	THE NETFLIX SEASON OF ARRESTED DEVELOPMENT
>	THAT HAPPENED FOR SOME REASON WASN'T GOOD,
>	WE ALL KNOW IT WAS STALE AND POORLY MADE,
>	BUT NO ONE CAN ADMIT IT
>	'CAUSE YOU HIPSTERS DRANK THE KOOL AID.

BETH/LINDSEY/JACOB/RICHARD:
>	DEVIN GARCIA AND JOLIE REEVES
>	ALSO COMMENTED ON DEVIN GARCIA'S POST.

>	*DEVIN is clearly offended but tries to be diplomatic. JOLIE is incensed.*

DEVIN:
>	WELL, I DON'T KNOW,
>	I THOUGHT THERE WERE FUNNY PARTS
>	THEY HAD A TEN YEAR BREAK AND IT WAS HARD TO MAKE
>	AND HOW CAN YOU NOT LIKE THE DECEMBERISTS?
>	CHECK OUT THE CRANE WIFE.
>	THAT ALBUM CHANGED MY LIFE.

JOLIE:
>	BUT WHY ARGUE WITH SOMEONE
>	WHO LIKES TO BE CONTRARIAN?

DID SOMEONE ASK YOU TO CHIME IN
AND EDUCATE US UNREFINED BARBARIANS?

DEVIN AND JOLIE:
EVERYONE'S ALLOWED TO SPEAK THEIR MIND
AND SHARE THEIR EVERY THOUGHT
BUT IF YOU'RE MEAN AND BITTER ALL
YOU'LL EVER DO IS STIR THE POT
NASTY COMMENTS ARE NEVER FUN
OPINIONS ARE LIKE ASSHOLES, SO DON'T BE ONE!
ALL YOU'LL DO IS MAKE YOUR FRIENDS AND YOU
AND EVERYONE UNHAPPY IN THE LONG RUN

GARON:
THANKS FOR YOUR AMATEUR PSYCHOLOGICAL
ASSESSMENT, I'LL BET YOU FIFTY BUCKS
THAT EVEN IF I WERE TO PROVE YOU WRONG
WITH EVIDENCE,
YOU BOTH WOULD STILL BE PATRONIZING FUCKS.

DEVIN: Whoa...

JOLIE: Jeez.

They both unfriend him.

RICHARD/JACOB:
UNFRIEND.

DEVIN: What the hell.

JACOB enters and earnestly addresses his online community. He is a sweet, sensitive metrosexual young man with lots of friends, online and otherwise.

JACOB:
IF YOU HAVE PRAYERS AND GOOD VIBES,
SEND THEM ALL MY WAY.
I'VE GOT SO MUCH RIDING ON WHAT'S HAPPENING TODAY!

JACOB's friends beam at him as they gracefully dance around him in a circle, liking his status and sending him positive vibes.

ALL:
    LIKE, LIKE, LIKE, LIKE, LIKE
    LIKE, LIKE, LIKE, LIKE, LIKE
    AHHHHHH

JACOB:
    LOVE YOU ALL!!!

GARON:
    WOULDN'T IT BE EASIER AND WAY MORE HONEST JUST TO SAY YOU'RE NUTS AND YOU NEED EVIDENCE THAT EVERYBODY LIKES YOU?
    I GUARANTEE THEY LIKE YOU LESS WITH EACH PATHETIC, SELF-INDULGENT POST, I DON'T KNOW IF THAT EVER REALLY STRIKES YOU
    AND WHY NOT JUST SAY WHAT YOU'RE DOING LATER ANYWAY?
    OR ARE YOU SWORN TO SILENCE BY THE FUCKING CIA? THERE'S NO WAY YOUR AFTERNOON IS AS IMPORTANT AS YOU'RE MAKING IT OUT TO BE
    IF I EVER GET THIS NEEDY, WILL YOU PUNCH ME IN THE THROAT AND PUT A GAG ON ME?

JACOB: Are you kidding me?

RICHARD:
    WHO IS THIS ASSHOLE, JACOB?

LINDSEY (*overlapping*):
    WHO WOULD EVEN SAY THAT?

RICHARD (*overlapping*):
    JESUS CHRIST.

JOLIE/BETH (*overlapping*):
    DON'T LISTEN TO HIM, JACOB.

LINDSEY (*overlapping*):
    WHAT'S YOUR PROBLEM, DUDE?

DEVIN/RICHARD:
    BUT ARE YOU REALLY FRIENDS?

LINDSEY/JOLIE/BETH:
    ARE YOU REALLY FRIENDS?

RICHARD/LINDSEY/JOLIE/BETH/DEVIN:
    IS THIS GUY YOUR FRIEND??

JACOB:
    THANKS FOR YOUR SUPPORT, YOU GUYS.
    DON'T MIND THE HATEFUL DOUCHE.
    I HAVEN'T SEEN HIM SINCE 2006.
    IT'S PROBABLY TIME TO CUT HIM LOOSE!

ALL:
    UNFRIEND.

RICHARD steps forward with a loudspeaker and urgently addresses the audience.

RICHARD:
    DUE TO THE FACT THAT FACEBOOK
    HAS CHOSEN TO INCLUDE SOFTWARE
    THAT WILL ALLOW THE THEFT OF MY PERSONAL
    INFORMATION, I STATE, AS OF THIS DATE,
    PURSUANT TO ARTICLES L. 111, 112, AND 113
    OF THE CODE OF INTELLECTUAL PROPERTY,
    I DECLARE THAT MY RIGHTS ARE ATTACHED
    TO ALL MY PERSONAL DATA, PHOTOS, VIDEOS, ETC.
    THOSE WHO WISH TO CAN DO
    A COPY AND PASTE ONTO THEIR OWN WALL
    THIS WILL ALLOW THEM TO PLACE THEMSELVES
    UNDER PROTECTION OF COPYRIGHT

GARON:
> THIS ISN'T REAL!
> YOU'VE GOTTA BE PARANOID AS FUCK TO BELIEVE
> THAT FACEBOOK IS STEALING YOUR FACE.
> IF THEY WANTED TO TAKE YOUR IDENTITY,
> DO YOU THINK THEY'D BE SCARED OF A COPY-AND-PASTE?
> AND IF YOU'RE SO CONCERNED WITH YOUR PRIVACY,
> WHY DO YOU EVEN USE FACEBOOK?
> CAN'T YOU SEE THE IRONY?
> IT'S NOT LIKE YOU'RE ILLUMINATI,
> YOU JUST TAKING PICTURES OF YOUR MANICOTTI!

ALL:
> UNFRIEND.

GARON: Fine, then.

Random Facebook friends start coming forward and sharing things.

LINDSEY:
> I WANT TO TAKE A MINUTE JUST TO SAY
> MY BOYFRIEND ROCKS AND I'M A LUCKY LADY!

GARON:
> HE'S TOO OLD FOR YOU, HE'S SUPER SHADY.

MIKE:
> THE BRONCOS NEED TO GET ANOTHER PEYTON
> MANNING OR THIS SEASON WE'LL BE DEAD.

GARON:
> OR YOU COULD READ A FUCKING BOOK INSTEAD.

SUSAN:
> SEVEN YEARS AGO TODAY, I SET OUT ON A JOURNEY
> WHEN I TOOK MY FIRST PILATES CLASS...

GARON:
> SO NOW WE ALL SHOULD KISS YOUR ASS.

> ROB and CARLY gently come forward, holding up a picture of a car seat.

ROB AND CARLY:
> NOTICE IN THIS PICTURE
> THERE'S AN EMPTY BABY CAR SEAT
> COMING SOON, NEXT YEAR IN FEBRUARY

Everybody gushes.

GARON:
> IF YOUR BABY IS AS LAME AS THIS POST,
> I HOPE YOU MISCARRY.

CARLY: Whoah!

JACOB/RICHARD/LINDSEY:	SUSAN/ROB/CARLY:
EVERYONE'S ALLOWED	UNFRIEND,
TO SPEAK THEIR MINDS	UNFRIEND,
AND SHARE THEIR EVERY	UNFRIEND
THOUGHT.	THAT WAS SO UNCALLED FOR
BUT IF YOU'RE MEAN AND	UNFRIEND,
BITTER ALL YOU'LL EVER DO	UNFRIEND,
IS STIR THE POT.	UNFRIEND
NASTY COMMENTS ARE	THAT WAS REALLY
NEVER FUN.	FUCKING MEAN
OPINIONS ARE LIKE	GET A HOBBY,
ASSHOLES,	JEEZ.
SO DON'T BE ONE!	I'M DONE,
ALL YOU'LL DO IS MAKE	I'M DONE
YOUR FRIENDS AND YOU	ALL YOU ARE IS MEAN AND
AND EVERYONE	BITTER AND OFFENSIVE IN
UNHAPPY IN THE LONG RUN.	THE LONG RUN

GARON:
> I THINK I'M DONE.

The following six parts are sung simultaneously

CARLY/ROB:
> EVERYONE'S ALLOWED TO SPEAK THEIR MINDS
> AND SHARE THEIR EVERY THOUGHT
> BUT IF YOU'RE MEAN AND BITTER,
> ALL YOU'LL EVER DO IS STIR THE POT
> NASTY COMMENTS ARE NEVER FUN
> OPINIONS ARE LIKE ASSHOLES, SO DON'T BE ONE!
> ALL YOU'LL DO...

JACOB:
> WHAT KIND OF COWARD GOES ONLINE
> AND THROWS HIS BILE AROUND?
> WHAT KIND OF BASTARD TAKES SUCH JOY
> IN BRINGING PEOPLE DOWN?
> YOU SHOULD BE ASHAMED,
> YOU SHOULD BE ASHAMED
> IT'S ON YOU...

LINDSEY:
> FUCK YOU, FUCK YOU, FUCK YOU
> FUCK YOU, FUCK YOU, GO FUCK YOURSELF
> FUCK YOU, FUCK YOU...

BETH:
> CAN WE PLEASE STOP CALLING EVERYONE NAMES?
> CAN WE CUT THE UGLY ALPHA MALE GAMES?
> YOU'RE NO PHILOSOPHER KING
> YOU'RE JUST A SAD LITTLE THING
> LOOK AT YOU...

RICHARD:
> YOU OUGHT TO KNOW THAT YOU'RE A SAD DISGRACE
> YOU BETTER HOPE WE NEVER MEET UP FACE TO FACE
> I'LL KICK YOUR ASS, LITTLE GUY
> YOU'VE GOT NO CLASS, LITTLE GUY
> SCREW YOU...

There is a scary, ominous sound and everybody disappears, leaving GARON all alone.

OFFSTAGE VOICE: Your account has been disabled for misuse of the site. It is a violation of Facebook's Terms of Use to harass users on the site, whether through unsolicited messages, friend requests, pokes or other features. We will not be able to reactivate your account for any reason. This decision is final.

GARON scoffs, puts his phone down on the bed and giggles to himself. He instinctively picks the phone back up again, then remembers what just happened and puts it back down. As the loneliness sets in, he realizes what he has done and stares longingly at his phone.

GARON:
    LOVE YOU ALL.

END

THE HIPSTER SISTER

Book, Music, & Lyrics by *Andy Roninson*

The cast of *The Hipster Sister* at Theatre Now's SOUND BITES 3.0.
(Back Row, Left to right): Pedar Benson Bate, Meredith Lark, Andrew Garret Karl, Mattie Kaiser, Meg Vandervort, Gizem Yucel, Brian Thompson, Aaron Drescher and Will Melones *(Front Row, Left to right)*: Tiffany Topol, Christiana Cole, Jeff Theiss

SYNOPSIS

33-year-old actuary Chelsea comes home to her nice Brooklyn apartment to find her 30-year-old sister Jacqueline banging pots and yell-singing, *"WE'LL NEVER BE THE SAME"*. On top of that, she finds that the vase her boyfriend just got her is smashed to pieces because Jacqueline knocked it over.

Frustrated, Chelsea goes to her bedroom to vent to her boyfriend Walter. Walter reminds her that she, Chelsea, was the one who invited Jacqueline to stay on their couch while she gets her life back together. Besides, Jacqueline is such a sweetheart. Chelsea has heard this her whole life, that *"JACKIE'S A SWEETHEART"*. and she bemoans that nobody ever sees how Jacqueline's irresponsibility is a burden on those who love her.

Chelsea goes to the living room to confront Jacqueline about moving out. But Jacqueline keeps avoiding the subject and keeps asking to play Chelsea her new song. Finally, Chelsea says, "Damn it, Jacqueline, why can't you ever just talk like a person?" And Jacqueline says, "Because I can't. What I can do is play you this song." Chelsea relents and listens to Jacqueline play *"THE UKULELE SONG (PART 1)"*. In the song, Jacqueline mentions not only that she may have stolen the ukulele, but that the ukulele is all she has as her one comfort in a life she constantly screws up. Well, not her only comfort. She also has her older sister.

Touched, Chelsea says she can let Jacqueline stay a few more weeks and that she'll help Jacqueline find a new job. A very happy Jacqueline plays the rest of *"THE UKULELE SONG (PART 2)"*—and Chelsea joins in to sing harmony at the very end.

PRODUCTION HISTORY

The Hipster Sister, written by Andy Roninson, had its first reading at Muchmore's in Brooklyn, February 2015.

It was then produced as episode #13 of the audio podcast TAKE A TEN which was presented as part of Manhattan Musical Theatre Lab's in New York City on July 23, 2015, with direction by Emmy-winner Matt Cowart. The cast was as follows:

CHELSEA	Natalie Charle Ellis
JACQUELINE	Tiffany Topol
WALTER	Pedar Benson Bate

The following year it had its first full stage production at Theatre Now's SOUND BITES 3.0 at The 47th Street Theater in New York on January 18, 2016. It was directed by Andrew Garret Karl with musical direction by Jeff Theiss. It was produced by Thomas Morrissey and Stephen Bishop Seely with associate producer, Zan Vailento. The cast was as follows:

CHELSEA	Christiana Cole
JACQUELINE	Tiffany Topol
WALTER	Pedar Benson Bate

In 2018 there were numerous productions:

Two productions took place as part of the Alberta High School Drama Festival in Canada: Lloydminster Comprehensive High School in Lloydminster, with direction by Simon Stang and at Memorial Composite High School in Stony Plain, with direction by Kevin Tokarsky.

Bard Early College High School in Queens, NY as part of their One Act Play Festival, with direction by Whitman Clark.

Minnesota State University in Mankato, MN with direction by John Nichol.

The One Act Festival at the Imperial Theatre in Ontario, CA with direction by Marcia Case.

CHARACTERS

CHELSEA   33 years old, an actuary.

JACQUELINE   30 years old, a singer-songwriter and former barista.

WALTER   35 years old, Chelsea's well-meaning boyfriend.

VOICES   The voices that join in at the end.

SETTING

A well-kept apartment in Williamsburg, Brooklyn, NY. Late February 2015.

MUSICAL NUMBERS

"We'll Never Be The Same"	Jacqueline
"Jackie's a Sweetheart"	Chelsea, Walter
"Happy Bat Mitzvah, Dana"	Jacqueline, Chelsea
"The Ukulele Song (Part 1)"	Jacqueline
"The Ukulele Song (Part 2)"	Jacqueline, Chelsea, Voices

AUTHOR'S NOTE

This play is autobiographical in the sense that I am both Chelsea and Jackie. Sometimes, I am the airheaded songwriter who doesn't want to do anything but lie on the couch all day. Sometimes, I'm the perfectionist with deadlines who wants to live up to my full potential. Neither is the hero or villain.

This play is based not only on myself but on all my beautiful, awful artist friends who prioritize creativity over dependability. These are my friends who can write a song on a banjo they just found that'll make you cry, but totally forget about the plans you've been arranging for weeks. They work in cafés, they live in vans, they wear tie-dye thirty years too late. In fact, this whole generation of hipsters of the 2000s and 2010s will soon seem silly and quaint much as the hippies of *Hair* do (and I love *Hair*), which is why this show is set firmly in 2015.

This play is also based on a theme I keep coming back to: familial contempt. It's the kind of relationship between siblings where you're used to fighting or arguing, but god help the poor fool who picks on your little brother. "He's my little brother, I'm the only one who can pick on him!" As the middle child of three, I've been the baby and the sitter, the pest and the caretaker. For some of us, it's not easy being in a family. But it's not supposed to be easy. That's why it's so meaningful to continue your obligations, even when it feels like you can't go further.

In your production, make sure not to let either Chelsea or Jackie become flat. Chelsea is not an uptight nag. Remember: She just came from a long day at work, dealt with all the noise and stench of the NYC subway, and is looking for the tiniest of respites when she gets home, especially from her sister, whom she voluntarily took in and has cared for the last three months. Jackie is not a dope. It's especially important that Jackie doesn't become too cutesy. Yes, the ukulele is a very cute instrument, but Jackie approaches it as a concert pianist would approach a Steinway. It is a door to a new world of music, a new way to express oneself sincerely. The sisters share various personality traits, both from genetics and from just growing up together.

If at all possible, Jackie should accompany herself on the ukulele. Yes, it is not the simplest of parts to play, but it is designed to be performed by a beginner.

- Andy Roninson

At a well-kept apartment in Williamsburg, Brooklyn, NY in 2015, CHELSEA, 33, comes home from work. She opens her front door and hears a cacophony of metal clanking and primal screaming.

CHELSEA: What the...?

> *SHE walks over to the kitchen door, opens it, and sees JACQUELINE, 30, banging pots and pans.*
>
> *Song begins - "We'll Never Be The Same"*

JACQUELINE (*improvising loudly*):
    OOH, AHH, WE'LL NEVER BE THE SAME! SAID-A
    OOH, AAH, WE'LL NEVER EVER BE THE SAME!

CHELSEA: Jacqueline!

> *JACQUELINE stops.*

What are you doing?!

JACQUELINE (*"duh"*): Writing a song. Actually, Chelsea, I need you to sing backup.

CHELSEA: I told you, I don't sing anymo—

> *She steps on a piece of broken glass.*

Oh my god, is this the vase Walter just got me for Valentine's? How did it break?

JACQUELINE (*"again: duh"*): The floor was lava.

CHELSEA: You are thirty years old! Why would you—

> *JACQUELINE bangs the pots and pans again.*

JACQUELINE:
    I SAID-A OOH, AHH, WE'LL NEVER BE THE SAME!

NO WE WON'T, NEVER EVER EVER EVER EVER EVER
(*etc.*)

CHELSEA: Ergh!!

CHELSEA slams the door behind her and goes to her bedroom. Her boyfriend, WALTER, 35, is looking in the mirror and trying on a tie.

WALTER: Hey, honeybear, what do you think of this tie?

CHELSEA: Walter, I can't take it anymore!

WALTER: Okay, no tie.

CHELSEA: Three months on my couch is enough, ok? She needs to move out already!

WALTER: Jacqueline?

We hear JACQUELINE offstage, working on her "song," it sounds more like a siren.

CHELSEA: Yessss! It's like a French ambulance is plowing through my kitchen.

WALTER: It makes me feel like we're in Paris.

CHELSEA: Walter, I need you on my side.

WALTER: But weren't you the one who offered her the couch in the first place?

CHELSEA: Well—yeah, but only because she had just gotten fired—again—and Zach had just dumped her, and she and mom had that big fight...

WALTER: She needs her big sister.

CHELSEA: She needs to grow up!

WALTER: Hey, Chels, c'mon, everyone's got their own path, right? Besides, she's been nothing but sweet.

   Song begins - "Jackie's a Sweetheart"

CHELSEA:
 WE'RE TALKING ABOUT MY SISTER, RIGHT?
 WE'RE TALKING ABOUT MY SISTER, RIGHT? RIGHT?

 JACKIE'S A SWEETHEART,
 THAT'S WHAT THEY SAY

 WALTER tries to calm Chelsea.

WALTER:
 AND SHE'S JUST A LITTLE BIT ODD

CHELSEA: I don't think you realize how long this has been going on.

 She sings:

 I MEAN, THIS IS A GIRL WHO HAS ALWAYS BEEN LATE.
 ON HER OWN GRADUATION, SHE GOT THE WRONG DATE.
 AND IF SHE MAKES YOU WAIT
 THEN SHE'LL WORK REALLY HARD
 ON A PERSONAL CARD

 CHELSEA pulls out the card and hands it to WALTER.

 THAT'LL HAVE LITTLE FLOWERS
 AND POEMS AND UNICORNS AND SHIT
 AND IT'S LIKE, FLOWERS ARE GREAT,

 WALTER points at the inside of the card, admiring those well-drawn flowers!

 BUT SHE SAID 3:15 AND IT'S QUARTER PAST EIGHT

 JACKIE'S A SWEETHEART,

> EVERYONE SEES THAT
> BUT SHE'S JUST A LITTLE BIT ODD

WALTER: Aw, you were kids then!

CHELSEA: You mean last week?

She sings:

> LIKE WHEN HER BOSS CALLED,
> SAID, "YOU GOTTA COME GET HER"
> SHE WAS BAWLING IN THE CORNER
> BLOWING SNOT INTO HER SWEATER
>
> AND WHEN I ASKED HER WHAT UPSET HER
> SHE SAID THAT SHE KNEW SHE COULD DRAW
> THAT LEAF IN THE LATTE SO MUCH BETTER
>
> I MEAN, THIS IS A GIRL WHO ADOPTED
> A DOG AND A CAT
> AND A PIG AND A RAT --
> AND NAMED THEM ALL TED.
> AND PAINTED ALL THEIR TOENAILS RED
> YEAH, EVEN THE RAT'S TOO
> AND YOU CAN GUESS WHO
> PICKED UP ALL OF THE POO

WALTER:
> JACKIE'S A SWEETHEART—

CHELSEA:
> JACKIE'S A SWEETHEART,
> I KNOW, I KNOW

WALTER AND CHELSEA:
> BUT SHE'S JUST A LITTLE BIT ODD

WALTER:
> SHE ALWAYS TRIES TO BE NICE

WITH EVERYONE THAT SHE MEETS

CHELSEA:
    LIKE STRANGERS DOWN ON THE STREETS
    INVITING THEM TO FREESTYLE ON HER
    "SUPER DOPE"\ BEATS

    I GET SHE WANTS TO BE NICE
    BUT NICE IS NEVER ENOUGH
    WHEN THE WORLD IS SAYING, "BE TOUGH,"
    YOU CAN'T BE MAKING PAINTINGS OUT OF
    MARSHMALLOW FLUFF

    AND ALL I WANT
    IS JUST TO KNOW
    SHE'S OKAY,
    THAT SHE CAN GO
    ONE MORE DAY
    ON HER OWN

    JACKIE'S A SWEETHEART
    JACKIE'S A SWEETHEART
    HOW LONG CAN SHE PLAY PRETEND?

WALTER:
    BUT JACKIE'S YOUR SISTER

CHELSEA:
    AND SCREW IT, MY FRIEND.

WALTER: Go talk to her.

CHELSEA: She is going to hate me.

WALTER: If she's really your friend, she'll understand.

CHELSEA: And I'm not a bitch?

WALTER: Chels, I love you, and I love how much you care for your sister. You deserve space, and she deserves a life of her own.

CHELSEA: Okay. (*beat*) This is gonna suck.

WALTER: No! A little.

CHELSEA: What, no, come on, you can't say that—

WALTER (*overlapping*): Ok, go, you have to go now, our reservations are for seven!

> WALTER pushes CHELSEA out the door. She's now in the living room with JACQUELINE who is lightly strumming on a ukulele.

CHELSEA: Okay... Hey, Jacqueline?

JACQUELINE: It's Jay-Kwellen now.

CHELSEA: Right, so, um... How was your day?

JACQUELINE: Super dope! I busked in the Bedford stop for seven hours. Made sixteen bucks!

CHELSEA: Oh, wow, yeah, that's... Have you talked to your boss at Coffees N' Smiles about getting your job back?

JACQUELINE: Mm, no, been busy. Hey, you wanna hear this song I've been working on? There's even a part for you.

CHELSEA: You know I don't do that anymore.

JACQUELINE: You haven't sung with me since Dana's bat mitzvah! Remember:

> Song begins - "Happy Bat Mitzvah, Dana"

HAPPY BAT MITZVAH

BOTH:
   DAAANA.

CHELSEA (*immediately*): Yeah, I remember...

JACQUELINE (*overlapping*): And Sammy Burstein kept trying to stick his tongue in your mouth like BLAAAHH—

CHELSEA: Ew, no, look! I came in here to talk to you about moving out. The neighbors are complaining, the living room is basically unlivable, and I'm starting to worry about you—

JACQUELINE: Hey, can I play you this song I've been working on?

CHELSEA: God! Jackie, why can't you ever just talk to me, like a person?

JACQUELINE (*honestly*): Because I can't. What I can do is play you this song. Can I please play you this song?

CHELSEA: Okay.

   Song begins - "The Ukulele Song (Part 1)"

   JACQUELINE accompanies herself on the ukulele.

JACQUELINE:
   YESTERDAY, I BOUGHT THIS UKULELE.

CHELSEA: Really? Where did you get the money?

JACQUELINE:
   WELL, ACTUALLY, I STOLE THIS UKULELE.

CHELSEA: What? Are you kidding? I can't tell if you're kidding.

JACQUELINE:
   THE STRINGS FELT SO SOFT,
   AND THE WOOD FELT SO HARD,
   AND I FELT SO ALIVE,

SLIPPING PAST THE SECURITY GUARD.

AND AS I MADE IT OUT THE DOOR,
THE SKY OPENED UP WITH A MIGHTY ROAR,
AND LAVA POURED ALL AROUND THE FLOOR.
AND I THOUGHT, "WELL,
I FUCKED UP AGAIN."

AND ALL I COULD SAY WAS,

BA BA BA BA
BA BA BA BA
BA BA BA BA BA.
YEAH ALL I COULD SAY WAS,
BA BA BA BA
BA BA BA BA
BA BA BA BA BA.

THE ONLY THING I OWN'S THIS UKULELE.
OH, BY THE WAY, I THINK HER NAME IS DANA.

CHELSEA: Oh, god.

JACQUELINE:
    AND SHE SINGS TO ME AT NIGHT,
    AND SHE TELLS ME I'M ALL RIGHT,
    AND I FEEL SO ALIVE,
    PLUCKING ON HER G-STRING ALL OF THE NIGHT.

CHELSEA chuckles.

BUT WHEN YOU'RE TOLD TO ACT YOUR AGE,
AND YOU CAN'T EVEN EARN JUST A MINIMUM WAGE,
AND EVERYBODY'S ON YA FROM YOUR MAMA TO OBAMA
AND ALL THE WORLD'S A CAGE,
IT MAKES YOU WANNA RAGE:

BA BA BA BA
BA BA BA BA

BA BA BA BA BA.
AND ALL YOU CAN DO IS
BA BA BA BA
BA BA BA BA
BA BA BA BA BA.

AND I KNOW
I'M A MESS
AND I KNOW
HOW TO FAKE MY HAPPINESS
BUT I KNOW
HOW LUCKY I AM
TO HAVE ONE THING IN THIS WORLD
WELL, ACTUALLY, TWO
MY UKULELE AND YOU

YOU, YOU, YOU
MY UKULELE AND YOU
YOU, YOU
YOU.

CHELSEA: One more week.

JACQUELINE: Ok.

CHELSEA: And we're gonna return the ukulele tomorrow.

JACQUELINE: I'm just holding it for a friend!

CHELSEA: I'll help you look for a job too, ok?

JACQUELINE: Love you, Chelsss.

CHELSEA: You too, Jacqueline.

JACQUELINE: Jay-Kwellen.

CHELSEA (*quickly*): Jay-Kwellen.

JACQUELINE: Wanna hear the rest of the song?

CHELSEA: There's more?

Song begins - "The Ukulele Song (Part 2)"

JACQUELINE begins playing the same song, but faster. Each instrument she mentions manifests in the orchestration. Throughout CHELSEA ad libs reactions to what Jacqueline says with a mixture of love and slight skepticism.

JACQUELINE: Okay, so then it picks up like this, right? And then the bass comes in. And then maybe some piano right here. And then the drums kick in like—

She imitates the drums.

POOPTY POOPTY PANTS!
BP, CH, BP, CH, BP, CH...

And it really builds here, and all the voices come in with:

BA BA BA BA
BA BA BA BA
BA BA—

And then strings come in!

BA BA BA BA
BA BA BA BA
BA BA BA BA
BA (etc.)

Come on, sing!

CHELSEA: No, I really don't want to—

JACQUELINE:
BA BA BA BA,

Sing! Sing!

CHELSEA: No, please, Jackie—

JACQUELINE: Here it is, right now!

BA

CHELSEA: Okay, okay, okay!

CHELSEA nervously takes over as the orchestra suddenly cuts out.

BA BA BA BA
BA BA BA BA
BA BA BA BA
BA

BOTH *(in harmony, still acapella)*:

BA BA BA BA
BA BA BA BA
BA BA BA BA
BA.

Blackout.

END

THE ONLY THING THAT MATTERS

Book, Music & Lyrics by *Chris Kerrigan*

Brooke Wetterhahn, Paige Berkovitz, and Lauren Baez in *The Only Thing That Matters* in Theatre Now's SOUND BITES 6.0.

SYNOPSIS

At an upper middle class home in Brentwood, California, Kerri, a fragile recovering alcoholic with only two weeks sobriety has just arrived to have dinner with her two sisters, Ally and Mystie. Ally is a nonstop young suburban mother, multi-tasking, picking up toys and setting the table. Mystie is an attractive career woman who seems to get everything right in life. Kerri sits on a stool and ponders to herself how much more fun these dinners used to be before her sisters grew up and became strangers to her *"TEN YEARS AGO"*. Ally and Mystie proceed to probe her with questions about her life and make not-so-subtle judgments about her relationship, her work ethic, and her general failure to thrive. When this reaches a fever pitch, Kerri excuses herself to go outside and smoke a cigarette while Ally and Mystie commiserate about their difficult sister.

Out on the sidewalk, Kerri leaves a voicemail for her current boyfriend Raymond, melancholy over how uncomfortable the dinner has been so far *"SAD PARIAH"*. She composes herself, marches back into the house, and decides to pour herself a glass of wine. Dinner is served, and Ally and Mystie begin to discuss family stuff while Kerri quickly and quietly drinks a whole lot of wine to get through the rest of the dinner *"THE ONLY THING THAT MATTERS"*. Eventually, the subject turns to a Netflix documentary about a man falsely accused of sexual assault, and Ally and Mystie opine about the overreach of the #MeToo movement and agree that it has turned into a witch hunt.

Kerri, quite drunk now, is enraged by this conversation and her sisters' stance on the issue. She curses at them, calls them uninformed, and rattles off rape statistics *"TWO MEN"*, all of which falls on deaf ears; her sisters are more concerned with her use of profanity and her tone than what she is saying. Finally, Mystie gently suggests that the reason Kerri is so worked up about this is because of things that happened to her when they were younger *"THE SENSITIVE ONE"*. Through tears, Kerri reminds them that nobody believed her after her assault and she was left all alone. She storms out, leaving Ally and Mystie to shake their hands, repeating that she "was always the sensitive one."

PRODUCTION HISTORY
The Only Thing That Matters written by Chris Kerrigan, first premiered during the Theatre Now's SOUND BITES 6.0 Festival on April 2, 2019 at the Merkin Hall at the Kaufman Music Center in New York City. It was directed by Rebecca Kenigsberg. It was produced by Chris Giordano, Thomas Morrissey, and Liz Doyle. The cast was as follows:

KERRI	Lauren Baez
ALLY	Paige Berkovitz
MYSTIE	Brooke Wetterhahn

CHARACTERS

KERRI — Female identifying, early 30s, recovering alcoholic with two weeks sober. Vulnerable, reactive, damaged by past traumas.

ALLY — Female identifying, late 30s, upper middle class suburban mother. Always moving, highly judgmental, privileged.

MYSTIE — Female identifying, late 30s, career woman, lives life on her own terms, highly judgmental, somewhat bratty.

SETTING
A suburban home in Brentwood, California. The present.

MUSICAL NUMBERS
The Only Thing That Matters is a musical performed as one continuous piece of music.

AUTHOR'S NOTE

I got sober in the Fall of 2007. One evening in my last two-month stretch of drinking, my older sister had a dinner party at her house at which she served homemade sangria. As a result of growing family disapproval, I vowed to not drink that night but ended up drinking most of it and making a scene. Today, after over twelve years of continued sobriety and relative life progress, I am still the member of my family voted most likely to drink all the sangria and make a scene.

While *The Only Thing That Matters* does manage to touch upon a few different themes (sibling rivalry, alcoholism, the #MeToo movement), it is essentially a musical about the roles that we play in our family and how these dynamics affect our social and political beliefs when we leave the nest and how they follow close behind us every time we return to the nest. Sometimes we happily volunteer to play these roles. More often, they are branded on us by our parents, siblings, etc. and we are confined to play them out no matter how hard we work to break free of them in our daily lives away from our families.

- Chris Kerrigan

A kitchen and adjacent dining room area in a white suburban home. ALLY is hosting an informal dinner get-together with just her two sisters. There is a high chair facing upstage with an assumed baby in it, unseen to us. ALLY is super mom, always on the move, finishing up dinner and feeding the baby, all while carrying on conversations. MYSTIE is setting the table; she is a petite and attractive career woman in her early 30's who seems to do everything right. KERRI, the third sister and black sheep of the family is sitting cross-legged on a stool by the kitchen counter, uneasy and fidgeting. She has brightly dyed hair, lots of tattoos, and looks unwell. MYSTIE begins to uncork a bottle of wine.

MYSTIE: Hey sis, do you want red or white?

KERRI: Neither, thanks. I'm not drinking. Remember?

MYSTIE: Oh, that's right. It changes so often, I can never remember where we are with that.

KERRI addresses the audience.

KERRI:
    I REMEMBER TEN YEARS AGO ME AND MY SISTERS
    COULD HANG OUT AND MAKE INAPPROPRIATE JOKES
    BUT NOW THEY HAVE HUSBANDS
    AND HOUSES AND HEADBOARDS
    AND NOBODY SAYS WHAT THEY'RE THINKING
    AND NOBODY SMOKES.

    THE DINNERS AND THE DULL SENSATIONS
    THE UNDERWHELMING CONVERSATIONS
    IT'S ALMOST LIKE WE'VE NEVER MET AND WE'RE
    FORCED INTO BONDING LIKE WE'RE AT A
    CORPORATE RETREAT.
    I USED TO LOOK FORWARD TO TIME WITH MY FAMILY
    BUT NOW IT'S THIS THING WHERE YOU SIT THERE AND EAT.

ALLY:
    HEY SIS, DID YOU GET THE VIDEO I SENT YOU
    OF LUCAS IN HIS TALENT SHOW?

KERRI:
>   I DON'T KNOW. I MIGHT HAVE.
>   I'M PRETTY BAD AT CHECKING EMAIL, THOUGH.

ALLY:
>   I SENT IT A WEEK AGO.

MYSTIE (*admiring the furniture*):
>   SIS, WHERE DID YOU GET THIS ADORABLE SHELF?

ALLY:
>   GOT THE IDEA ON PINTEREST AND MADE IT MYSELF.

KERRI:
>   YOU'RE SUCH A BADASS!

ALLY:
>   SHH! COME ON, KERRI.

KERRI:
>   SORRY, SIS.

ALLY:
>   MY SON DOES NOT NEED WORDS LIKE THAT IN HIS
>   VOCABULARY.

MYSTIE:
>   SO WHAT'S BEEN GOING ON WITH YOU THESE DAYS?
>   THE FALL SEMESTER MUST BE STARTING SOON.

KERRI:
>   I TRIED TO REGISTER FOR INTRO TO DESIGN,
>   BUT NOW I GOTTA WAIT IN LINE
>   AND CRASH THE CLASS ON MONDAY AFTERNOON.

ALLY:
>   YOU'VE HAD SINCE THE END OF JUNE…

KERRI:
> I KNOW BUT MY WHOLE SCHEDULE WAS UP IN THE AIR.

ALLY:
> YOU MADE TIME TO SKETCH SUNSETS
> AND COLOR YOUR HAIR.

KERRI:
> IT'S NOT YOUR BUSINESS.

ALLY:
> DON'T GET DEFENSIVE.

KERRI:
> LET IT GO.

ALLY:
> I HOPE YOU'RE SAVING UP FOR BOOKS,
> THEY'RE GETTING SO EXPENSIVE.

MYSTIE: Hey!
> ARE YOU STILL DATING THAT CREEPER
> YOU MET AT THE FLATS?

KERRI:
> HIS NAME IS RAYMOND
> AND I WISH YOU WOULDN'T CALL HIM THAT.

MYSTIE (*laughing*):
> I'M SORRY, SIS.

ALLY:
> THE GUY'S A REAL LIVE WIRE.

KERRI:
> LET IT GO.

MYSTIE:
> IT'S JUST I THINK YOU NEED TO SET YOUR SITES
> A LITTLE HIGHER...

KERRI:

> *Heads for the door.*
>
> I'LL BE RIGHT BACK.

MYSTIE:
> WHERE ARE YOU GOING? WE'RE ABOUT TO SIT-

KERRI:
> I'M JUST GOING OUTSIDE.

MYSTIE:
> OUTSIDE TO SMOKE?
> YOU PROMISED MOM YOU WOULD QUIT.

KERRI:
> CAN I JUST GO OUTSIDE? I'M THIRTY-THREE YEARS
> OLD!

MYSTIE:
> GOD.

ALLY:
> GO OUTSIDE,
> JUST SHUT THE DOOR SO IT DOESN'T GET COLD.
>
> *KERRI goes outside. ALLY and MYSTIE look at each other.*
>
> DO YOU REMEMBER TEN YEARS AGO,
> KERRI HAD TWO STEADY JOBS,
> AND WE TOLD OURSELVES SHE'D BE OK?
> BUT TEN YEARS OF BOYFRIENDS
> AND DRINKING AND DRIFTING,
> SHE'S STUCK IN THIS HIGH SCHOOL CHARADE

    AND SHE CAN'T BREAK AWAY.

ALLY/MYSTIE:
    THE WORRY AND THE CONSTANT TENSION,
    THAT BIG DRAMATIC INTERVENTION.

MYSTIE:
    AND SHE DOESN'T CARE.

ALLY:
    THAT'S NOT FAIR.

MYSTIE:
    FINE, SHE CARES,
    BUT IT'S JUST YOU AND ME WHO ARE DEALING WITH IT.
    MOM AND DAD ARE CAUGHT UP
    IN THEIR OWN SELFISH DRAMA,
    SHE'S FINE FOR A STRETCH, THEN IT ALL GOES TO SHIT.

KERRI texts her boyfriend out on the front porch while she nervously sucks down a cigarette.

KERRI:
    HEY BABE, I FEEL LIKE I'M SHRINKING.
    I DON'T KNOW WHAT I WAS THINKING.
    JESUS, I WISH I WAS DRINKING.
    ARE YOU HOME?

    ALLY THINKS HER KID IS THE NEW MESSIAH,
    AND MYSTIE IS AS THIN AS A TWIG.
    BOTH MY SISTERS THINK I'M THIS SAD PARIAH,
    AND EVERY WORD THEY SAY IS A DIG.
    CALL ME WHEN YOU'RE HOME AND I'LL COME HOME, TOO.

She puts her cigarette out, composes herself, and comes back inside.

KERRI:
    I THINK I WILL HAVE A GLASS OF WINE.

ALLY:
    OH HEY, YOU'RE BACK, IT'S TIME TO EAT.

KERRI:
    I THINK I'LL POUR MYSELF A GLASS OF WINE.

ALLY:
    GET YOURSELF A PLATE.

KERRI:
    IF YOU'RE BOTH GOING TO HAVE ONE,
    MAYBE I'LL JUST GO AND GRAB ONE...

MYSTIE (*annoyed*):
    OK FINE! HAVE A GLASS OF WINE!

ALLY (*overlapping*):
    HAVE A GLASS OF WINE!

KERRI: Thanks.

She pours herself a glass of red wine and quickly tosses it back. Throughout the following, MYSTIE and ALLY spoon penne and salad onto their plates while KERRI quietly continues to refill and consume two more glasses of wine, as if on a mission.

MYSTIE:
    THANKS FOR DINNER, SIS.
    DELICIOUS AS USUAL.

ALLY:
    I'M JUST GLAD WE COULD GET TOGETHER.
    IT'S BEEN TOO LONG!

MYSTIE:
    I KNOW, IT JUST FEELS WRONG.

Notices what KERRI is doing with the wine.

    YOU OK, KERRI?

KERRI: Yep.

ALLY:
    AT THE END OF THE DAY,
    FAMILY'S THE ONLY THING THAT MATTERS.

She sighs and starts to make a plate for KERRI.

    WHEN YOU THINK OF ALL THE ENERGY WE PUT INTO
    OUR DAILY MOVEMENTS,
    OBSESSED WITH FORWARD MOTION AND OUR SELF-
    IMPROVEMENT,
    WE LOSE SIGHT OF WHERE WE CAME FROM.
    SO CRUCIAL THAT WE GET TOGETHER.
    AND TRY TO GET ALONG.
    I MEAN, IT'S BEEN TOO LONG.

She puts a plate of food in front of KERRI, who is still quickly drinking lots of wine.

    YOU OK, KERRI?

KERRI: Yep.

ALLY:
    'CAUSE WHEN YOU STRIP IT ALL AWAY...

ALLY/MYSTIE:
    ...FAMILY'S THE ONLY THING THAT MATTERS

KERRI gets a corkscrew out of a drawer and begins opening the second bottle.

ALLY:
    AND IN AN INSTANT IT CAN ALL BE TAKEN AWAY
    IT'S GONE AND YOU'RE AN EMPTY SHELL.
    AFTER WATCHING THAT THING ON NETFLIX
    IT'S A POSSIBILITY WE KNOW ALL TOO WELL

MYSTIE: Oh my God, right? That poor guy.

ALLY: I know, and those poor kids.

KERRI: What's this?

MYSTIE: The documentary series about that family in Florida, you didn't see it?

ALLY:
> THIS GUY WAS CHEATING HIS WIFE BUT THEN SHE
> FOUND AND HE SWORE TO MAKE AMENDS
> HE WENT TO SEX ADDICTS ANONYMOUS, ACCEPTED FAULT
> THE WOMAN HE'D BEEN CHEATING WITH WENT OFF
> HER MEDS AND WHEN HE BROKE IT OFF
> SHE ACCUSED HIM OF SEXUAL ASSAULT

MYSTIE:
> AND EVEN WITH NO EVIDENCE,
> THERE WAS NO ASSUMPTION OF INNOCENCE
> THE WHIRLWIND IN THE MEDIA OVER RAPE
> HAD GOTTEN SO INTENSE
> HE WAS SENTENCED TO FIVE YEARS,
> HE LOST EVERYTHING HE HAD
> HE COULDN'T BE A HUSBAND AND
> HE COULDN'T BE A DAD
> HE MISSED THE BIRTH OF HIS THIRD SON,
> HE WAS COMPLETELY CAST ASIDE.

ALLY:
> HE'D SERVED TWO-THIRDS OF HIS SENTENCE WHEN
> THEY FOUND OUT SHE HAD LIED,
> 'CAUSE THEY LEARNED ABOUT HER REPUTATION.
> IT WAS NOT HER FIRST FALSE ACCUSATION.

ALLY/MYSTIE:
> JUST GOES TO SHOW (JUST GOES TO SHOW)
> HOW ALL THE "ME TOO" PEOPLE TAKE THINGS TOO FAR,
> WITH HYSTERIA AT THE FOREFRONT.

MYSTIE:
    AND NOW THE WHOLE THING IS A WITCH HUNT.
    IT STARTED OUT GREAT,
    IT RAISED AWARENESS OF SEXUAL HARASSMENT IN
    THE WORKPLACE.

ALLY:
    NOW WE WON'T BE SATISFIED 'TIL EVERY MAN IS
    DISGRACED.

ALLY/MYSTIE:
    INSTEAD OF STANDING UP FOR WOMEN BEING BRAVE,
    WHICH WAS THE WHOLE POINT IN THE FIRST PLACE.

KERRI (*incredulous*): What???

MYSTIE:
    AND THE WORST PART IS, IT MAKES US LOOK WEAK,
    LIKE SOME GUY FLIRTING IS TRAUMATIC

ALLY:
    RIGHT!
    THAT'S WHY I UNFOLLOWED FEMINISTS OF BRENTWOOD.
    THEY'RE GETTING SO OVERDRAMATIC.

ALLY/MYSTIE:
    'CAUSE EVEN THOUGH IT'S HARD TO ADMIT
    MISOGYNY IS HERE TO STAY
    AND WE HAVE TO WORK AROUND IT.

KERRI:
    THAT'S THE MOST PATHETIC THING I'VE EVER HEARD.
    I CAN'T BELIEVE YOU JUST CALLED IT A WITCH HUNT.

MYSTIE: It is.

KERRI:
    HAVE YOU EVEN READ THE FUCKING STATISTICS?

ALLY: Language!

MYSTIE: What statistics?

KERRI:
    THEN YOU'RE AN UNIFORMED CUNT!

ALLY/MYSTIE: Kerri!

KERRI takes out her phone and urgently searches for information that she then reads out loud.

ALLY: You can't talk like that in my house!

KERRI: No, listen to this...

    "THREE HUNDRED TWENTY-TWO THOUSAND
    AMERICAN WOMEN ARE VICTIMS OF RAPE EVERY YEAR.
    WITH NINETY-NINE PERCENT OF ALL SEXUAL
    PREDATORS WALKING THE STREET FREE AND CLEAR.
    NINETY-FOUR PERCENT OF THEIR VICTIMS WILL
    SUFFER FROM POST-TRAUMATIC STRESS."

    BUT TELL ME MORE ABOUT
    THIS POOR LITTLE MAN WHO IS SO OPPRESSED.
    SINCE FOR EVERY HUNDRED WOMEN WHO ARE
    SEXUALLY ABUSED, TWO MEN ARE FALSELY ACCUSED!

ALLY:
    OK, CALM DOWN, STOP CURSING AT ME

ALLY/MYSTIE:
    WE CAN JUST AGREE TO DISAGREE

KERRI: Fuck that.

    IF YOU KNEW ABOUT HISTORY YOU WOULDN'T SPOUT
    ALL THIS STATUS QUO BULLSHIT AGAIN AND AGAIN
    YOU'RE UNDERCUTTING A MOVEMENT THAT LIFTS

WOMEN UP AND PROTECTS THEM FROM TERRIBLE MEN
YOU SOUND LIKE MOM AND THESE SAD BABY
BOOMERS WHO THINK WE SHOULD SUFFER
'CAUSE THEY DID TOO
IT'S BAD ENOUGH HEARING THIS SHIT FROM
DEFENSIVE MEN BUT IT'S WORSE WHEN IT COMES
OUT OF YOU
'CAUSE IT LETS THEM SHAME AND HAUNT US
IT PUTS US RIGHT BACK WHERE THEY WANT US

THE REVOLUTION STILL IS IN THE EARLY STAGES,
IT'S NOT PERFECT, IT GETS MESSY
MAYBE NOT EVERY PUNISHMENT FITS EVERY CRIME
BUT INSTEAD OF WHINING AND BLAMING THE VICTIMS
WE ALL COULD STAND TOGETHER
AND WORK OUT THE NUANCES
RATHER THAN LISTENING TO BITCHES LIKE YOU
WHO ARE WASTING OUR TIME!

MYSTIE:
    OK, THAT'S ENOUGH
    LET'S HONEST ABOUT WHERE
    ALL OF THIS IS COMING FROM
    YOU CALLED US NAMES, YOU SHOUTED ABOUT FEMINISM,
    YOU SHUT US DOWN WITH YOUR SHARP TONGUE.
    BUT EVERYONE KNOWS YOUR OVER-THE-TOP ACTIVISM
    IS JUST BAGGAGE FROM WHEN WE WERE YOUNG.

ALLY:
    YOU WERE ALWAYS THE SENSITIVE ONE
    SCARED OF LIVING BEFORE WE HAD EVEN BEGUN
    SO TRUSTING OF EVERYONE
    YOU WERE ALWAYS THE SENSITIVE ONE

She tries to hug KERRI, who slips away.

ALLY/MYSIE:	
YOU WERE ALWAYS THE SENSITIVE ONE	KERRI: DON'T TOUCH ME.

CRYING IN YOUR ROOM   DON'T TOUCH ME.
  WHILE THE REST OF US
  WERE HAVING FUN

ALLY/MYSIE:
  SCARED OF MEN AND THINGS THEY HAD DONE
  YOU WERE ALWAYS THE SENSITIVE ONE

KERRI:
  IF THAT'S THE WAY YOU PERCEIVE ME,
  WHY DID YOU BOTH FUCKING LEAVE ME,
  BACK THEN WHEN NO ONE BELIEVED ME?

  MOM SAID I WAS OVER EXAGGERATING
  AND BLAMED IT ON THE DRESS THAT I WORE
  NO ONE EVER BOTHERED INVESTIGATING,
  AND KIDS AT SCHOOL CALLED ME A WHORE.
  AND WHERE THE HELL WERE YOU TWO?

MYSTIE (*gently*): Kerri.

KERRI:
  I'M GOING HOME.

She scrambles to get her things, stopping to take one last big sip from her glass.

ALLY: Kerri, come on. That was a long time ago, we were away at college. You know that.

KERRI:
  LEAVE ME ALONE, I'M DONE.

She storms out. ALLY and KERRI look at each other.

ALLY/KERRI:
  SHE WAS ALWAY THE SENSITIVE ONE.

Blackout.

END

WHAT'S YOUR WISH?

Book, Music, & Lyrics by *Thicket & Thistle*

Kyle Acheson and Sam De Roest in *What's Your Wish?* at Theatre Now's SOUND BITES 2014.

SYNOPSIS

On the night of his 16th birthday, Nicholas celebrates in their attic with his mother, sister, and his best friend Brian. The boys are left alone and they discover an old book *"WHAT'S YOUR WISH?"* that sucks them in and transports them to a magical forest called Death Forest. The boys approach a nearby house that is inhabited by an Enchantress *"SECRETS ON THE WIND"* who asks them for help. She traps them and exclaims that she needs their virgin blood to bring back her powers *"DARK SPIRIT OF THE ANCIENT SOIL!"* While the Enchantress goes out to collect the ingredients needed for her potion, the boys are advised by the Fairy in the Cage to *"MAKE A WISH"* to get them out of their situation. Upon the Enchantress' return, the boys wish to go back to the real world ten minutes ago! They are swooped back into the real world to Nicholas' attic.

PRODUCTION HISTORY

What's Your Wish?, written by Thicket & Thistle, was first performed as a 10-minute musical at The 47th Street Theater in New York, NY for Theatre Now's SOUND BITES 2014 on December 8, 2014. The production was directed by Jonathan Foster. It was produced by Thomas Morrissey, Rebecca Nell Robertson, and Stephen Bishop Seely, with associate producer, Charles Quittner. The cast was as follows:

NICK	Kyle Acheson
BRIAN	Sam De Roest
FAIRY IN A CAGE	Nyssa Duchow
ENCHANTRESS	Corley Pillsbury

The show was awarded Best Music and Actor (Sam De Roest) in that year's festival.

Then the show went through four developmental readings and productions in 2015 & 2016, expanding to a 90-minute musical into a full length. They were all directed by Jonathan Foster and produced by Sarah George. The first reading was at Access Theatre in New York. The cast was the same as listed above with the addition of Joshua Stenseth playing a new character named OLD VERN.

The second, third, and fourth productions happened at The New York International Fringe Festival in the Al Fresco division, the Michael Chekhov Festival and remounted at Access Theatre. The cast remained the same from the previous reading with the exception of the character FAIRY, played by Lindsay Zaroogian.

In December 2017, the 90-min version of the show returned to Theatre Now as part of their Alternating Rep Series in a nine performance run at the West End Theatre in New York, NY. It was produced by Tom Morrissey and Chris Giordano, and Sarah George representing Thicket & Thistle. It was directed again by Jonathan Foster with choreography by Mia Crivello, set design by Rodrigo Escalante, lighting design by David Sexton, costume design by Genevieve Beller, sound design by Jessica McIlquham, music supervision by Ellie Kahn, stage managed by Molly McCarthy, and wardrobe supervision by Ashley Benson. The cast was as follows:

NICHOLAS	Kyle Acheson
BRIAN	Sam De Roest
FAIRY	Lindsay Zaroogian
ENCHANTRESS	Corley Pillsbury
OLD VERN	Joshua Stenseth

In July 2018, the 90-min version of the show made it's Off-Broadway debut in five performance run at the Acorn Theatre on Theater Row as part of the 15th Annual New York Musical Festival. Jonathan Foster and Sarah George returned as director and producer respectively with set design by Travis George, lighting design by Kate McGee, costume design by Genevieve Beller stage managed by Erin Cohen, and general management by Simpson & Longthorne Theatrical. The cast remained the same from the previous production with the exception of the character ENCHANTRESS, played by Julianna Wheeler.

The show was nominated for Outstanding Direction (Jonathan Foster), Best Lead Actor (Joshua Stenseth), Outstanding Ensemble, and Outstanding Musical Orchestrations.

CHARACTERS

NICHOLAS WILKE — Smart, gullible, cautious, 16.

MCKENZIE WILKE — Unapologetically weird sibling of Nicholas, goth, 15.

DIANA WILKE — Single, harried, caring parent, mid-30s.

BRIAN — Down-to-earth, impulsive, Nicholas's best friend, 16.

WITCH — A powerful, power-hungry Enchantress, with long, billowing robes and a beautiful visage. Appears to be in her 30s.

FAIRY — All wings and sparkles, she is a Fairy with a rebellious streak. Appears to be about 17. A servant to the Witch, she is trapped in a cage.

NOTE: The same actor can play DIANE and WITCH and the same actor playing MCKENZIE can also play FAIRY. The character names/descriptions fit the original casting; however, all parts can be played by any gender. Rename Nicholas to Chrysalis, Brian to Bree-Ann, and Diana to Devin.

SETTING

A suburban home and a magical storybook land, the present.

MUSICAL NUMBERS

"Overture"	Instrumental
"What's Your Wish?"	Nicholas, Brian
"Secrets On The Wind"	Witch
"Dark Spirit Of The Ancient Soil"	Witch, Nicholas, Brian
"Make A Wish"	Fairy
"Dark Spirit (reprise)"	Instrumental
"Overture (reprise)"	Instrumental

AUTHORS' NOTE

When What's Your Wish was originally conceived to be a part of SOUND BITES, it was Thicket & Thistle's first collaboration. In the original production and subsequent productions, the actors were also the musicians with the acoustic palette of accordion, mandolin, flute, banjo-ukulele and guitar; using their instruments as props, playing, while singing and dancing. Using actor-musicians is not mandatory, however what is mandatory is that you have fun using DIY chutzpah and old-fashioned theatre magic to bring the world of this show to life. Adhering to a "suitcase theatre" tenet, everything used for the original production could be packed into the trunk and backseat of a car. The staging was simple in effect and we manipulated the set by using a rolling rack with two sides - a forest and an the interior of the enchantress' house. This piece is full of wit and whimsy and should not be taken too seriously!

- Thicket & Thistle

SCENE 1 - The Attic. Ten minutes to midnight. The attic of a house overlooking a forest.

Music begins - "Overture"

As the overture is played, the actors enter the space. DIANE holds a cupcake with a lit candle. She stands center, with NICHOLAS stage right and BRIAN stage left; and taking a big breath, NICHOLAS extinguishes the candle. Lights up to full.

DIANA, MCKENZIE, & BRIAN: Happy Birthday!!!

BRIAN: What'd you wish for?

NICHOLAS: Brian, I can't tell you, or it won't come true!

MCKENZIE: Do you really believe that? About wishes?

NICHOLAS: That's how wishes work, dummy.

MCKENZIE: Wishes don't work butthead!

NICHOLAS: Mom!!

DIANA: Your sister's right, Nicholas, wishes don't work. I should know. Well I will just be in the living room not wallowing in a pit of despair. Happy birthday.

She eats the cupcake and exits.

MCKENZIE: Bye Brian.

SHE blows a kiss in BRIAN's direction.

BRIAN (*shudder*): Dude, I think your sister has a crush on me.

NICHOLAS: She does that to all of my friends.

BRIAN: You have other friends?

NICHOLAS: Yes!

BRIAN: Then why aren't they at your birthday party?

NICHOLAS: Because they were all busy.

NICHOLAS and BRIAN look around the attic.

BRIAN: This attic kinda gives me the creeps.

NICHOLAS: Yeah, it's super haunted. So Brian, don't touch—

BRIAN: Woah! Check this out!

BRIAN pulls the blanket off the chest, sending dust swirling in the air.

NICHOLAS: Brian, that is literally haunted!

BRIAN opens the trunk and removes a BIG LEATHER-BOUND BOOK. HE blows dust off the cover.

BRIAN: Reeee-laaax. What do we have here? (*reading*) "To Grant Wishes." Who's Grant?

NICHOLAS: No, idiot, it's a storybook. It belonged to my grandfather.

BRIAN opens the book, which emits an eerie light. THEY read from the book.

Song begins - "What's Your Wish?"

BRIAN: Once upon a time.

NICHOLAS:
ONCE UPON A TIME...
IN DARKNESS

BRIAN: There lived a beautiful enchantress who would grant wishes to young boys. But over time the forest grew sick, and the enchantress became a witch. And some who sought her powers were never seen again.

NICHOLAS:
IN A COOL AND SHADY GLEN
AND SOME WHO SOUGHT HER POWERS WERE NEVER SEEN AGAIN

BOTH:
SHE'LL GRANT YOUR WISH UPON THE WIND TO YOU
GRANT YOUR WISH UPON THE WIND
THE EARTH WILL FABRICATE A PERFECT COMPASS ROSE FOR YOU
WHAT'S YOUR WISH?

BRIAN:
THOUGH THE PATH IS FRAUGHT WITH DANGER
THOUGH THE FEAR IS IN YOUR HEART
THOUGH THERE IS NO HOPE OF TURNING BACK
ONCE YOU START—

NICHOLAS: Dude, that sounds scary!

BRIAN: Nicholas, this could be the greatest adventure of our young lives!

NICHOLAS:
MY FRIEND, MY FRIEND,
IT'S CLEARLY JUST A LEGEND
LET'S GO. NO MORE. NO MORE.

BRIAN:
MY FRIEND, MY FRIEND
DON'T BE SO CONVINCED CAUSE YOU DON'T KNOW
AND WHAT IF IT WERE TRUE?

BRIAN: When you blew out the candle, what did you wish for?

NICHOLAS: I can't tell you or it won't come true-

BRIAN: Come on, what was it?

NICHOLAS: Alright fine! I wished for a used car something sensible like a Camry.

BRIAN: Oh my god, dude, you wasted a wish! We have to think bigger...

BRIAN:
    WE COULD WISH FOR POWER AND RICHES

NICHOLAS:
    WE COULD WISH FOR PERFECT LOVE

BRIAN:
    WE COULD WISH FOR—

NICHOLAS:
    —MORE WISHES!

BOTH:
    FOR WINGS TO WHEEL ABOUT ABOVE!

BRIAN: What's the worst that could happen?

BOTH:
    SHE'LL GRANT YOUR WISH UPON THE WIND TO YOU
    GRANT YOUR WISH UPON THE WIND
    THE EARTH WILL FABRICATE A PERFECT COMPASS ROSE
    FOR YOU
    WHAT'S YOUR WISH?

"Shhhhhhhhhh..." sound and the boys travel into the storybook.

Scene 2 - Death Forest. Lights up on BRIAN and NICHOLAS, at the door to the WITCH's shed. Vines curl around the structure, it looks weathered and neglected. In a small garden, adjacent, sprout vile, magical-looking plants and herbs. The forest is dark and forbidding.

NICHOLAS: Did we get sucked into the book?

BRIAN: Looks like it.

NICHOLAS: You got us sucked into the book. How could this get any worse?

BRIAN pulls vines away from a sign, which reads "DEATH FOREST."

NICHOLAS: Bravo Brian, you got us sent to Death Forest. Of all the things we could have done on my 16th birthday, you brought me to a Forest of Death!

BRIAN: Well I am sorry! I didn't mean to get us sucked in. If you had wished for something better than a Camry maybe we wouldn't be here at all!

NICHOLAS: Shh! What's that sound?

We hear the beginning of the WITCH's haunting song.

Song begins - "Secrets on the Wind"

WITCH:
SECRETS ON THE WIND
SKY FULL OF STARS
LISTEN, YOU CAN HEAR THEM SINGING
MELANCHOLY TUNE
DEATH COMES ALL TOO SOON.

NICHOLAS: Brian! Where are you going?

BRIAN: Maybe she knows how to get us back home!

WITCH:
SECRETS ON THE WIND
HEARTS ALL AFIRE
CRACKLING LIKE A SAPLING, FRESH CUT.
YOUTH IS BUT A RUSE
TRAGEDY'S AMUSING
WHAT HAVE I TO LOSE BUT THIS EPHEMERAL FLESH?

She ends the song softly crying.

BRIAN: What's wrong?

WITCH: Oh! I didn't see you there! How did you get in here?

NICHOLAS: Well we wanted to knock but you were singing.

BRIAN: It sounded sad.

WITCH: It's just... my enchanted forest is dying. And each moment it grows weaker... I grow... weaker...

NICHOLAS: Well if there's anything we can do...

BRIAN: I'm really strong.

NICHOLAS: And I am also... —I am a good listener.

WITCH: Well, as it happens, I am missing one ingredient for my spell that only you can provide.

BOTH: What is it?

WITCH: The blood of two virgins.

BOTH: Well—sorry. We are not virgins. I mean we have totally had you-know-what before,—well not us, but—

WITCH: Silence!

WITCH draws a long ceremonial dagger and begins her incantation.

Spiritus mali in sanguine virginis!
Spiritus mali in sanguine virginis!

Song begins - "Dark Spirit of the Ancient Soil"

WITCH:
    MY MY MY POOR LITTLE BOYS
    TREMBLING IN THE FACE OF THE
    CHOICE TO BE SAVIORS OF THE LAND
    I'LL MAKE IT AS PAINLESS AS I CAN
    DON'T FRET DON'T CRY MY POOR LITTLE BOYS
    NOBODY CAN HEAR YOUR PITIFUL
    NOISE YOUR BLOOD SMELLS SO PURE
    GRADE A VIRGIN TO THE CORE
    OH DARK SPIRIT OF THE ANCIENT SOIL

NICHOLAS & BRIAN:
    OH NO OH NO!

WITCH:
    RECEIVE THIS SACRIFICE OF BLOOD UNSPOILED

NICHOLAS & BRIAN:
    PLEASE LET US GO

WITCH:
    MY BODY WILL BURN LIKE A RIVER OF OIL
    RELEASE THESE POOR LOST BOYS

NICHOLAS & BRIAN:
    RELEASE THESE POOR LOST BOYS

WITCH:
    FROM THEIR MORTAL COILS
    OOOHHOOHH!

WITCH: Oh fiddlesticks! Somebody forgot the Moon-Kissed Soil.

    WITCH eyes FAIRY, a beautiful fairy with an ugly name.

FAIRY: Sorry.

WITCH: It's like I have to do everything myself. I'll be right back, don't go anywhere.

The WITCH exits, cackling.

Ahahaha!!

BRIAN and NICHOLAS are left alone, trapped, helpless.

NICHOLAS: We have to get out of here now! She is going to kill us!!

BRIAN: I'm sorry, this is all my fault—

FAIRY: Listen!

Song begins - "Make a Wish"

FAIRY:
WHEN LIFE HAS GOT YOU FEELING LOW,
NO ESCAPE, NOWHERE TO GO.
THE WORLD HAS GOT YOU REELIN'
THOUGH YOU'RE STUCK IN A CAGE
OUT OF LUCK? TURN THE PAGE...

AND MAKE A WISH.
MAKE A WISH AND LET YOUR WISH COME TRUE!
YOU KNOW I WISH YOU WOULDN'T BE SO BLUE
THERE'S WISHES WISHING FOR SOME WISHING TO DO
YOU ARE A WISH, AND THAT WISH, WELL IT'S YOU...
SO MAKE A WISH

The instrumental break is interrupted, when The WITCH bursts into the room, cackling evilly. The BOYS scream!

WITCH: I'm baaaack!! Ick, it smells like youthful optimism in here. Lucky for me, no one feels very youthful after a blood sacrifice! Fairy in the Cage, my theme!

The WITCH strikes up the band and begins singing her incantation, circling the boys who are trapped!

Music begins - "Dark Spirit Reprise" (underscored)

BRIAN: "No not again!!"

NICHOLAS: "Brian! If we wished ourselves into the book, maybe we can wish ourselves out!"

BRIAN: "Then wish us home!"

NICHOLAS: "I wish we were free!"

> *The music stops. The WITCH's spell is interrupted. The BOYS look at each other hopefully. Then it all resumes.*

BRIAN: It didn't work!

NICHOLAS: I already made a wish today—I must be out of wishes! Brian... YOU have to make a wish!

BRIAN: I wish we were free! Uh, I wish we were in the attic! I wish I had fifty thousand dollars" This is: ridiculous, wishes aren't real!

NICHOLAS: You weren't being sincere enough!

BRIAN: Sincerity is subjective!

NICHOLAS:
WE ARE GOING TO DIE!!

> *The WITCH finishes her incantation, moves in with her dagger.*

WITCH: Any final words?

BRIAN *(closing his eyes)*: I wish it was ten minutes ago!

> *The WITCH screams, the BOYS scream, everything swirls in chaos, sheets are thrown over their objects, and we arrive safely, back in the attic.*
>
> *Scene 3 - Back in the attic. The BOYS are breathing very hard,*

Downstage while DIANA enters, with a burning candle on top of a cupcake.

BRIAN: We are back in the attic!

NICHOLAS: Your wish worked! We made it out alive!

THE BOYS hug.

DIANA: Blow out your candle, Nicky!

The BOYS scream.

MCKENZIE: Before we die please?!

DIANA: Your sister is right. We don't have forever.

NICHOLAS: I know exactly what I'm going to wish for.

NICHOLAS extinguishes the candle. Lights out.

Music begins - "Overture (reprise)"

Actors bow, then play themselves offstage.

END

WELCOME TO RIDGINGTON

Book & Lyrics by *Jordan Silver*
Music by *Luke Steinhauer*

Kristin Serafini, Laura Shoop, Barrett Riggins, and Greg Carter in *Welcome to Ridgington* at Theatre Now's SOUND BITES 5.0

SYNOPSIS

A traditional family unit of four, Patrick (father), Karen (mother), Hailey (daughter), and Ben (son) cheerfully, absently, sing in perfect harmony *"THE RIDGINGTON PLEDGE"*. Patrick and his children participate in a call and response *"OPENING"* about their societal responsibilities ending with a call to a cleansing day. A day different than every other in the commune of Ridgington, on cleansing day, they have permission to speak the truth. After drawing sticks, Hailey begins the ritual *"GROW UP"* with the energy of a firework, relentlessly berating her family with each minor and major annoyance they cause her throughout the year. Then Patrick's reproach begins *"WHAT FOR?"* with a depressed sense of longing that transforms into violent threats towards his daughter Hailey. Now it's Karen's time to cleanse, but she refuses to participate, *"ONLY LOVE"* insisting the family doesn't need the outdated ritual, but rather only love. Karen's noncompliance causes Ben to question the ritual, *"I THINK I'M DONE"* leading into Patrick's biblical recanting of Ridgington's cleansing day *"DO WHAT I SAY"* which consequently allows the children to see the story in a new, nonsensical light. "Why don't we leave the town and try something new?"

PRODUCTION HISTORY

Welcome To Ridgington, written by Jordan Silver, and Luke Steinhauer, premiered at The Irene Diamond Stage at The Pershing Square Signature Center for Theatre Now's SOUND BITES 5.0 on May 28, 2018. The production was directed by Andrew Rasmussen with musical direction by Luke Steinhauer. It was produced by Thomas Morrissey, Chris Giordano, and Stephen Bishop Seely. The cast was as follows:

KAREN	Laura Shoop
PATRICK	Greg Carter
BEN	Barrett Riggins
HAILEY	Kristin Serafini

Laura Shoop was awarded Best Actress for the role of KAREN in that year's festival.

CHARACTERS

KAREN   A middle-aged "Stepford" housewife.

PATRICK   A suit and tie middle-aged dad.

BEN   The son and older brother.

HAILEY   The daughter and younger sister.

SETTING

The town of Ridgington is the most successful, rapidly growing commune in North America. It's cleansing day. Present day.

MUSICAL NUMBERS

Welcome To Ridgington is a musical performed as one continuous piece of music. However, the music can be broken down into the following sections:

"The Ridgington Pledge"	Company
"Opening/Ritual Oo's"	Company
"Grow Up"	Hailey

"I Love You/Ritual Oo's"	Company
"What For?"	Patrick
"Ritual Oo's (reprise)"	Patrick, Hailey, Ben
"Only Love"	Karen
"I Think I'm Done"	Company
"Do What I Say"	Company
"Rain Happens"	Company
"Finale"	Company

AUTHOR'S NOTE

Welcome to Ridgington is about questioning the unquestionable. Ridgington is technically a commune, but it represents any society with religions or rituals and how those ideas look from the untainted perspective of the youth. The traditional family in Ridgington comments on how a patriarchal society from the past remains prevalent in today's current state of affairs. The man in power, whether it be Henry Ridgington or the dad, Patrick, does not want to lose his supremacy and will hold onto it with every bone in his body. The show holds up a mirror to the face of any culture and demands us to reassess and reevaluate pervasive conventional wisdom. Are these ideas still relevant? Do they hold their weight or are they used as a means to subjugate and suppress others? A cleansing day is a special holiday in Ridgington where all families have permission to let it all out, and speak the truth, usually containing secret information or withheld aggression. This implies that on every other day of the year, everyone must smile and nod in obedience, keeping the family in agreement, which in turn makes for a happy society. Of course, to most, this idea seems far fetched, but all different ways of life appear that way unless it is your own.

- Jordan Silver

Lights up on a family. PATRICK, a suit and tie middle-aged dad. KAREN, a middle-aged Stepford housewife. BEN, the son and brother. HAILEY, the daughter and younger sister.

Music begins - "The Ridgington Pledge"

ALL:
    WE GIVE OUR THANKS TO RIDGINGTON,
    A FLOURISHING COMMUNITY.
    BUILT ON EQUAL SHARE OF WEALTH
    AND UNITY OF FAMILY.
    IF YOU FOLLOW FUNDAMENTAL RULES AND REGULATIONS,
    PROVIDED IN RETURN IS FOOD AND SHELTER.
    RIDGINGTON, OH RIDGINGTON
    WE GIVE OUR THANKS TO YOU!

Music transitions into - "Opening"

PATRICK:
    WHY DO WE BRUSH OUR TEETH?

BEN & HAILEY:
    TO KEEP THEM CLEAN.

PATRICK:
    WHY DO WE GO TO SLEEP?

BEN & HAILEY:
    TO ENERGIZE.

PATRICK:
    WHY ARE WE POLITE?

BEN & HAILEY:
    TO PROTECT OUR LIES.

PATRICK & KAREN:
    BUT ONCE A YEAR IN RIDGINGTON WE CELEBRATE

ALL:
    WHAT MAKES US GREAT.

BEN & HAILEY:
    A CLEANSING DAY
    EACH FAMILY
    SPEAKS THE TRUTH TODAY.

PATRICK: Better than Christmas!

ALL:
    A CLEANSING DAY
    EACH FAMILY
    SPEAKS THE TRUTH TODAY.

Patrick is passing around a gauntlet for each person to take their stick. The shortest stick goes last, the longest goes first.

PATRICK: What makes today different than any other?

HAILEY: We let it all out!

BEN: Damn right!

KAREN: Language, Ben.

PATRICK: Control your feelings before they control you. Except today. Everyone has their stick and is now comparing size.

HAILEY: One.

PATRICK: Two.

KAREN: Three.

BEN: I'm always last.

He sings:

IT'S NOT YOUR TYPICAL MORNING.
YOU WON'T GET ANY WARNING.

ALL:

SO EXPECT THE TRUTH
AND NOTHING LESS
AND NOW IT'S OUR TIME TO CONFESS
WHAT WE PENT UP ALL YEAR.

BEN:

A CLEANSING DAY
EACH FAMILY
SPEAKS THE TRUTH TODAY.

Patrick prepares the blue paint and smears it on Hailey's mouth.

Music transitions into - "Ritual Oo's"

ALL:

OOOO, OOOO, OOO...

KAREN *(to HAILEY)*: Now honey, remember that we love you.

BEN: We're strong, we can take it.

PATRICK: That's my boy!

Music transitions into - "Grow Up"

HAILEY:

MOM THAT WAS REALLY REALLY NICE
BUT SO AMICABLE IT COULD ALMOST KILL ME.

I've been studying for the SAT can you tell? Amicable.

WHERE DO I EVEN WANNA START?
BEN, YOUR OBSESSION WITH CALL OF DUTY IS ALMOST
AS EMBARRASSING AS THE WAY THAT YOU DRESS.
ABERCROMBIE AND VIDEO GAMES?

PEEING ON THE TOILET SEAT IS NEVER OK.

BEN: You don't have a penis, you don't know what it's like!

HAILEY: Wipe it up, it's not that hard.

WHEN ARE YOU GONNA GROW UP?
I'M SUPPOSED TO BE THE YOUNGER SIBLING.
WHEN AM I GONNA GROW UP AND GET RID OF YOU?
NOW ON TO YOU...

PATRICK: Alright, let's go.

HAILEY:
DAD YOU GAINED SO MUCH WEIGHT.
CAN YOU AT LEAST PRETEND
TO LOOK HALFWAY MEDIOCRE?
WHERE DO YOU GO WHEN YOU SAY
YOU'RE GOING TO THE GYM?

PATRICK: What are you implying? Say it!

HAILEY:
I THINK THAT I'VE OUTGROWN
YOUR CONDESCENDING TONE.
YOU'RE SO CLICHE, GETTING FAT
AND TALKIN BOUT THE GOOD 'OL DAYS.

And that's the truth.

The family wipes HAILEY mouth's clean with a towel.

Music transitions into - "I Love You / Ritual Oo's"

ALL:
I LOVE YOU.
I LOVE YOU.
THAT'S WHY WE SPEAK THE TRUTH.

PATRICK: Don't you feel better?

HAILEY: I think so!

> *HAILEY prepares the blue paint and smears it on PATRICK's mouth.*

ALL:
OOOO, OOOO, OOO...

BEN: Alright, Dad. Let's go.

> *Song begins - "What For"*

PATRICK:
LET'S START WITH THE LOVE OF MY LIFE KAREN.
I REMEMBER THE DAY THAT WE MET
ON THE FOURTH OF JULY
YOU WERE HOLDING A SPARKLER
AND OH BOY YOU WERE SPARKLING BRIGHT!

KAREN: That was lovely, wasn't it?

PATRICK:
IT'S SAD TO THINK THE FLAME HAS GONE
AND NOW YOU SEEM DISTANT AND DARK
I WORK ALL DAY AND I THINK WHAT FOR?

KAREN: I'll always love you.

> *He turns to BEN.*

PATRICK:
BEN, YOU'RE MY FAVORITE CHILD.
YOU HAVE SO MUCH POTENTIAL, I WISH THAT YOU
WOULD USE IT
HAILEY'S RIGHT, PUT THE PLAYSTATION DOWN,
PUT ON A BUTTON DOWN.

PATRICK:
>YOU HAVE SO MUCH POTENTIAL
>I WISH THAT YOU WOULD USE IT

BEN: I want to make you proud.

>HAILEY,

HAILEY: Oh god...

PATRICK:
>OH HAILEY,
>I REMEMBER WHEN YOU WERE A LITTLE GIRL
>AND NOW YOU'RE SNEAKING AROUND THE HOUSE
>WITH YOUR BOYFRIEND

>You think I don't have eyes?

>IF YOU DO IT AGAIN , I'LL KILL YOU AND YOUR FRIEND!

KAREN (*scolding*): Patrick!

PATRICK:
>YOU LOVE YOUR MOTHER MORE THAN ME
>BUT CAN'T YOU SEE I LOVE DIFFERENTLY.
>I WORK ALL DAY AND I THINK WHAT FOR...

>And that's the truth.

>*BEN & HAILEY wipe PATRICK's mouth clean with a towel.*

>*Music transitions into - "I Love You (reprise)"*

ALL EXCEPT KAREN:
>I LOVE YOU.
>I LOVE YOU.

BEN: Mom?

PATRICK: Honey... let's do it again.

KAREN: No.

Music transitions into - "Only Love"

She sings:

I'VE NOTHING BAD TO SAY.
THERE'S NO NEED FOR ME TO DO SO.
ONLY LOVE. I WANT ONLY LOVE.

BEN: What's she doing?

KAREN:
NO MATTER WHAT THE DAY,
I KNOW WE'LL BE OKAY
IF WE COME BACK TO ONLY LOVE.
WHEN THERE'S SO MUCH HATE OUTSIDE OUR TOWN,
WE SHOULD FIND A WAY I KNOW THERE IS A WAY
TO ONLY LOVE, I WANT ONLY LOVE.

PATRICK: No, no, no, no.

KAREN: That's the truth.

BEN: You're doing it wrong!

HAILEY: If I did it, we all have to!

PATRICK: You'll be so pent up, one day you'll explode!

KAREN:
WHEN I HAVE PAST, WHEN I AM GONE,
WHEN MY BONES AND BRAIN SHAVE FAILED ME
AND I DON'T KNOW WHAT'S GOIN' ON,
I WANT ONLY LOVE. ONLY LOVE.

PATRICK: Forget it. Ben, it's your turn.

Music transitions into - "I Think I'm Done"

BEN:
    I THINK I'M DONE.

PATRICK:
    YOU CAN'T KEEP IT PENT UP.

BEN:
    NO, I KNOW I'M DONE.

KAREN:
    WE CAN'T ALWAYS DO THINGS
    THE WAY THAT YOU LIKE.

PATRICK: It's not the way I like. It's the way it is.

HAILEY:
    IF YOU DON'T LIKE IT, THEN WHY DO WE DO IT?

PATRICK:
    THERE ARE MANY THINGS IN LIFE, I DON'T ENJOY.

KAREN:
    THIS IS NOT THE ONLY WAY.

HAILEY:
    THEN TELL US A BETTER WAY.

KAREN: This day doesn't make me feel any better. It never did.

BEN:
    HEARING THESE AWFUL THINGS
    I CAN'T DO IT ANYMORE.

HAILEY:
    SHOULD WE BE THIS HONEST ALL THE TIME?

BEN:
> THAT'S WHAT THEY DO EVERYWHERE ELSE, RIGHT?

HAILEY: Is that true?

PATRICK:
> OUR COMMUNITY WORKS ON A SYSTEM OF NICETIES.
> IF WE CAN'T UPHOLD THEM,
> THEN WHERE DO WE BELONG?

Music transitions into - "Do What I Say"

BEN: In the year of 1892, a man by the name of Henry Ridgington saved our small town from poverty, disease, and near extinction.

PATRICK:
> IF YOU DO WHAT I SAY
> THEN I'LL FIX THE DROUGHT.
> IF YOU DO WHAT I SAY
> THEN I'LL FIX YOUR HOUSE.
> IF YOU DO WHAT I SAY
> THEN I'LL FIX THE TOWN.
> DO WHAT I SAY DO WHAT I SAY.

KAREN: And they did what he said. One week later, the rain poured down.

ALL:
> DON'T FORGET WHERE YOU CAME FROM.
> A TOWN THAT WAS RUBBLE AND RUN DOWN.

PATRICK: Now, the crops were thriving and the people were thankful. Mr. Ridgington had their trust, so he gave them simple instructions like what to wear and what to eat and exactly how to cook their meat.

> FOLLOW THE LAWS I'VE WRITTEN.
> IF YOU TURN AWAY
> YOU'LL PLAGUE THE TOWN

AND LOSE WHAT LITTLE LUCK YOU'VE FOUND
SO DO WHAT I SAY!

A cleansing day is one of the laws. The rain represents our honesty. It should only pour once a year to cleanse our sinful thoughts.

BEN: I haven't heard this story in years. It feels different.

HAILEY: It could've just rained because it was gonna rain anyway.

Music transitions into - "Rain Happens"

BEN:
YEAH. RAIN HAPPENS. IT'S PRETTY STANDARD.

PATRICK: Henry Ridgington was a prophet.

HAILEY: Or he was lucky.

KAREN: Hailey!

PATRICK: Even discussing this

He sings:

WE COULD PLAGUE THE TOWN
PUTTING EVERYONE IN DANGER.

KAREN:
WE STILL NEED TO BE UPHOLD THE LAW.

PATRICK: See what you did?

KAREN: We have a good life here, I just want to make it better.

She sings:

I WOULD NEVER BETRAY.

PATRICK: For how else should we act? Look at the world around us. Look how they communicate. War, conflict, and bloodshed. When we follow the rules, the rules of our commune, we live in peace and harmony.

HAILEY: No we don't.

KAREN: The grass is always greener, Hailey. Trust me.

PATRICK: If we don't uphold this tradition, then what about the others? We can't just pick and choose which rules apply.

BEN: Why not?

Music transitions into - "Finale"

HAILEY & BEN:
    WHY DO WE HOLD OUR TONGUE?

PATRICK:
    BECAUSE I SAY.
    HAILLEY & BEN:
    WHY DO WE LISTEN?

PATRICK:
    BECAUSE I SAY.

Patrick exits and Karen runs after him.

See what you did?!

KAREN:
    I WOULD NEVER BETRAY!

HAILEY & BEN:
    WHY DON'T WE LEAVE THE TOWN
    AND TRY SOMETHING NEW?

END

THE SOUND BITES FESTIVAL OF 10-MINUTE MUSICALS 2013 TO 2019 PRODUCED BY THEATRE NOW

SOUND BITES 2013
Monday December 9, 2013
The 47th Street Theatre, NYC

SLAM!
Book and Lyrics by Danielle Trzcinski, Music by Jonathon Lynch

THE GIVER
Book and Lyrics by Nathan Christensen, Music by Scott Murphy

JEALOUS HUSBAND RETURNS IN FORM OF PARROT
Book and Lyrics by Nathan Brisby, Music by Matt Patrick Walsh

SOME PLACE LIKE HOME
Book, Music & Lyrics by Adam Gwon

JUICE: BASED ON THE O.J. SIMPSON TRIAL
Book & Lyrics by Patricia "Bebe" McGarry, Music by Gabe Greene

A RELATIVE RELATIONSHIP
Book, Music, & Lyrics by Timothy Huang

FINDING THE WORDS
Book & Lyrics by Chris Critelli, Music by Andy Roninson

THE CHARM
Book & Lyrics by Christiana Cole, Music by David Shenton

THE OEDIPUS PROJECT: ANTIGONE
Music & Lyrics by Kyle C. Norris

SINGING DIXIE: A COUNTRY JUKEBOX MUSICAL
Written and Produced by Caitlin Gallo

SOUND BITES 2014
Monday December 8, 2014
The 47th Street Theatre, NYC

AVAC MEMORIES
Book & Lyrics by John Herin, Music by Frederick Alden Terry

COOKIE SOIREE: A SWEET NEW MUSICAL SHORT
Book & Lyrics by Justin Anthony Long, Music by Ge Enrique,
Concept by Jonny Lee Jr.

DUST
Book & Lyrics by Maggie Herskowitz, Music by Douglas Makuta

GILGAMESH & THE MOSQUITO
Book & Lyrics by Sam Chanse, Music by Bob Kelly

GRINDR! THE MUSICAL
Book by Bryce Cutler, Music & Lyrics by Jacob Tischler

PELLETS, CHERRIES, AND LIES: THE PAC MAN STORY
Book, Music, & Lyrics by Erik Przytulski

TAKE ME AMERICA
Book & Lyrics by Bill Nabel, Music by Bob Christianson

THE ANSWERING MACHINE
Book & Lyrics by Kevin Hammonds, Music by Andy Roninson

THE BOY, THE KING, AND THE FLOWER
Book & Lyrics by Maggie Herskowitz, Music by Neil Douglas Reilly

WHAT'S YOUR WISH
Book, Music, & Lyrics by Thicket & Thistle

SOUND BITES 3.0
Monday January 18, 2016
The 47th Street Theatre, NYC

A CAPPELLA LOVE
Book by Mark Browning Milner, Lorrie Kole & Nelson Kole, Music by Nelson Kole, Lyrics by Mark Browning Milner

BAKED GOODS
Book by Charles Cohen, Music by Helen Park, Lyrics by Christyn Budzyna,

BURNING UP
Book by Pamela Weiler Grayson and Rick Bassett, Music by Rick Bassett, Lyrics by Pamela Weiler Grayson

FICTITIOUS
Book, Music & Lyrics by Tom Hyndman & Paul Cozby

GORGONZOLA: A CAUTIONARY SICILIAN TALE
Book & Lyrics by Gregory Bonsignore, Music by Nolan Livesay

HOUDIN
Book, Music, & Lyrics by Marcus Pelegrin

ON YOUR MARK!
Book & Lyrics by Danny K. Bernstein, Music by Aaron Kenny

THE HIPSTER SISTER
Book, Music, & Lyrics by Andy Roninson

TOO MUCH COFFEE MAN OPERA
Book by Shannon Wheeler, Libretto by Shannon Wheeler and Damian Willcox, Music by Daniel Steven Crafts

WE HAVE APPLES
Biik, Music, & Lyrics by Rachel Griffin with additional Music by Aron Accurso

SOUND BITES 4.0
Monday May 29, 2017
The Irene Diamond Stage, The Pershing Square Signature Center, NYC

A MOST AVERAGE MUSICAL
Book & Lyrics by Jonathan Keebler, Music by Bob Kelly

CONNECTED
Book, Music, & Lyrics by Alanya Bridge

EXPRESS (1946)
Book, Music, & Lyrics by Janine McGuire & Arri Lawton Simon

FRANKLIN PIERCE: DRAGON SLAYER
Book & Lyrics by Preston Max Allen, Music by Will Buck

HAPPENSTANCE
Created by Caitlin Gallo & Jimmy Burgio

SUPERHOTS!
Book & Lyrics by Blair Bodine, Book & Music by Joel Esher

THE FACEBOOK FIGHTER
Book, Music, & Lyrics by Chris Kerrigan

THE MEDIUM...THE MUSIC...AND ME!
Book, Music, & Lyrics by DonnaD Lipari

THE POUND: A MUSICAL FOR THE DOGS
Book, Music & Lyrics by Phil Darg and Julie Ana Rayne

THE WILD & WONDERFUL WHITES OF WEST VIRGINIA
Book & Lyrics by Justin Anthony Long, Music by Ge Enrique

SOUND BITES 5.0
Monday May 18, 2018
The Irene Diamond Stage, The Pershing Square Signature Center, NYC

BYSTANDER
Book & Lyrics by Ed Levy, Music by Eric Grunin

COOKING FOR TWO
Book & Lyrics by Charlie O'Leary, Music by Karl Hinze

DEAD FLOWERS
Book, Music, & Lyrics by Michael Finke

DINOSAUR
Book, Music, & Lyrics by Zach Spound

END OF THE LINE
Book by Howard Ho, Lyrics by Chris Edgar, Music by Kristen Rea

HOSPITAL KIDS
Book & Lyrics by Lisa Mongillo, Music by Jake Chapman

JABEZ AND THE P.P. GANG
Book, Music, & Lyrics by Tom Hyndman

RUN THIS TOWN
Book & Lyrics by Cindy Sideris, Music by Assaf Gleizner

THE ALMOST IN-LAWS
Book & Lyrics by Greg Edwards, Music by Andy Roninson

WELCOME TO RIDGINGTON
Book & Lyrics by Jordan Silver, Music by Luke Steinhauer

SOUND BITES 6.0
April 2, 2019
Merkin Hall at Kaufman Music Center, NYC

ANT AND GRASSHOPPER
Book & Lyrics by A.J. Freeman, Music by Dimitri Landrain

BEHIND THE BAR
Book & Lyrics by Audrey Martells, Music by Audrey Martells & Etienne Stadwijk

BITTERSWEET LULLABY
Book by Will Lacker, Music & Lyrics by Dylan Glatthorn

BLEEDING KANSAS
Book by Anderson Cook, Music & Lyrics by Ben Lapidus & Amanda D'Archangelis

BOOK LOVERS
Book & Lyrics by Talaura Harms, Music by Jonathan Bauerfeld

EIGHTH GRADE PRESIDENT
Book & Lyrics by Jacey Powers, Music & Lyrics by Ashkon Davaran

GOLEM OWNED A TROPICAL SMOOTHIE
Book, Music, & Lyrics by Ethan Crystal and Garrett Poladian

JACK & JILL
Book & Lyrics by Zackry Childers, Music by Patrick Thompson

MAYA & ME
Book & Music by Cheeyang Ng, Book & Lyrics by Kathy Ng

THE ONLY THING THAT MATTERS
Book, Music, & Lyrics by Chris Kerrigan

RIGHTS AND PERMISSIONS

For professional/stock, amateur and educational live performance rights for any of these titles, please contact Music Theatre International (MTI). For more information please visit www.mtishows.com, email licensing@mtishows.com or call (212) 541-4684. All other rights in and to the musical stage plays appearing in this volume, under copyright and otherwise, are reserved by the respective authors thereof.

All titles are reprinted with permission of the authors. All Rights Reserved.

A RELATIVE RELATIONSHIP © 2009 by Timothy Huang.

A MOST AVERAGE MUSICAL © 2015 by Talia Berger, Jonathan Keebler and Bob Kelly.

ANT AND GRASSHOPPER © 2019 by A.J. Freeman and Dimitri Landrain.

BITTERSWEET LULLABY © 2019 by Will Lacker and Dylan Glatthorn.

BOOK LOVERS © 2018 by Talaura Harms and Jonathan Bauerfeld.

BYSTANDER © 2017 by Eric Grunin and Ed Levy.

COOKIE SOIREE © 2020 by Justin Anthony Long.

COOKING FOR TWO © 2014 by Karl Hinze and Charlie O'Leary.

DEAD FLOWERS © 2018 by Michael Finke.

DINOSAUR © 2018 by Zach Spound.

END OF THE LINE © 2015 by Howard Ho, Chris Edgar, and Kristen Rea.

FRANKLIN PIERCE: DRAGON SLAYER © 2017 by Preston Max Allen and Will Buck.

FINDING THE WORDS © 2013 by Andy Roninson and Chris Critelli.

ON YOUR MARK! © 2016 by Danny K. Bernstein and Aaron Kenny.

PELLETS, CHERRIES, AND LIES: THE PAC MAN STORY © 2014 by Erik Przytulski.

RUN THIS TOWN © 2019 by Assaf Gleizner and Cindy Sideris.

SUPERHOTS! © 2016 Blair Bodine and Joel Esher.

THE ALMOST IN-LAWS © 2015 by Greg Edwards and Andy Roninson.

THE ANSWERING MACHINE © 2014 by Kevin Hammonds and Andy Roninson.

THE CHARM © 2013 by Christiana Cole and David Shenton.

THE FACEBOOK FIGHTER © 2017 by Chris Kerrigan.

THE HIPSTER SISTER © 2015 by Andy Roninson.

THE ONLY THING THAT MATTERS © 2019 by Chris Kerrigan.

WELCOME TO RIDGINGTON © 2018 by Jordan Silver and Luke Steinhauer.

WHAT'S YOUR WISH? © 2017 by Thicket & Thistle.

CONTRIBUTORS

PRESTON MAX ALLEN is a playwright, composer, and lyricist whose work has been performed at the New Amsterdam Theatre, Signature Theatre, Lincoln Center, Chautauqua Institution, The PIT, Joe's Pub, Musical Theatre Factory, and Feinstein's/54 Below. He conceived and wrote the book, music, and lyrics for *We Are The Tigers* (Off-Broadway; Theatre 80), *Never Better, Agent 355* (co-book/dramaturgy by Jessica Kahkoska), and *Carrie 2: The Rage, An Unauthorized Musical Parody* (Jeff Nominee, Best Musical). Preston is an LA Ovation winner for Best Lyrics/Composition (*We Are The Tigers*), member of the Ars Nova Play Group (2019/2020), and an alumni of the BMI Musical Theatre Workshop. @prestonmaxallen

JONATHAN BAUERFELD is a New York based musical theater composer, orchestrator, and music director. Selected credits: INTERNATIONAL: *Legacy: The Book of Names* (Composer, Edinburgh Fringe); *Limbo: The Twelve* (Composer, Edinburgh Fringe). OFF-BROADWAY: *If Sand Were Stone* (Arranger/Orchestrator, NYMF); *The Pout-Pout Fish* (Music Director/Arranger, New Victory Theater); *Single Rider* (Music Director/Orchestrator, The Player's Theater). CHICAGO: *Short Shakespeare! The Comedy of Errors* (Composer, Chicago Shakespeare Theater). Graduate of Northwestern University, and a proud member of Advanced BMI Musical Theatre Workshop and Theatre Now's Musical Writer Lab. www.jonathanbauerfeld.com.

WILL BUCK is a composer, lyricist, and pianist. His musical *Only Anne* (book and lyrics by John Dietrich) was featured in Goodspeed Opera House's Festival of New Musicals in January 2016. His short piece, *Franklin Pierce: Dragon Slayer* (written with Preston Max Allen), was featured in the 2017 SOUND BITES Festival in New York and 2018's City Theatre Summer Shorts in Miami, where it was a finalist for the National Award for Short Playwriting. Other writing credits include: *Toybox* (with Teresa Lotz), *Go* (with Cory Conley), and the upcoming *Larry And Larry And Me* (with Deb Poppel), *Nureyev* (with Dietrich) and *Powerless*. He is an alumnus of Northwestern University and the NYU Musical Theatre Graduate Writing Program, and is a current member of the BMI Workshop. www.willbuck.com

TALIA BERGER is an LA-based writer and director. Talia studied film at Pennsylvania State University where she directed and produced her senior thesis film: *A Most Average Musical* (with Bob Kelly and Jonathan Keebler). Talia's directing credits include: *High School Musical*, *Reefer Madness*, *In the Heights*, *Pride and Prejudice*, *The Phantom Tollbooth* and *Urinetown*. Talia directed the staged production of *A Most Average Musical* for Theatre Now's SOUND BITES 4.0 in the summer of 2017. Since graduating, Talia has worked in film and television in both New York and Los Angeles. Her television credits include: *Madam Secretary* (CBS), *Insecure* (HBO), *Lady Dynamite* (Netflix), and *Baskets* (FX). Talia is a member of IATSE Local 871, currently working as a writer's assistant on HBO Max's *Doom Patrol*.

DANNY K. BERNSTEIN is an award-winning composer/lyricist, director, music director and pianist. His music and lyrics have been heard Off-Broadway, Feinstein's 54 Below, Green Room 42, Club Cumming, Prohibition, and all over New York City. NYC: Far From Canterbury (Book, Music, Lyrics) - Outstanding Overall Musical, 2015 New York International Fringe Festival, The Bishops (Book, Music, Lyrics), Danny has Friends! At The Green Room 42 (Music, Lyrics), Procrasticomposer (Music, Lyrics) Danny K Bernstein in Concert at 54 Below (Music, Lyrics). TV: Broadway At The White House. 2019 and 2017 Jonathan Larson Award Finalist, 2014 Winner, New Voices Project, New Musical Inc., through Walt Disney Imagineering, Los Angeles. Proud member of ASCAP and the BMI Advanced Musical Theatre Workshop.

BLAIR BODINE is a lyricist, performing songwriter and teaching artist. Recipient of the Grand Prize for Lyric Writing from *American Songwriter Magazine*, Blair tours nationally, performing her storytelling songs at venues such as Lincoln Center, World Cafe Live, and Nashville's Bluebird Cafe. She is the winner of the Falcon Ridge Folk Festival, and a songwriting finalist in the Telluride Bluegrass Festival and NewSong Music Competition. Blair's musical theater work has been developed at BMI Lehman Engel Musical Theatre Workshop, Theatre Now (SOUND BITES Festival) and Dixon Place (Puffin Foundation). B.A. Columbia University.

CHRISTIANA COLE (They/Them) is a writer, composer, performer, and teacher. Credits: *Bombshell Baby* (book/lyrics/music with Rachel

Felstein and Matthew Anchel), a WW2 epic about a drag queen who fights Nazis, produced at Ensemble Studio Theatre; *Make the Earth Great* (book/lyrics, with composer Rona Siddiqui) at the Prospect Theater Lab; and lyrics for a slew of cute children's shows: *Peanut Butter and Cupcake, Sparkle Spa, The Frog Prince,* and many more. Christiana is an experienced book consultant. They served as dramaturg on Christopher Cerrone's opera *Invisible Cities* (nominated for the Pulitzer Prize). Member: BMI Workshop, Ring of Keys, Maestra, Dramatists Guild.

CHRIS CRITELLI resides in New York City, where he balances his time between acting, whether it's voicing cartoons or getting beat up by superheroes, writing all kinds of stuff, and drawing, where he's just wrapped up illustrating his second book - a sequel compendium of political limericks, 'Trumpericks 2', available through Amazon!

CHRIS EDGAR is a composer and songwriter writing music for film, theater, TV, and digital series. He has scored award-winning films, including *Ghost in the Gun*, which won numerous film festival awards for Best Original Score; the movie musical *The Breakout: A Rock Opera*; and the animated musical *Steve's Quest*, which won numerous awards including the International Academy of Web Television's Best Animated Series Award and the Best Original Score Award at the Hollyweb festival. He has also toured as a drummer, and worked as an orchestrator, with signed recording artists. Last and probably least, he is an attorney who specializes in commercial litigation and entertainment law, although he is in the process of leaving that behind to fully focus on music.

GREG EDWARDS wrote the script for *Application Pending* (Off-Broadway, Drama Desk nomination) and *Craving for Travel* (Off-Broadway); lyrics for *Neurosis* (Off-Broadway), and book and lyrics for *Evelyn Shaffer and the Chance of a Lifetime* (Samuel French OOB Festival winner, City Theatre National Award for Short Playwriting, Take a Ten Podcast). Greg's essays appear in Avidly (LA Review of Books) and McSweeney's, and his game *Jessica Plunkenstein and the Dusseldorf Conspiracy* (NYT "Best Adventure Game of the Year") was published by PC Gamer UK. Greg is an alumnus of Yale (Phi Beta Kappa), the BMI Workshop (Harrington Award), and the Dramatists Guild Fellows. www.greged.com

GE ENRIQUE (They/Them) is a New York based actor, singer, writer, composer, music director, and piano bar entertainer, as well as a connoisseur of all things baked and an expert in cookies. Their favorite are, of course, Samoas. Ge has written music for three 10-minute musical performances with Justin Anthony Long: *Cookie Soirée* (Winner of the 2012 Ken Davenport 10-minute play/musical competition, 2014 Theatre Now's SOUND BITES Audience Choice Award), *Jake and Lindsay* (Ken Davenport 10-minute musical finalist), and the opening number to a concept of *The Wild and Wonderful Whites of West Virginia* (2017 SOUND BITES Audience Choice Award). They also won Outstanding Music at the 2008 Midtown International Theatre Festival for their additional music to *Twist: The Musical* (Book and lyrics by Gila Sand, Music by Paul Leschen). You can find more info about Ge on their website: www.geenrique.com

JOEL ESHER is a NYC-Based Music Theater Writer and Educator. Off-Broadway: *PharmaBro, an American Douchical*! (Music/Additional Lyrics). *Folk Wandering* (Music/Additional Lyrics). NYC: *Joey and Ron* (Music/Lyrics), *Bagels from Benny, Sammy Spider* (Music) *Superhots!* (Book/Music). Music Supervisor/podcast songwriter for the Story Pirates. Joel's work has been developed at: Goodspeed Musicals, The Johnny Mercer Songwriter Project, Fresh Ground Pepper BRB, Music Theater Factory, BMI-Advanced Writing Program. B.M, Northwestern. Educational Partnerships: Disney Theatrical Group, Carnegie Hall, Trinity Wall Street, Metropolitan Opera Guild, Dreamyard Project, Little Orchestra Society, Boston Lyric Opera.

MICHAEL FINKE is an award-winning New York based musical theatre writer. He's had his work performed at Lincoln Center, Feinstein's/54 Below, Joe's Pub, the Christmas Day telecast on ABC, the Bowery Poetry Club, and more. He's written the book, music and lyrics for musicals such as *Reporting Live, Caroline and George, Surrounded By the Water, Powerline Road,* and the musical short *Dead Flowers*. Michael's a winner of the New Voices Project with Disney Imagineering and New Musicals Inc. and is a proud member of ASCAP and the Dramatist Guild.

A. J. FREEMAN is a writer, director, and performer originally from Los Angeles and now based in New York. She is a lyricist in the BMI Lehman Engel Musical Theatre Workshop, and a cabaret performer, championing brilliant but forgotten music of the 1920s and '30s. She has worked for over 12 years in educational theatre, directing dozens of full scale productions, and running her own literacy-based musical theatre program for low income students in schools all over Los Angeles. Through this program, *The Troupe*, thousands of children received free reading books. *The Troupe*'s free theatre workshops and assemblies inspired students from all backgrounds to use their gifts and talents through visual and performing arts.

DYLAN GLATTHORN is a Brooklyn based composer & lyricist. His music has been described by the New York Times as "assured" with the "steaminess and drive of Janacek" and the "harmonic allure" of Debussy. Original musicals include: *Edison, Republic, Bittersweet Lullaby*, and *The Way It Goes*. Co-composer and arranger for Diana DeGarmo's album *GEMINI*. Music director/arranger for Alexa Green's *So Good* (released on Broadway Records, named "Best New Solo Recording of 2016" by Broadwayworld.com). He has written music for dozens of critically-acclaimed and award-winning films, as well as for world-renowned brands like Nickelodeon, Oakley, Alessi, Red Bull, and PBS. He is the recipient of the 2019 New Hampshire Theatre Award for Best Sound Design, the Clive Davis Award for Excellence in Music in Film, Best Original Score at First Run Film Festival, and a two-time recipient of the Alan Menken Award. Dylan is a proud member of both ASCAP and The Dramatists Guild of America, Inc. dylanglatthorn.com

ASSAF GLEIZNER was born and raised in Israel and has been working as a composer, musical director, orchestrator, and arranger both in NYC and around the world for the past ten years. Select credits include: Broadway: Stephen Schwartz 70th Birthday Concert- Featuring Ben Platt, Renee Fleming, Lindsey Mendez, & Andrew Lippa (Hudson Theater)- Orchestrator, Arranger. Arts For Autism- Featuring Kelli O'Hara, Julia Murney, & Christopher Jackson (Gershwin Theater)- Orchestrator, Arranger. Off-Broadway: *Friends the Musical Parody*)- Composer, Orchestrator. *90210! The Musical*- Composer, Orchestrator. *Full House* Musical Parody- MD, Orchestrator. Regional: The Swingaroos (Florida Studio Theater)- Composer, MD. Other: *The Astonishing Times of Timothy Cratchit* (The Workshop Theatre, NYC)- Cast Recording Featuring Adam Kaplan & Emily Skeggs. *You're the Pest:* The Web Series- Composer, Music Supervisor. Assaf is also a member of the BMI Lehman Engel Musical Theatre Workshop.

ERIC GRUNIN is a composer, lyricist, and book writer. Recent work includes full-length musicals Brooke Astor's Last Affair (Music; Chicago Musical Theater Festival, 2019; Emerging Artists Theater, 2013) and Our Woman, Frank Thompson (Music & Lyrics; Musical Theater Factory/Playwrights Horizons Downtown, 2017). Also music for short musicals Bystander (Sound Bites 2018, winner "Best Music"; Hudson Guild, 2017, winner "Best Short Musical") and We're Still Here (Lincoln Center, 2019). Also book for Dybbuk of the Opera (Lincoln Center, 2019) and RansomWHERE? (Lincoln Center, 2017). He has contributed songs to MuseMatch (Feinstein's/54 Below, 2018), and The Resistance Cabaret (The Tank, 2016 & 2017); blogged for Ryan Scott Oliver's CrazyTown; and reviewed for TheaterScene. He is an alumnus of the BMI Musical Theater Workshop, and holds a Doctorate in Composition from Juilliard.

KEVIN HAMMONDS is a two-time winner of the BMI Jerry Harrington Award for Outstanding Creative Achievement (2015-Lyricist; 2017-Librettist). Most recently, his musical with composer Kristin Bair, *Up and Away*, premiered at Pittsburgh CLO Cabaret Theater where it enjoyed a remarkable 16-week run. It then had its west coast premiere in Portland, Oregon at the Broadway Rose Theatre. Previously, he and composer Charles Miller had a successful run of their musical *When Midnight Strikes* at Upstairs at the Gatehouse in London (original cast recording available on iTunes). Their musical *Brenda Bly: Teen Detective* received critical acclaim at London's Bridewell Theatre, and was published by Samuel French. His other musicals with Charles Miller - *When Midnight Strikes*, *No One in the World*, *Hope* and *Mr. Christmas* have been published by Rodgers & Hammerstein UK. The same four musicals have been translated into German and published by Gallissas Theaterverlag. His short musical *The Answering Machine* (music by Andy Roninson) won "Best Musical" and "Best Lyrics" at the Theatre Now's 2nd Annual SOUND BITES 10-Minute Musical Theatre Festival. Kevin is a member of the BMI Lehman Engel Musical Theatre Advanced Workshop.

TALAURA HARMS is a New York City based writer and actor. As a writer, her work has appeared at ESPA Detention and Across A Crowded Room at NYPL Performing Arts, and in print in "105 Five Minute Plays." As an actor, she has performed in readings, workshops, and productions with Primary Stages, The Pearl, Ensemble Studio Theatre, The Lark, Stable Cable, among others. She is the Playbill.com Vault Manager and a BMI Lehman Engel Musical Theatre Workshop lyricist. Proud member AEA and Dramatists Guild. www.talauraharms.com

KARL HINZE is a composer and playwright in NYC. He has been a member of the BMI Workshop since 2013, and his original musical *210 Amlent Avenue* with playwright Becky Goldberg was an Official Selection of the Next Link Project at the New York Musical Festival. His play *Prophesy* premiered at the 2018 Fresh Fruit Festival and won awards for best acting, production, and direction. Other collaborations include *Are They Edible?*, an experimental puppet show by Jeanette Yew at La MaMa; *Shackled Spirits*, a multi-media dance drama by Lynn Kremer presented at the Bali Arts Festival; and *Big Picture*, with lyricist Patrick Spencer and book writer Susan Murray. Karl has a Ph.D. in Music Composition from Stony Brook University. karlhinze.com

HOWARD HO is a playwright and composer. His short musical *End Of The Line* (co-written with Kristen Rea and Chris Edgar) was in The Samuel French Off-off-Broadway Short Play Festival and Theatre Now's SOUND BITES 5.0. His play *Various Emporia* was a 2017 O'Neill National Playwrights Finalist. His musical *Pretendo* was featured in the Center Theatre Group (CTG) Library Reading Series. He was a 2016 CTG Literary Fellow and a 2013 NY State Summer Writers Institute Scholarship recipient. His work has been developed with East West Players, Playwrights' Arena, Company of Angels, Kaya Press, New Musicals Inc., Playground-LA, Santa Monica Playhouse, Here and Now, and The Vagrancy. His popular Youtube videos analyzing the musical *Hamilton* (youtube.com/HowardHoMusic) have been recognized by Lin-Manuel Miranda and have garnered millions of views collectively. He holds a musicology degree from UCLA and a Master of Professional Writing from USC.

TIMOTHY HUANG's works have been produced at Prospect Theater Company, NYTB, and Baayork Lee's National Asian Artists Project (Andy Pickets, 2 to Wakefield, Crossing Over respectively) He is the creator of the one person musical *The View From Here* and his song "Everything I Do, You Do" was recorded by Sutton Foster for the charity album *Over the Moon: The Broadway Lullaby Project*. His full length

American Morning was the recipient of the 2016 Richard Rodgers Award, the 2015 New American Musical Award, the 2015 NAMT Festival of New Musicals, ASCAP Musical Theater Workshop, and the BMI Master Class hosted by Stephen Sondheim. Other works: *And the Earth Moved*, *Death and Lucky*, *LINES: A Song Cycle*, *Missing Karma* (Finalist Sam French OOBF 2015, City Theater of Miami 2016) and *A Relative Relationship* (Best Musical, *2013* SOUND BITES Festival). Dramatists Guild Council, MacDowell Fellow, BMI Advanced Workshop. www.timothyhuang.net

JONATHAN KEEBLER is a lyricist and book writer based in New York City. Select musicals include *Gay Card* (music by Ryan Korell) and *Truth Or Lie* (music by Bob Kelly), as well as short works including *Worlds Apart* (music by Ryan Korell) and the short musical film, *A Most Average Musical* (screenplay by Talia Berger, music by Bob Kelly). His work has been seen at the Piccolo Spoleto Festival, SOUND BITES 4.0, UC Irvine's 4@15, the North Raleigh Arts and Creative Theatre, the College of Charleston, and Rollins College, as well as performed at Feinstein's/54 Below and Joe's Pub. His work has been developed at the Johnny Mercer Writers Colony at Goodspeed Musicals, as well as by Hajjar Entertainment at the New York Theatre Workshop. He was a finalist for the Jonathan Larson Grants and is a proud member of the Dramatists Guild.

BOB KELLY is a NY-based composer/songwriter, pianist, music director, and orchestrator/arranger. Works of musical theatre include: *gilgamesh & the mosquito* (with Sam Chanse), *Waiting... a song cycle* (with Kelly Pomeroy), and *Truth or Lie* (with Jonathan Keebler). His work has been supported by the National Alliance for Musical Theatre, the Yale Institute for Music Theatre, The Gallery Players, Prospect Theater Company, NY Theatre Barn, Leviathan Lab, Theatre Now NY, NYU CDP Series, New Musicals Inc., and the Festival of New American Musicals in Los Angeles. Bob is from the Twin Cities, MN, and is a graduate of St.Olaf College and the NYU Graduate Musical Theatre Writing Program. He was the 2013 recipient of the ASCAP Foundation Max Dreyfus Scholarship for musical theatre composition, and is a member of Local 802 AFM, ASCAP, and the Dramatists Guild. More info at bobkelly-music.com

AARON KENNY is an Australian composer based in New York, featured by ASCAP as a "composer to watch". Composing for film, television, theater, and the concert hall, he was nominated for Best Song at the Hollywood Music in Media Awards (2019), as well as being awarded Australian Young Composer of the Year. His theatrical writing debut happened in 2016 with *On Your Mark!*, a contemporary musical adaptation of "The Tortoise and the Hare." Aaron is a current member of the BMI Lehman Engel Musical Theatre Advanced Workshop. He has also previously been selected for the ASCAP Foundation's Broadway Conductors Program (NYC 2012), and the ASCAP Musical Theater Workshop (NYC 2017). He is also the Music Assistant to Disney Legend and Broadway composer Alan Menken, and has worked on *Beauty and the Beast* (2017 film), *Hercules* (Stage) and the upcoming *The Little Mermaid* (film).

CHRIS KERRIGAN is a musical theatre actor, singer/songwriter, and playwright living and working in Los Angeles. He is the head of the theatre department at STAR Education, a far-reaching after school program that serves over a hundred schools in the greater Los Angeles area. He has written nine full-length children's musicals (*Two Sides to Every Story, Screen Time: The Musical!, The Toy Store*, and *Reading is Rad*, to name a few) that have been performed in elementary schools far and wide. He has performed in several regional productions including *Parade* (Hugh Dorsey), *Violet* (The Preacher), *Assassins* (John Wilkes Booth), *American Idiot* (Tunny), *Jekyll & Hyde* (Jekyll/Hyde), and *Avenue Q* (Brian), to name a few. He plays piano/keyboards in several LA bands as well.

WILL LACKER is a New York City based playwright originally from St. Petersburg, Florida. Original Works: Bittersweet Lullaby, Catch the Westbound, Edison, The Invasion, Chupacabra, The Custodian, Republic, and Trials of a Scientific Mind. His works have been produced at The Player's Theatre, Merkin Concert Hall, The Flea, NYC Fringe, Gene Frankel Theatre, Manhattan Repertory Theatre, Woodstock Fringe, Alexandra Film Festival, and Gen Con Film Festival. Will earned a BA from Marymount Manhattan, an MFA from Queens College, and is a graduate of the UCB improv school. Member: Dramatists Guild. Honors and Awards: Best Book, Best Director: SOUND BITES 6.0, Best One Act: Central PA Theater Fest, Players Theatre Short Play Festival, Manhattan Repertory One Act Fest.

DIMITRI LANDRAIN is an NYC-based composer and Jazz pianist from Paris, France. He is an alumni from Berklee College of Music, CCM (University of Cincinnati), holds an MFA from NYU/Tisch Graduate Musical Theatre Writing Program and attended the BMI Lehman Engel Musical Theatre Workshop. His work is featured on a solo piano album titled *September, NYC* and on French singer Liane Foly's platinum album *Entre Nous*.

JONNY LEE JR. is an Asian American actor, singer, and writer. As a writer, Jonny co-wrote the music, lyrics, and book to the new musical *Welcome To Shoofly*, a selection in ASCAP/Dreamworks Workshop with Stephen Schwartz presented at the Wallis Annenberg Center in Beverly Hills. Jonny also co-wrote and starred in the musical web-series, *City of Dreams*, which has been featured in The New York Times, USA Today, Playbill and BroadwayWorld. Other writing works include music for the CBS Diversity Showcase, *Take Out* (AAFL Top 10), and *Benjamin Franklin And the Legend Of the Vajra*, a winning entry for LiveReadLA. Some acting credits include, Ito in *Mame*, Ching Ho in *Thoroughly Modern Millie*, Henry in *Next to Normal*, Thuy in *Miss Saigon*, and Lit in *Gold Mountain*.

ED LEVY wrote the libretto and lyrics for *Bystander* (Best Short Play or Musical; NY Summerfest, Hudson Guild Theater, 2017, Theatre Now's SOUND BITES 5.0, Best Music; Signature Theater). He wrote the lyrics for *Uncomfortable Sex* (Players Theater Short Play Festival, 2017). He has had 3 short musicals produced at Lincoln Center (*Across a Crowded Room*, 2017 and 2015). In August of 2018, his ten minute play *Picket Line, 1936* was produced at the Association for Theater in Higher Education conference. Ed studied lyric writing at BMI Lehman Engel Musical Theater Workshop. He is a member of the Dramatist Guild, the Directors Guild of America, and BMI.

JUSTIN ANTHONY LONG's writing includes the comedy feature *Benjamin Franklin & the Legend of the Vajra* (LiveReadLA Winner), the musical web-series *City Of Dreams* (NY Times, USA Today, IndieWire, Playbill), the comedy musical *Welcome To Shoofly* (ASCAP/DreamWorks Musical Theatre Workshop with Stephen Schwartz), the short film *Take Out* (Top 10 AAFL), the short musical *Jake & Lindsay* (Davenport Finalist), and an original opening musical number for the CBS Sketch

Comedy Diversity Showcase. With some of his collaborators, Justin made his songwriting debut at Feinstein's/54 Below in *The Opposite of Cool: The Songs of Lee, Long, & Burns*. Also an actor, Justin has "gracefully" graced the stage and screen. Some credits include *Mutt House* (Center Theatre Group), *Joseph & The Amazing Technicolor Dreamcoat* (3-D Theatricals), *The Brat Pack* (For the Record), *Mary Poppins* (MPAC), the musical parody of Stephen King's *IT* (Rockwell), and Martin Scorsese's Oscar nominated film, *The Wolf Of Wall Street*. More info at www.JustinAnthonyLong.com, @justinanthonylong

CHARLIE O'LEARY is an alumnus of the Project Y Playwrights Group, the Brooklyn Generator, the Advanced BMI Workshop, Crashbox Theatre Company's Write Play Launch, the 24 Hour Plays: Nationals, and the Fornés Playwriting Workshop. His plays have been developed and presented by the Flea Theater, Middle Voice at Rattlestick, Jersey City Theater Center, Dixon Place, Crashbox Theater Company, Pipeline Theatre Company, Project Y Theatre, Theatre Now New York, Loading Dock Theatre, the Tank, the PIT, the Habitat, the Artist Co-op, the Dare Tactic, and the University of Notre Dame. He has been a finalist for the Seven Devils Playwrights Conference, the DVRF Playwrights Program, Sanguine Theatre Company's Project Playwright, and the Woodward/Newman Drama Award; a semifinalist for the O'Neill National Playwrights Conference and Ars Nova Play Group; and recipient of a New York Innovative Theatre Award and an Iowa Arts Fellowship. His song "A Date" (music by Helen Park) was a selection of the BMI Workshop Smoker; ; his songs have also been performed at places like 54 Below, Don't Tell Mama, the West End Lounge, and the Duplex. He is currently pursuing his MFA at Iowa Playwrights Workshop. www.charlieholeary.com

ERIK PRZYTULSKI is a composer, writer, and producer whose works include: *A Song for Christmas, Thumbelina,* and *Christmas In Neverland*. His show, *Princesses,* was presented at the 2012 ASCAP/Dreamworks Musical Theatre Workshop hosted by Stephen Schwartz. *Pellets, Cherries, and Lies: The Pac Man Story* marked his Off-Broadway debut and was soon followed by the NYC premiere of the award-winning *Alien Vs. Musical* in early 2019. Upcoming projects include *Marian – A New Musical*, an updated adaptation of the Robin Hood legend, and *BugBandKids*, a new educational music series premiering in 2020. (www.pretzylmusic.com) (@pretzylmusic)

KRISTEN REA is a former dancing french hornist turned musical theater book writer, lyricist & composer. After over a decade performing in the Tony and Emmy award-winning theatrical production, *Blast!* and *Blast! The Music of Disney*, throughout the US and Japan, Kristen shifted to the creative side and studied Music and Lyrics at New Musicals, Inc. and BMI Lehman Engel Musical Theater Workshop. Original works include *End of the Line* (Samuel French Off-off-Broadway Short Play Festival, Theatre Now's SOUND BITES 5.0 Festival, NMI), *New Horizons* (BMI Workshop), *North Pole High* (NMI Got Musical, NMI New Works Staged Reading), *Sombrellu* (CITYstage), and *In The Hall* (with Lori Jaroslow). Kristen grew up in Placerville, CA - the epicenter of California's Gold Rush, and holds a B.M. in French Horn Performance from the University of Southern California and an M.F.A. in Brass Performance from California Institute of the Arts. She currently resides in New York City where she works in musical theatre publishing and licensing and tries to make your favorite musicals' scores and parts look pretty.

ANDY RONINSON is a composer, lyricist, orchestrator, and music director living in New York City. He is a recipient of the 2019 Jonathan Larson Grant, a 2019-2020 Dramatists Guild Foundation Fellow, and a participant in the 2017 Johnny Mercer Foundation Songwriters Project. As a member of the BMI Lehman Engel Musical Theatre Writing Workshop, he was awarded the Robert B. Sherman Scholarship and the Harrington Award for Creative Excellence. For more, visit AndyRoninson.com. He is the creator, host, and co-writer of *TAKE A TEN*, the all-original ten-minute musical podcast. Recorded episodes featured Broadway voices like Laura Osnes, Rob McClure, George Salazar, and more. Episodes have been produced live around the world and have won numerous awards including Best Musical twice at Theater Now's SOUND BITES Festival, the 2016 City Theater National Award for Short Playwriting, and the top place at the Samuel French Off-Off-Broadway Short Play Festival. To hear every episode for free, visit TakeATenMusicals.com.

DAVID SHENTON is an English-born pianist, violinist, composer, and arranger based in New York City. As pianist/music director David has worked with renowned members of the music profession in all genres, and has written music for Broadway, West End, and Hollywood films.

David enjoys touring with his groups, Empire Trio and Uptown Girls, as well as teaching and educating children both in the United States and in Africa where he and his wife, soprano Erin Shields, frequently volunteer.

CINDY SIDERIS has been working as a writer and creative producer for nine years. She began her training with the Upright Citizens Brigade, completing their Improv and Advanced Sketch Comedy Writing programs. Her sketch comedy musical *West Side Story Remade* had a sold-out run at The PIT. Other: *Run This Town* (Theatre Now's SOUND BITES 5.0 Festival, Signature Theatre). Cindy holds an MBA from NYU with a focus on Entertainment, Media and Technology, and works as an Associate Producer for the annual NYU Tisch Gala. She is a proud member of The Dramatists Guild and The BMI Musical Theatre Advanced Workshop.

JORDAN SILVER is a NYC based playwright/lyricist. He graduated from Ithaca College in 2016 in BFA Musical Theatre. Since graduating, he's had multiple developmental readings of his full-length play *Nobody Gives a $#!T About You (and the power that comes with knowing it)* produced by Dan Stone (Dear Evan Hansen, H2$, Catch Me if You Can, etc...) and directed by David Perlow. This past summer, *Nobody Gives* was presented at The Manhattan Repertory Theatre. In addition to playwriting, which he studies at Primary Stages, Jordan is also a lyricist/book writer. Jordan presented *Welcome to Ridgington* at Theatre Now's SOUND BITES 5.0 Festival. In 2018, Jordan was invited to attend the ASCAP musical theatre workshop in LA. He's collaborated with composers, Alexander Sage Oyen (Dramatist Guild Fellow), Chris Urquiaga, Greg Good, Luke Steinhauer, and Jake Landau. You can also hear Jordan Silver's original music available on iTunes and Spotify.

ZACH SPOUND is a New York based composer-lyricist, arranger, orchestrator, and actor. He has written two full-length musicals; *Leap* (NMI/Disney New Voices Award), *What The Fuck Is Going On*, and is currently writing and developing his third musical, *In This Body*. His short musical, *Dinosaur*, has won numerous awards including Best Lyrics and Audience Choice Best Musical at Theatre Now's SOUND BITES 5.0 Festival and the 2019 City Theatre National Award for Short Playwriting. He also participated in the 2016 Johnny Mercer Foundation

Songwriters Project. He is the music supervisor, arranger, and orchestrator of *Cruel Intentions: The 90s Musical*, which ran Off-Broadway and completed its 1st National Tour. He is also the English lyricist of *Nikola Tesla- Infinite Energy*. As an actor, he has been seen Off-Broadway in *The Other Josh Cohen* and has performed at regional theatres such as the Cape Playhouse, South Coast Repertory, and the Geffen Playhouse.

LUKE STEINHAUER is a New York based composer, actor, and vocal coach originally from Pittsburgh, Pennsylvania. He recently made his 54 below debut with Jordan Silver in *The Songs of Silver & Stein* and his compositions have been performed at Signature Theatre, The Green Room 42, and various stages across the country. Selected acting credits include: The Muny, Theatre Aspen, Music Theatre Wichita, Pittsburgh CLO, Unquowa Rep, Theatre by the Sea, Casa Manana, and Pittsburgh Public Theater. He is a graduate of The University of Michigan Musical Theatre Program, a proud member of Actors Equity, and an Estill Master Trainer. He is a YoungArts Winner in Musical Theater and attended Stagedoor Manor for several years.

THICKET & THISTLE is a troop of theatre makers who weave their multidisciplinary creative skills, imaginative storytelling, and humble virtuosity to create original, charming, and accessible musical theatre in which the actors are also the musicians playing multiple instruments while singing, dancing, and acting. Formed in early 2014, the current members are: Kyle Acheson, Julianna Wheeler, Jonathan Foster, Sam De Roest, Lindsay Zaroogian, and Joshua Stenseth. Thicket & Thistle's first creation was a ten minute musical, *What's Your Wish?*, for Theatre Now New York's SOUND BITES 2.0 festival. They then developed *What's Your Wish?* to a full musical and performed it at the NY Fringe Fest in 2015, Access Theatre in 2016, The Michael Chekhov Festival in 2016, and NYMF in 2018. In 2015, Thicket & Thistle performed *The Waterman* at Ars Nova for their Summer ANT Fest, and the following year, they began developing their 3rd original musical, *Death Cruise* which played at Access Theatre and the PIT in 2019. Thicket & Thistle has enjoyed residencies with Access Theatre, The PIT Theatre, and are currently participants in Theatre Now New York's Musical Theatre Writers Lab.

www.ingramcontent.com/pod-product-compliance
Lightning Source LLC
Chambersburg PA
CBHW020932180426
43192CB00036B/546